Fast Fulfillment

Fast Fulfillment

The Machine that Changed Retailing

Sanchoy Das

BUSINESS EXPERT PRESS

Leader in applied, concise business books

Fast Fulfillment: The Machine that Changed Retailing

Cover design by Charlene Kronstedt

Interior design by Exeter Premedia Services Private Ltd., Chennai, India

First published in 2021 by
Business Expert Press, LLC
222 East 46th Street, New York, NY 10017
www.businessexpertpress.com

ISBN-13: 978-1-63742-076-8 (paperback)
ISBN-13: 978-1-63742-077-5 (e-book)

Business Expert Press Marketing Collection

Collection ISSN: 2169-3978 (print)
Collection ISSN: 2169-3986 (electronic)

First edition: 2021

10 9 8 7 6 5 4 3 2 1

Description

The fulfillment machine is the delivery side infrastructure of an online business, and it is the physical and digital innovations which make it possible to immediately deliver customer orders. Customers want to order everything, while sitting on their couch and they want immediate fulfillment. Fast fulfillment is happening, and everyone knows that, but most are scared of it.

Many experts describe the wonders of online retail, but none explains what fast fulfillment is or propose a solution to building a fast fulfillment machine. Managers are frustrated just reading about how great Amazon is, and how startups are innovating fantastic technology driven processes. Here is the book, written in a simple, easy-to-read style which unravels the technical mystery of the fulfillment machine. It levels the knowledge field, reveals the secrets of fast fulfillment, and helps the reader construct a plan to innovate and be ready to face the disruptors.

What is happening in retail is contagious across industries, there are no wide moats. Managers and engineers are rushing to redesign their supply chains into fast fulfillment machines. This book provides insights and process details of how to design and build disruptive innovations, so that you are not flying blind or just throwing darts in an effort to pivot/expand to the online order fulfillment world. The book does not story-tell the fast fulfillment machine, it is informative and instructive.

Keywords

e-commerce operations management; omni channel; Amazon logistics; supply chain engineering; lean supply chain; e-commerce process design; warehouse logistics

Contents

For additional material and supporting information please visit the accompanying website www.fastfulfill.org

Foreword

Amazon has radically changed the way we shop, and everybody knows it's the leading online retailer in the world. But only a few of us know that Amazon and a few other companies have built an amazing fulfillment machine that switches on whenever we click, *Submit Order* on our mobile devices, and only stops when we get that *Delivery Completed* alert. The development of the fulfillment machine was not accidental, a lucky strike, or a divine intervention. It was engineered by teams of smart and innovative people who saw the incapability of the current systems, foresaw the seismic shifts in the buying behavior of consumers, and visualized the solution as opportunities provided by technology and mathematical modeling.

I have three objectives in this book. First, to provide you with a detailed view and learning perspective of the fulfillment machine, including an analysis of why it's so efficient. Second, to explain how the innovation was catalyzed and implemented to create this large-scale intelligent machine. Third, show how your business can design-build a fast fulfillment machine. None of the information or knowledge is secret, or confidential, or requires special access to facilities or managers. Surprisingly, it has been readily and easily available to the public, and it still surprises me that the largest U.S. retailers waited so long to respond. I have neither intimate knowledge of Amazon operations nor have I spent long hours talking to fulfillment engineers at Amazon or any other online retailer. I study supply chains and mathematical models and using this expertise the book explains first, why the Internet killed the mall; second, the unique analytics driven design of the physical machine; third, the digitally embedded intelligent fuel that propels the machine, and finally presents innovation methods to build the zero-infinity fulfillment machine.

Underlying every business is an operational machine that delivers a product or service to the customer, and at the end of the day, this machine determines performance, customer growth, and profitability. This book focuses on the retail fulfillment machine, but the concepts, analysis, and approaches can be applied to any business operations machine. One of the most impactful business books in recent times is *The Machine That Changed the World*, the authors skillfully and simply told the story of the Toyota production machine. The book spawned the lean production approach, which then was adopted by businesses throughout the globe. The Internet allows every business to directly access every customer and vice versa, which means almost every legacy business operation is obsolete. Incremental improvements or business process cost reductions are not sufficient solutions. The goal of the book is to motivate you and facilitate your team in developing disruptive process innovations that position you and your company to succeed and lead in the Internet age. The book is organized into four sections that describe the physics of the machine, the knowledge to be learned, and how to apply it to your business fulfillment processes.

OMG! The Internet Killed the Mall: For as long as we know, the market, the store, and the mall have been the exchange point of retail trade. Goods and payments were exchanged at the sales counter and the transaction was completed. Common retailer performance metrics were the number of stores, sales per square foot, and the stock market's favorite, same-store sales. But today, the retail landscape has changed, and store closings are common. Classical marketing techniques are not working, and the store manager tweets: *Houston we have a problem!* and the problem is a nondescript warehouse 300 miles away in the middle of nowhere. In this section, we explain how the fulfillment machine blindsided retailers, and faster delivery speeds changed consumer shopping behavior.

The Physical Machine: Behind every great company, there is an efficient machine producing a valuable product or service. Behind that machine is an efficient process, and behind that process is a bunch of brilliant innovators. In the digital economy, the innovators masterfully blend physical processes, mathematical analysis, and computing to achieve breakthrough levels of performance. In this section, we explore how transfer functions are used to seed and grow innovative ideas. These ideas evolved into machines that disrupt and disintermediate existing machines. We talk about Alpha, Sigma, and Gamma automation, and how you can integrate those wonderful technologies: AI, Robotics, and Smart Computing in your processes.

The Intelligent Fuel: An amazing feature of the fulfillment machine is the decision granularity. By controlling the flow of the smallest transactional unit, one can design and build systems that were previously infeasible or even unthinkable. No decisions are trivial or random, each is analytically optimized to achieve a defined objective. Expanded customer options result in a high degree of process flow uncertainty, which in turn implies an explosion of operational decisions. The decision space is beyond human memory and cognition. In this section, we explore how the innovators have harnessed computing power, streaming data models, and decision distribution to create these amazing machines. The tools already exist, the innovative challenge is how to visualize the granular flows and create an optimizable model around them. Data analysts are the foot soldiers of the intelligence war, you need to tell them what to predict and when.

Zero-Infinity Fulfillment: What is the fulfillment utopia? A business offers an infinite catalog of products/services and promises delivery in zero time. Disruptive innovators are building fast fulfillment machines, and you need to match their speed or better still, race past the disruptors. In this section, we present a plan to assemble teams that investigate process innovations and design-build the fast fulfillment machine.

Acknowledgments

As an educator, I have had opportunity to discuss, argue, and learn from a wonderful group of smart people. This has included: students, industry professionals, academic colleagues, and conference attendees. I thank them all for the small and large bits of information I gathered from these encounters.

For the last 15 years, I have taught the Supply Chain course at the New Jersey Institute of Technology (NJIT) and want to give a big thanks to the hundreds of students who attended those classes and helped me assemble the ideas, concepts, and tools presented in this book. My biggest gratitude is to my three amazing NJIT doctoral students, Sevilay Onal, Jingran Zhang, and Wen Zhu, with whom I researched and discovered the inner workings of the fulfillment machine.

Finally, a big thanks to my wife and son, Rajyasri and Rohit, for their patience and support.

CHAPTER 1

Paradigm Shift in Retailing Logistics—Fulfillment

Discover how innovative storage and distribution concepts have changed the delivery side of retailing—the supply chains that move goods from warehouses to customer doorsteps in hours. The disruptors have weaponized these innovations into a pivoting enabler—using fast fulfillment to capture and pivot customers from brick-and-mortar to online. Fulfillment machines are rapidly disrupting all industries and no product or service is immune to these innovations.

An Enormous and Amazing, (Humongous! Massive! Gargantuan! Take your pick) change has occurred in how consumers buy the things they need, and in the last 10 years, this change has been explosive both in terms of the number of people and the number of products affected. Wow! You no longer need to go to the store to see, buy, and pick-up the products you want. Instead, you can review, select, and pay for the product online, and do it whenever you want and from wherever you wish. Then, in a few hours or a day or so, the product is delivered to your doorstep. Most people, particularly millennials, already know this, and the narrative is frequently repeated in media outlets, textbooks, and social conversations. It goes by many names, online retail, and electronic commerce being the two most commonly used. What is surprising, though, is that many of the successful online retailers are new companies. Of these, the most well-known is Amazon, accounting for close to 50 percent of all U.S. online sales in 2017. Why were traditional retailers not online pioneers? Did they not see the change coming? Did they not know how to respond? Were they too deeply vested in their existing retailing infrastructure? Many would argue they just could not innovate fast enough, and strangely brick-and-mortar became a synonym for an old and fading retailing model. This is the new normal, the customer is unleashed from the information tether of the past, and now demands a highly responsive and superefficient fast fulfillment machine that delivers products to their door immediately. Get used to the trend and make it your friend. My job in this book is to position you with tools and knowledge to design-build a winning solution.

One thing is certain, online retail is very different from traditional retail; it is a chain of innovative ideas put together by some brilliant and futuristic people. They recognized that the age of information transparency had dawned, and built online retail businesses that leveraged this new consumer power. The online retail businesses they built had two distinctive parts:—*Sell Side:* Digital marketing and customer engagement, and *Delivery Side:* Order processing and fulfillment. The sell side is the more visible part and as customers, we have all experienced it and recognize the innovation. The delivery side, though, is behind the scenes and as customers, all we hear is the doorbell ring and a package delivered on our doorstep.

> *Online Order Fulfillment*—Starts from the receipt of a customer's online order and ends with parcel delivery. Fast refers to the time or speed with which the fulfillment is completed.

The fulfillment machine is the delivery side infrastructure of an online business and consists of the physical and digital innovations that make it possible to deliver customer orders in short time. Relative to the sell side, the delivery side or fulfillment process is more difficult to develop, and is both capital and technology intensive. Commonly, the delivery side is described as the supply chain and logistics infrastructure of the retailer and its partners. In this book, we investigate the delivery side innovations and identify what determines success. We learn from the innovations of the online retail leaders, mix it with traditional supply chain knowledge, and garnish it with technology trends. We present a pathway to innovating a fast fulfillment machine for your business.

What Does a Supply Chain Do?

A supply chain brings products from a manufacturer to the point-of-use, which could be your home, your office, or wherever. If you are buying cheese from the dairy across the road from you, well in that case there is no supply chain. If on the other hand, you are buying that fancy French brie at Whole Foods, then there is a significant and complex supply chain that makes this convenience possible. The many physical distribution facilities, transportation vehicles, and talented people together constitute the supply chain logistics infrastructure, which brings the brie to your home. Now let me let you into a little secret, you, the consumer, are also a part of this supply chain logistics and an unpaid participant. Every time you get in the car and drive to the retail store or mall, buy one more item and bring them home or somewhere else, you just completed the last leg of that supply chain. Why did you do that? Most likely you had no choice, drive to the grocery store or go hungry.

Over the decades, many innovations have tried to free you from this supply chain bondage: mail-order catalogs, shopping concierge services, and home delivery options. For the most part the convenience, immediacy, fun and excitement, and most importantly the economics of retail shopping have won, and these innovations were just footnotes. Then the Internet was invented, online shopping was born, and a bunch of really smart people made fast fulfillment a reality. Suddenly, many of the core advantages of retail shopping were challenged by an innovative logistics machine. The big gorilla in fast fulfillment, actually the T-Rex, is Amazon Fulfillment. Embracing every dimension of technology, they, and their partners, have defined a new form of retailing logistics. Lesson one, it's not a change, a modification, or an improvement, rather, it's new, it's a paradigm shift.

There are in general two types of supply chains: Manufacturing supply chains—a converging network of product movements that bring parts and materials to a factory; Retailer supply chains—a diverging network of flows that distribute finished products from the manufacturer to retail stores. With the growth of online retail, we are witnessing transformational changes in retailer supply chains, for the simple reason that more products are not being distributed to a store but forwarded instead to a fulfillment center. Retailer supply chains, global or local, are designed to move bulk volumes of products speedily and economically. Post-1980, and with the start of the Walmart era in retailing, supply chains became a competitive advantage for many retailers. Rapid developments in information technology allowed progressive retailers to build logistics networks that tracked shipments from distant manufacturers, many located in the far corners of the globe, all the way to the retail shelf. A stellar example of such a solution is Walmart's RetailLink system that collected cash register data from all stores into a central database. These data were then used to run powerful supply chain models that optimized their inventory usage. Similar IT-driven innovations were implemented by all retailers to improve the efficiency of their supply chain infrastructure. In the last decade, though, a host of innovations have led to the development of a completely new supply chain and logistics infrastructure. It is so radically different that it has made the old infrastructure a business handicap.

Eight Paradigm Shifts

So, what are the paradigm shifts that have driven the growth of a fast fulfillment infrastructure? Figure 1.1 lists several inventory storage and product distribution paradigms that are changing retail logistics. Next, we discuss each paradigm and explain why old systems cannot respond to online customer needs.

1. Online Shopping
2. Point-of-Use Delivery
3. Earlier Bulk Unitization
4. Free Shipping
5. Variety Multiplication
6. The Warehouse is the Store
7. Predictive Correlations
8. Supply Chain Subscription

Figure 1.1 Fast fulfillment—New paradigms

1. ***Online Shopping***—The growth of the Web and mobile devices allowed retailers to bring their product catalog straight to the consumer. Through online shopping, customers could then complete the sell-side activity entirely at home, which meant no visit to the store. Early on many assumed, mistakenly, that this was just a replacement for the mail-order business and would remain a niche market. Were they wrong! The ease and convenience of online shopping grew quickly and in 2017 accounted for 15 percent of all U.S. retail sales. The Pew Research Center reports[1] that 80 percent Americans are online shoppers and 15 percent buy online on a weekly basis. Unfortunately, online shopping was not compatible with a retailer's existing supply chain and logistics operations, making it difficult for them to organically expand into the online space.

   Why could they not just use their existing supply chains? Retailers hold inventory in two locations: stores and distribution centers, and their logistics networks are designed to efficiently bring the product to the store. During the 1990s, Walmart built a highly efficient network of cross-dock facilities to quickly replenish store inventories. Likewise, the apparel retailer H&M built warehouses, IT systems, and gathered a trucking fleet, for daily replenishment of store inventories. These are just two examples of the wonderful supply chain and logistics innovations that brick-and-mortar retailers had implemented. The problem is many of these innovations were a misfit for the logistics of online shopping, and for many retailers, their core competitive advantages did not transfer to the new economy. The shipment volumes, packaging, and destination are not just different, they are completely different. Even the customer is different, for a brick-and-mortar supply chain it is the store, for an online retail supply it is the actual customer. Sure, they could fulfill orders from their stores and distribution centers but it was not fast, and fast is what the online shopping customer wanted.

   Almost no retailers are safe from the shift to online shopping. Products that we would have assumed could not be sold online are now being successfully sold and delivered. Take the case of Casper, which is selling mattresses online and shipping orders within

24 hours. The product is designed certainly for comfort, but also for shipping ease, and requires no special delivery service.

2. ***Point-of-Use Delivery***—Retail supply chains come to a screeching halt at the store, then you the consumer drive to the store, pick up the item and take it to the point-of-use. In logistics vocabulary, the consumer is performing their last-mile delivery. Online shopping changed this process; customers wanted their purchases delivered to their home, office, dorm room, or anywhere. The range of delivery options and delivery speed are key determinants of online shopping convenience, and these may at times trump other factors such as price and quality. Dominos is very likely not the best pizza in your town, but more than likely it's the highest revenue pizza store. Why, because of the convenience and reliable efficiency of its delivery infrastructure, both of which are key business differentiators for Dominos. Sure, the gourmet family owned pizzeria can hire a delivery driver for the evening rush, but the strategy is not scalable. The pizzeria is focused on its store customer and is never able to match the speed and reliability of the Dominos delivery service.

Retailers are not in the point-of-use delivery business, except when the product is too large or heavy, even then it is usually an outsourced service. For any retailer the logistics impact of point-of-use delivery was enormous, a massive supply chain focused on brick-and-mortar stores would have to be rebuilt. The paradigm shift was radical, existing retail supply chains could not be just realigned, repositioned, or restructured; they would have to be built anew. Most Amazon shoppers today don't bother to check any other shopping websites, they have full confidence that Amazon's fulfillment system will deliver faster than anyone else.

3. ***Earlier Bulk Unitization***—Once a bulk pallet leaves the factory, it progressively gets broken down into a retail unit and the supply chain infrastructure is designed to optimize this breakdown process. In each movement link, the associated vehicles and logistics facilities are designed to handle and move packages of a specific size. A bulk warehouse will move pallet loads efficiently but not box loads and certainly not unit loads. Distribution centers are the central node in a brick-and-mortar supply chain, and typically pallet loads are

broken into box loads. Fulfillment centers provide a similar function in online retail, breaking box loads into unit loads.

In online retail, the bulk unitization process starts much earlier, and the supply movements handle much smaller packages (Figure 1.2). This also implies that a much greater number of packages must be moved and tracked, given a fixed sales volume. An efficient fulfillment center needs to cost-effectively move single units of a product. The operational impact of earlier unitization is significant. When a distribution center pretends to be a fulfillment, the economics can be disastrous and fast fulfillment is just not feasible. One innovative solution used by many distribution centers is task interleaving, which can improve operator utilization. But this works best when a high volume of full pallet loads is being moved and is of less value when the pallet loads are unitized earlier. The reality is that a distribution center cannot move and stock a single toothbrush, but a fulfillment center can. Let's say toothbrushes are bulk packed in boxes of 100 units and a pallet of 10 boxes. Then, for a throughput volume of 1,000 units, a distribution center requires 11 product movements, but in a fulfillment center, the same volume will require 1,010 movements. The distribution center is simply not designed or equipped to execute a 100× increase in product movements.

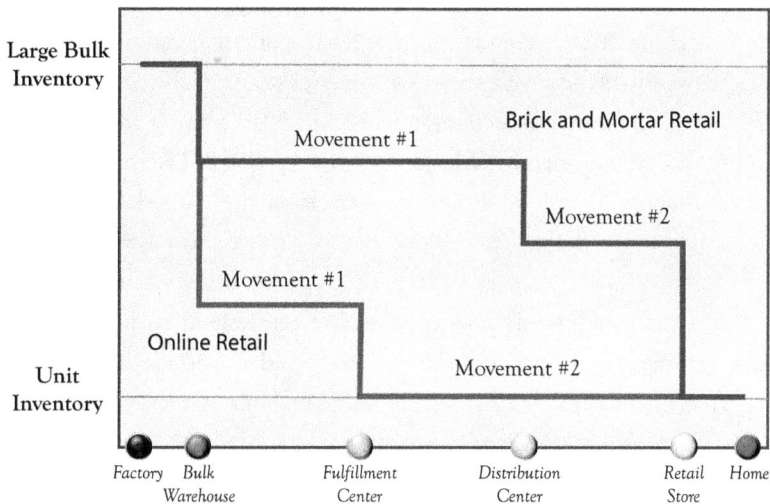

Figure 1.2 Breaking down bulk shipments through the supply chain

4. *Free Shipping*—A retailer's supply chain costs end at the store. Delivery to the home or last-mile delivery was only available at an additional cost. Delivery was offered as an external or add-on service and usually not an integral part of the retailer's supply chain and logistics infrastructure. The add-on delivery was provided by a third party, either a local company or with a national network. The three largest last-mile delivery companies in the United States are USPS, FedEx, and UPS. Their retail shipment rates are a function of speed, and a quick check reveals they are steep for guaranteed three-day delivery (Table 1.1). We can assume that negotiated wholesale shipping rates are a fraction of retail rates, but they certainly are not free. The shipping cost for online orders, whether fulfilled from the store or a central facility, is therefore dependent on the cost efficiency of a third-party service provider. All of this was OK as long as the customer was willing to pay for the service.

Table 1.1 Parcel shipping costs

2 lb. Parcel From/To	USPS	FedEx	UPS
Shipped from Los Angeles to New York	$10.30	$11.70	$12.30
Shipped from Houston to Chicago	$8.20	$10.40	$11.00

In 2002, Amazon started offering free shipping on orders above $99, but that in itself was not a novel concept, but certainly, it cracked the online shopping barrier for many customers. But in a brilliant move, Amazon Prime was launched in 2005, offering free shipping for an annual membership fee.[2] At the start of 2018, there were an estimated 70 million Prime subscribers in the United States. This single move dealt a fatal blow to many brick-and-mortar retailers. The perceived cost disadvantage of an online order was neutralized, and the paradigm of free shipping was a threshold requirement for customers. Retailers could no longer consider last-mile delivery as a recoverable supply chain cost, it had to be built into the price.

5. *Variety Multiplication*—Henry Ford famously said, "Any customer can have a car painted any color that he wants so long as it is black." His reasoning was simple, by having a single color, he could achieve economies of scale on the production side and supply chain efficiency

on the sell side. Likewise, shop floor sales metrics and supply chain efficiency limit the variety of products a physical store can offer. The variety includes options in multiple dimensions: brands, style, colors, product features, and accessory add-ons. Slow-moving items are not pushed out by fast-selling items. If we only sell only one of that weird looking iPhone case per month, it's just not economical to maintain in-store stock. But if the demand for that same iPhone case is aggregated for the entire retail market, it adds up to 20 a month. In that case, it is an economically viable product for an online retailer, who can then stock it at one of its fulfillment centers.

By stocking small quantities of a wider variety of product choices, an online retailer can attract customers who are not happy with the store choices. If the brick-and-mortar retailer tries to match the online retailer variety, a bunch of problems could arise. First, higher logistics cost to process the low unit volumes; second, lower revenues per square foot from slower selling varieties; and third, more clearances for unsold inventory. Online retail aggregates the dispersed insignificant customer into a significant one. Recognizing that they can effectively market low-demand items in an online channel, many manufacturers have already multiplied their product variety. The marketing advantage of "available online in 12 colors" compared to two colors in the store is clear.

Table 1.2 Available product variety of retailers

Retailer—Product	In-Store SKU Availability	Online SKU Availability	Amazon Prime Online SKU Availability
Home Depot – Centerset Bathroom Sink Faucets	41	191*/771	1392
Walmart – Camping Air Bed Built-in Pump	5	16*/69	103
Best Buy – Wireless Headphones	100	289	2000+
Macy's – Coffee Maker Coffee, Tea and Espresso	19	57	778
Foot Locker – Nike Women's Running Shoes	381	556	1344

* Two-day shipping SKUs.

Stock keeping units (SKUs) represent a unique product option, and the number of available SKUs is indicative of the stocked product variety. Looking at the in-store and online SKU availability for specific product classes at several brick-and-mortar retailers (Table 1.2), the variety multiplication effect is self-evident. The ratio of online/in-store SKUs ranges from 2 to 10+. When we extend the comparison to the variety on Amazon the multiplication continues, the online SKU ratios range from 2 to 6+. Yes, it's only four products, but we checked, and the ratios are consistent across many common product classes. From a marketing perspective, products are being de-commoditized in the online catalog. The supply chain impact is huge, successful online retail entails stocking more product options and shipping in smaller volumes.

6. ***The Warehouse Is the Store***—A couple of years ago, I visited a local wine store. The owner had recently launched a website for online orders and was offering attractive prices on mixed cases. Orders were pouring in! Open cases were scattered throughout the store, the owner and his two associates were running around with printouts, picking up bottles from shelves, and rushing to fulfill the orders. They had converted the store into a warehouse and collateral damage alienated their regular store customers. It was BOFS or Buy Online and Fulfill from a retail Store. But this is an inefficient solution when scaled up to process thousands of orders. Imagine if your neighborhood Walmart had to fulfill a couple of thousand orders every hour, shoppers would be tripping on boxes and bumping into pickers. A retailer's most valuable asset is their stores, and their online strategy frequently attempts to leverage this asset. But in a paradigm shift, the store has limited utility to an online retailer. Yes, Amazon has recently opened stores and bought Whole Foods. While many pundits have opined on this strategy, I believe few outsiders of Amazon know the end game of this plan. A recent article[3] describes a new class of retailers—*Online Retail Plus Showrooms*—sales are online but customers can visit physical showrooms to experience the product. Examples include Warby Parker and Bonobos. This is not a *store is the warehouse* strategy; the store functions only as a showroom for

the customer who needs to touch and feel the product before making that buy decision.

When customers visit a retail store, they browse through the aisles picking up the items they need. In online retail, this function is transferred from the customer to a picker in a fulfillment center. In a fulfillment center, items are stocked in single units throughout the facility, and an army of pickers respond to customer orders and collect the needed items. Depending on the operational design, a single picker could work on a single order or multiple orders, or multiple pickers could work on multiple orders concurrently. The warehouse has become the store, and a distribution center cannot be reconfigured to do this efficiently.

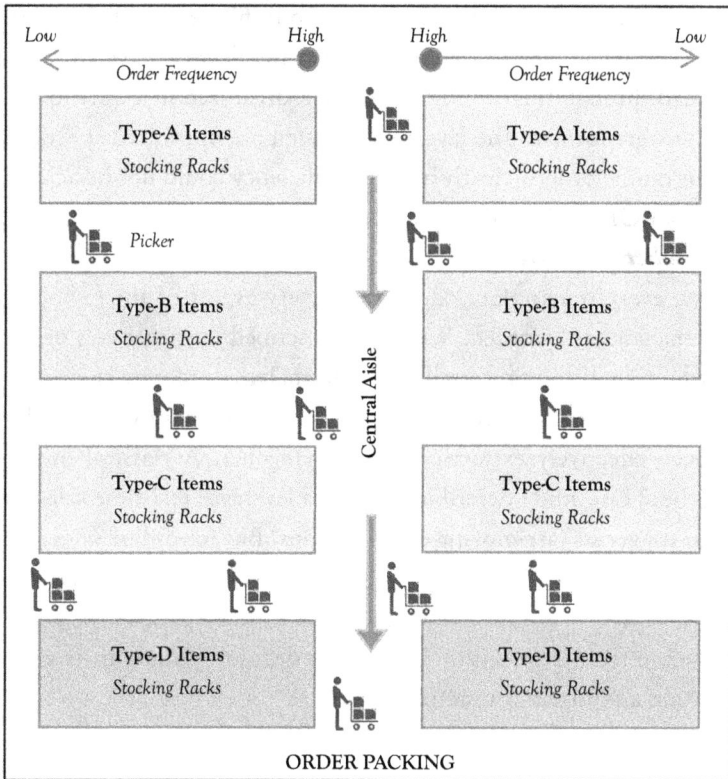

Figure 1.3 Warehouse designed for a storelike flow

An online grocer analyzes buyer behavior and decides to categorize its catalog into four groups (A-Packaged Goods, B-Liquid Items, C-Bulk Goods, and D-Others). The groups were selected such that 80 percent of customer orders include items from at least three groups. Figure 1.3 shows a warehouse design that facilitates order picking for fast fulfillment. Items with highest order frequency are located closer to the central aisle. The design looks more like a store and is radically different from a traditional warehouse. The online grocery pioneer Peapod illustrates this shift from brick-and-mortar to pure online. In new markets, Peapod fulfills orders from mini fulfillment centers or warerooms located within local grocery stores (owned by their parent company); when a market matures, they build a dedicated fulfillment center to accelerate the fulfillment efficiency. FreshDirect is a pure online grocer serving the metro New York market from two fulfillment centers. A 2012 New York Times[4] article documented the flow of a grilled salmon salad through their fulfillment center, organized in a warehouse in the store format. The layout and design are optimized specifically for online orders, clearly a similar efficiency could not be achieved by a BOFS solution.

7. *Predictive Correlations*—An online customer has no anonymity; every transactional detail and every aspect of their shopping behavior are recorded. We are all described in megabytes of data, which are being processed by a data analytics program somewhere. Retailers have been collecting point of sales data for years and have been effectively extracting sales intelligence. A classical business school case study describes how Zara leverages real-time sales data to trigger its fast-moving supply chains. But for online sales, these data are 10-fold larger in size and much richer in terms of the descriptive attributes. A deep analysis of these data allows a smart online retailer to optimize multiple decision points in its supply chain and logistics system.

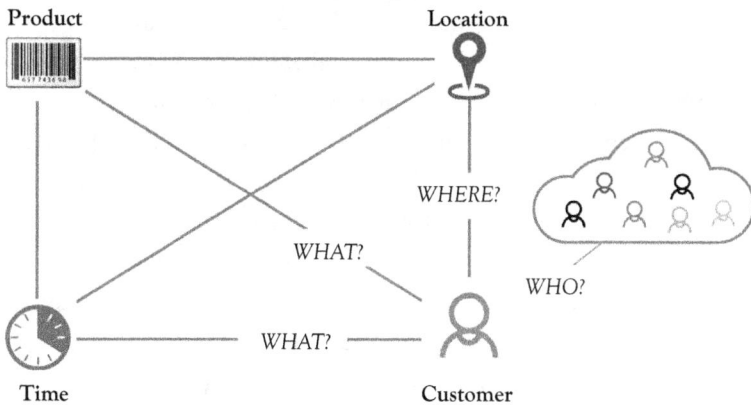

Figure 1.4 Entity relationships in an online order

Three entities link to an online customer's purchasing data (Figure 1.4): Product—what they bought; Location—where the product was delivered; and Time—when they made the purchase. By correlating this data with the millions of other customers in the database, we can identify who their online retail twins are. These correlations can then be used to make speculative predictions of future demand behavior. One of the earliest innovations on the Amazon bookstore was *customers who bought this also bought this*, that simple correlation has evolved into the data-driven marketing or product recommendation engine. Aside from their marketing value, these correlations can be exploited to achieve higher fulfillment efficiencies. If orders for an item are trending up in the New York metro area, then using the customer correlated data we can predict the behavior of that trend over the next few days. Inventory can then be accordingly positioned in nearby fulfillment centers. When an item is frequently bought with a basket of other items, then it can be stocked in closely clustered locations for faster order picking. Correlations are more significant in aggregate datasets, and many will not show up in individual store data. Predictive correlations allow the online retailer to design and operate an intelligence-driven supply chain.

8. ***Supply Chain Subscription***—Building a supply chain infrastructure whether for brick-and-mortar or online retail is a capital-intensive activity and only perfected over time. The supply chains of Home Depot and Walmart are legendary, and their methods are highlighted in textbooks and magazine articles. Product manufacturers gravitate toward retailers with efficient supply chains, knowing fully well that fewer stockouts and fast replenishments are good for business. When LG entered the U.S. home appliances market in 2003, they evaluated retailers for retail placement, intending to build their brand. In addition to Home Depot's broad retail presence, its strong supply chain and willingness to collaborate on logistics issues made it a preferred retail partner. Small or start-up retailers are typically shut-out of big-box retailers until their product is a proven success. One of the few exceptions, though, is Whole Foods that does embrace small manufacturers. The success of Whole Foods shows that a strong supply chain retail partner can enable success for a small producer or manufacturer with an excellent product. Their local leaning procurement strategies lets the small producers subscribe to the Whole Foods fulfillment system[5] with healthy profits and growth opportunities.[6]

Amazon changed the manufacturer–retailer relationship with the launch of the *Fulfillment by Amazon* service in 2006. For a monthly subscription fee, small businesses and individual sellers could use Amazon's fulfillment supply chain and its associated logistic facilities and software. The retail placement power of a retailer was effectively neutralized. A manufacturer, of any size, could in a matter of weeks have a superefficient online fulfillment supply chain. Instant Pot is the fairy tale story of this transition. Robert Wang and his team focused on inventing and manufacturing an exciting new product, and then in October 2010, they launched it on Amazon.[7] Success came quickly, in 2016 they sold and fulfilled 215,000 Instant Pots on Prime Day. By subscribing to the Amazon supply chain, they did not have to spend much effort on supply chain and logistics issues. Instead, they spent their time scanning customer reviews and reinventing the product. Wang proclaims, "every 12 months to 18 months, we introduce the next generation of Instant Pot incorporating feedback from our real customers." The supply chain has been democratized, and every inventor, every craftsman, and every entrepreneur can in an instant distribute their goods everywhere all the time.

Fast Fulfillment—The Pivoting Enabler

The eight paradigm shifts may seem obvious to some and not so amazing to others. The reality, though, is that in combination they have affected a tsunamic transition in the retailing industry. I have been studying supply chains and teaching supply chain courses for many years, and honestly, I could not have foreseen these changes. *A key enabler of this transition is fast fulfillment, the logistical capability to deliver products before the customer is inconvenienced by the lack of it.* Fast fulfillment requires a network of physical facilities and transportation vehicles, supported by intelligent information systems that control every decision in the network. Some call this the physical Internet, which strangely enough is behind the scenes, while the digital Internet in the form of shopping websites is at the forefront. The disruptors have weaponized these innovations into a pivoting enabler. If a product is readily available at a nearby retail store, and the price and quality are no different from an online store, then why would I the customer pivot from in-store to online? Two reasons, the convenience of shopping from my mobile device (no need to drive to the store) and the assurance it will be delivered fast (before I need to use it). This book is all about the second reason.

The Amazon fulfillment machine consists of several building types: Sortable fulfillment center, nonsortable fulfillment center, sortation centers, receive centers, specialty, and delivery stations.[8] By 2020, Amazon had built a U.S. network of 200 fulfillment centers and 55 Prime Now hubs from which it rapidly fulfills orders from customers across the country.[9] Considering that in 2005 there were only six such centers, the build rate is simply off-the-charts. This network functions as a fast fulfillment machine, which has been Amazon's stealth competitive advantage. All brick-and-mortar retailers now have an online store, but none have a fast fulfillment machine. To process millions of orders every day and deliver them anywhere in the United States, the very next day requires a highly engineered and capital-intensive solution. The few times I have had the opportunity to attend presentations from Amazon managers and engineers at business meetings, it was clear to me that they feared no competitor. They were safe in the assumption that they were several years ahead of all other retailers. Fast fulfillment is the pivot that makes online shopping the default choice for the millennial generation. Fast fulfillment also affects the labor force and is creating many new jobs. In 2005, there were 657,000 warehouse workers in the United States, and in 2017, there were about a million workers, a 46 percent increase.[10]

In this book, I present insights, structural details, and analytical conclusions about how this fast fulfillment machine operates and what it may look like in the future. There are two aspects to this machine, the physical facilities where products are stocked, picked, packed, and shipped, and the intelligent decision methods that control every movement in the machine. In addition to Amazon, there are many other new and innovative companies that have built fast fulfillment machines, and we learn from them too. These include Jet.com, Boxed, Peapod, Parcel, Wayfair, Flipkart, JD.com, and many others.

As mentioned earlier there is a sell side and delivery side of online retail. My knowledge of the sell-side is elementary, and this book only explores the delivery side of the business. There is a treasure trove of books and articles on the sell side and these explore many facets of online consumer behavior. Online marketing is a knowledge frontier and everyday smart marketers are proposing new concepts and implementing innovative ideas. Here we are concerned with what happens after the consumer clicks the <SUBMIT ORDER> button on the checkout page. I believe fulfillment machines are not unique to retailing but are rapidly transforming all industries. Whether you are a bank, hospital, restaurant chain, a manufacturer of office supplies, or almost any other business, my warning is that an exogenous innovative disruptor somewhere is building a fast fulfillment machine that is pivoting your customers away from you. So, what can your business do? Learn and understand how to use data, physio-digital innovations, and very large-scale data stream decision optimization models to embrace and party along with the disruptors.

A key part of designing and building a fast fulfillment machine is the idea of disruptive innovations, and throughout the book, we present, discuss, and analyze these innovations. To become a disruptor, you need to first understand what disruptive innovation is. The term was first introduced by Clayton Christensen[11] and described as innovations that make products and services more accessible and affordable.

> Disruptive innovation is the introduction of a technologically enabled product or service that potentially changes the way the world works. Innovation should displace industry incumbents, increase efficiencies, and gain majority market share. While the threat to existing businesses is grave, the long-term opportunities for companies and investors participating in this change could be measured in the trillions. Innovation must meet three criteria: (i) Experience dramatic cost declines and unleash waves of incremental demand, (ii) Cut across sectors and geographies, and (iii) Serve as a platform for additional innovations—ARK Investment Management.[12]

The fulfillment process is being disrupted every day, and you have to assume that your current process is not going to be competitive tomorrow. Not every idea is innovative and even fewer are disruptive. So, investigate, explore, and design-build intelligently.

The Fast Fulfillment Machine

A great product or service is the key to success. Customers come to you from far and wide and are willing to pay high prices. Consider a small restaurant in the middle of Alabama making with a secret recipe for making the world's best barbecue ribs, it has met the sufficient conditions for economic success. But if the business wanted to expand, the traditional way was to open new locations. However, with a series of process innovations, the restaurant could build a fast fulfillment machine that would disrupt the traditional way and expand its market.

A fast fulfillment machine collects customer orders for a specific product/service with a chosen delivery date and location; prepares the orders for delivery, and then delivers the product/service to the selected customer location at high speed.

At first glance, this description does not appear to be anything special; basically every wholesaler has been doing this for decades. But once you start analyzing how good or bad is a fulfillment machine, then you realize it is a machine and not just a business process. There are five fast fulfillment performance measures: (i) *Economic measure*: Cost per unit delivery; (ii) *Speed measure*: Cycle time per order; (iii) *Variety measure*: Range of offered products/service and customization options; (iv) *Scale measure*: Breadth of geographic area and customer categories that can readily access the machine; and (v) *Robustness measure*: Operational stability under market uncertainty.

Why do we call it a machine? Because it is a process where every detail has been rigorously defined and is supported by a series of physical and digital innovations that optimize operations across a range of uncertainties. While the book does focus on retailing, fulfillment machines are being built across industries and apply to both products and services. Here are two examples:

Rocket Mortgage—Quicken Loans: Home mortgages are a very old product/service, and loan approvals are often a notoriously slow process with tons of paperwork. Customers connect with mortgage lenders through legacy bank branches and pay a litany of inexplicable fees. The banker controlled the approval process and you were thankful if they approved your loan. Quicken created an assembly line style fulfillment machine for mortgage banking. Process innovations redesigned every step of the loan approval process, allowed it to approve loans more efficiently, and at a much lower cost. Rocket mortgage was launched in 2015 and one year later it had originated $7 billion in loans. Quicken already had a mortgage product, Rocket was a new innovative fulfillment machine to deliver the mortgage.

As we progress through the book, we explore how fulfillment machines can be designed and built for almost any product or service.

Chapter Summary

- Introduces the fulfillment process for online orders. Describes the critical role of fulfillment as the delivery side of e-commerce, and an increasingly important component of retail supply chains.
- Identifies and describes the eight paradigm shifts that have driven the growth of a fast fulfillment infrastructure.
- Explains why the fast fulfillment machine, or the logistical capability to deliver products before the customer is inconvenienced by the lack of it, is a key enabler of online retail growth and success.
- Highlights the growth of fulfillment machines across industries and its application to both products and services.

CHAPTER 2

The Evolution
of Online Retail

Starts from eBay and gang, then Amazon fulfillment followed by first responses from brick-and-mortar stores. Insightful data tells the physical and economic growth story of the fulfillment machine. Through four phases of evolution, the smart disruptors leveraged data, technology, and decision models into a customer delight. Identify the four traits of successful machine builders: prerequisites, timeliness, technology enablers, and a long view.

The Netscape web browser, launched in 1994, made it much easier for all of us to navigate the Internet. Almost immediately we were all looking for fun things to do while online. But few of us, including brick-and-mortar retailers, would have guessed that shopping would be on top of the list and better still a bunch of innovators would design, build, and operationalize solutions to satisfy that need. The history of online retail is recorded in many excellent books and articles, and you should read some of these to better understand how quickly online shoppers and retailers evolved. If you have the time for a leisurely review then read, *The Everything Store: Jeff Bezos and the Age of Amazon*[13], if you just want the short 10-minute review then a good option is *The Wired Guide to Online Shopping.*[14] But for a snapshot view, let's start with some online shopping history trivia, courtesy Wikipedia:

- *NetMarket* an online marketplace recorded the first online sale on August 11, 1994—someone from Philadelphia used a credit card to buy Ten Summoner's Tales, a CD by Sting.

- *eBay*, founded in the autumn of 1995, starts connecting buyers and sellers of unique, strange, and outright weird products. By 2000, it's the largest online auction buying company with $431 million in sales.
- *Amazon*, also founded in 1995, starts selling books online and the first sale occurs on July 16, 1995. Two years later, in 1997, the company processed its one-millionth order. By 2000, it was serving 20 million online customers with annual revenues of $2.75 billion.
- The Chinese e-commerce company *Alibaba* was founded in 1999, launching an eBay-style business-to-business marketplace. In 2003, it launches *Taobao*, an Amazon-style marketplace for third-party sellers.
- Starting from 2000, pure online retailers are launched in many different countries: *Jingding* or JD (China), *Rakuten* (Japan), *Flipkart* (India), *Otto* (Germany and France), *GMarket* (South Korea), *Zalando* (Germany), and *MercadoLibre* (Latin America).
- *Walmart* acquires *Kosmix* in 2011 and renames it Walmart Labs, making online retail a top priority for the first time in its history. In 2016, it acquires *Jet.com* to remake its fulfillment operations.
- *Jumia* was started in Nigeria in 2012 and soon became the largest online retailer in Africa. The company debuts its Initial Public Offering (IPO) in April 2019 with a $2 billion valuation.

Listed previously are only some of the successful innovator-led companies that have facilitated and validated the paradigm shifts listed in Chapter 1. Many lesser-known companies were also online retail builders; in many cases, these merged into larger rivals and some just ran out of capital or stopped growing. At least two legacy companies, UPS and FedEx, were also critical players in the build process and without their existing fulfillment infrastructure, most innovators would have struggled to get their ideas working. They are both supply chain inductees of the online retail hall of fame.

There were many players in the evolution of online retailing, but almost none came from within the ranks of established retailers. Even more remarkable, only a small percent of the individual innovators had any retailing experience. Note to self: Your machine-building team must include people with knowledge of the enabling technology and not everyone should be vested in the current machine. Success was not guaranteed to the early players and only a few survived the early years. Many of the players recognized some of the paradigm shifts and built their businesses to leverage the shift. But few, and possibly only one, saw all the shifts and they became online retail leaders. So why look at the evolution and not just study the machines they built. Because it is important to go through a discovery phase where you learn what worked and what didn't, what are the enabling technologies, and what are the paradigm shifts you missed.

Data, Data, and Data

Everybody on your project team, your executive team, and your formal/informal consultant teams claims to have data that explain the past and project the future. Do not take any of this at face value. Be sure to always remember that one of the downsides of the online era is that information is easily posted and readily available to everyone. The reality, though, is that a lot of data are not validated, likely tainted by a confirmatory bias, or even downright wrong. It is OK, rather a must, to question and investigate any publicly accessed data you plan to use in decision making or project planning. Fact check, authenticate, validate, call it what you want but don't forget to do it. So, let's review selected validated data that provide instructive insights on the evolution of online retail and the associated supply chains.

The first of the online paradigms is online shopping, anecdotally we all know this is happening, but studying the data tells us when online shopping first became significant and what the future trend is likely to be. In 2000, online retail accounted for only 0.9 percent of all U.S. online retail sales, and experts would opine that online was a niche retail channel and posed no threat to a traditional brick-and-mortar retailer. Over the next several years, all the paradigm shifts had occurred, and by the end of 2018, fully 10 percent of U.S. retail sales (Figure 2.1) were online.[15]

What are the future trends? Projecting the current growth rate of about 1 percent per year, we expect that 25 percent or fully one-fourth of all U.S. retail sales will be online by 2033. What does this mean for the fulfillment machine? It must more than double and possibly triple in capacity in the next 15 years. Manufacturers must strategically plan and execute a shift of their supply chains from a retailer to a direct online focus.

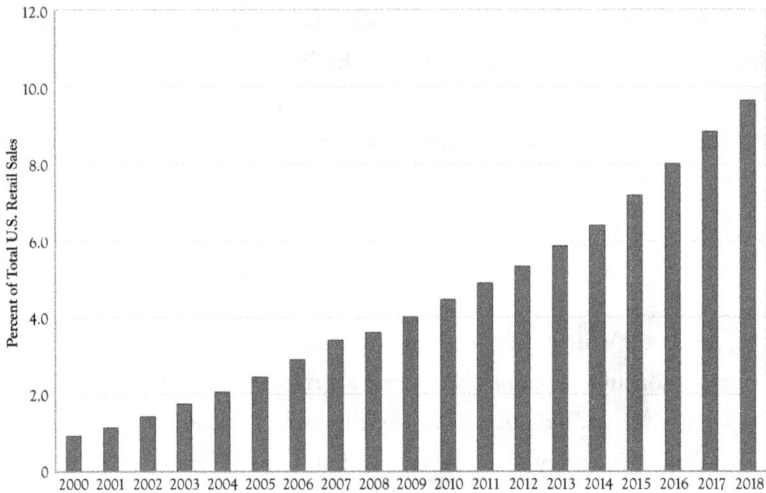

Figure 2.1 Online retail sales as a percent of annual U.S. retail sales

Next, let's investigate the revenue data for Amazon and investigate how it relates to the paradigms. Currently, Amazon reports sales in five categories: Online retail store; Physical stores (e.g., Whole Foods); Third-party seller services; Amazon web services; Subscription fees; and Advertising. Of these, the first two are product sales of Amazon-owned inventory, while the third represents sales of non-Amazon-owned products. It was only after 2010 that these categories were reported separately by Amazon, meaning total retail product sales or gross merchandise value (GMV) before 2010 will have to be estimated from the available data.[16] The third-party seller ratio, which is the share of physical gross merchandise sales sold on Amazon by independent third-party sellers, is reported since 2000. Combining this ratio and the likely historic growth of non-product revenues,[17] we can create a relatively reliable estimate of Amazon's annual GMV product sales since 2000 (Figure 2.2). Why are we focused on this sales number? Because these sales are directly associated with the value throughput of the fulfillment machine.

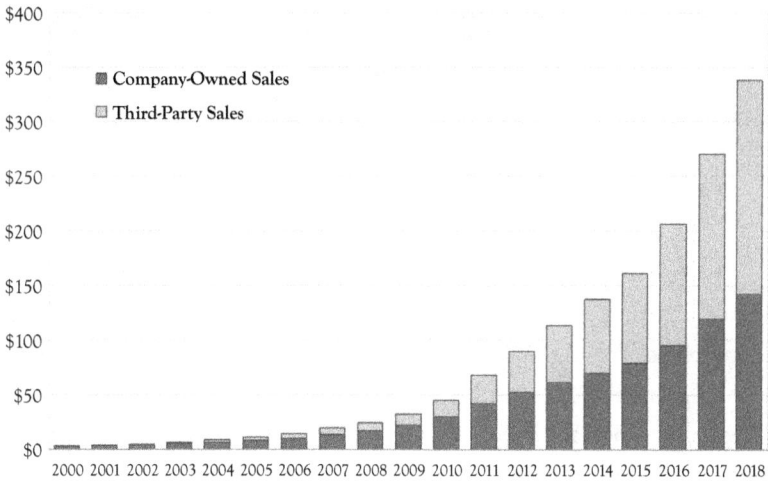

Figure 2.2 *Amazon annual GMV product sales (billions)*[17]

The GMV product sales growth rate is phenomenal with an 80-multiple increase from 2000 to 2018. Splitting the data into five-year snapshots, the annual growth rates were: 30 percent from 2003 to 2008, 36 percent from 2008 to 2013, and 25 percent from 2013 to 2018. Was there a threshold year? I would have to say it is 2005 when online product sales crossed $10 billion. At that point, the existing U.S. parcel fulfillment infrastructure was close to capacity, and future growth would have to be processed through a new fulfillment machine. Not surprisingly, the five-year period 2008–2013 has the highest growth rate, it's the period immediately following the launch of the iPhone, a product that accelerated the digitization of retail.

An interesting and significant trend in the sales data is the rapid growth in third-party sales, rising from 3 percent in 2000 to 58 percent in 2018. The data validate the online supply chain subscription paradigm. Many small- and medium-sized manufacturers were able to use Amazon's fulfillment machine to quickly and efficiently serve a world of online shoppers. Jeff Bezos opened his 2018 letter to shareholder[18] with a direct reference to this new fulfillment channel.

Third-party sellers are kicking our first party butt. Badly. The annual growth rate for our first-party business (1999 to 2018) is 25%. But in that same time, third-party sales have an annual growth rate of 52%. We helped independent sellers compete against our first-party business by investing in and offering them the very best selling tools we could imagine and build. There are many such tools, including tools that help sellers manage inventory, process payments, track shipments, create reports, and sell across borders.

—Jeff Bezos, 2018 Amazon Shareholder Letter[18]

The year 2014 was a pivotal year for the Amazon fulfillment machine, for the first time more than half the GMV product flow was from third-party sellers. Paradigm #8, supply chain subscription, was now rapidly changing the retailing world. Validation is a key step in data analysis, but an equally important step is to question whether any data segments are missing, else one could end up with conclusions from only a partial picture. If one had looked only at Amazon's company-owned product sales, the size and growth of the fulfillment machine would have been greatly underestimated.

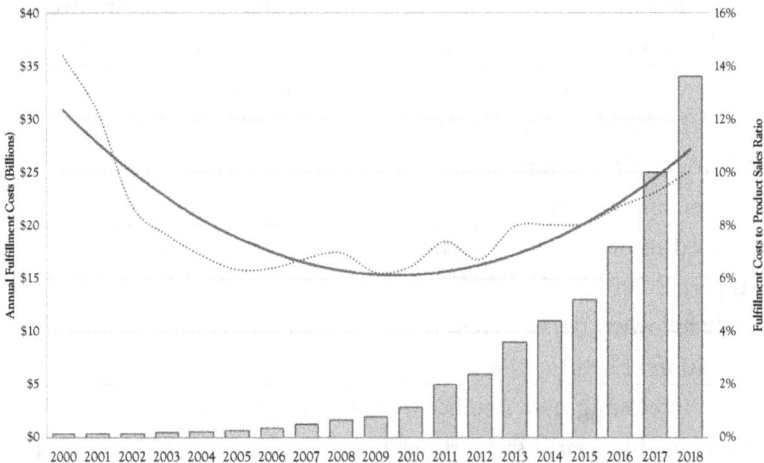

Figure 2.3 Amazon annual fulfillment costs

Building and operating the fulfillment machine are expensive, and the capital investments require a long-term view. The point-of-use delivery and free shipping paradigms require a cost-efficient fulfillment system that extends all the way to the customer address. Without cost efficiency, free shipping would be just a short term and ultimately suicidal business strategy. Figure 2.3 reviews Amazon's annual fulfillment costs over the past 18 years[19] and confirms the scale of the fulfillment machine and its progressive growth over the years. From 2000 to 2005, Amazon was building the first version of the fulfillment machine, and the fulfillment cost to GMV product sales ratio decreases from 14 percent to about 6 percent. The machine that changed retailing had a coming-out party, and Prime membership with free shipping was launched in 2005. For the next five years, the ratio remains relatively flat, but since 2010 it has been rising and in 2018 it hit 10 percent. Why this increase? Very likely the online shopping paradigm is growing faster than the fulfillment machine is evolving. Expect to see even more capital investments from Amazon, UPS, and the Walmarts of the world as they expand their fulfillment infrastructure to meet the continued growth of paradigm #1, online shopping. One view of the changing retail landscape classified retailers on an information and fulfillment matrix, four quadrants were proposed[3]: traditional, pure online, shopping and delivery hybrid, and online retail plus showrooms. Progressively, we would see a blending of these quadrants as the stronger retailers expanded into other quadrants.

The last data we want to review are the current state of online retail, and a snapshot view is provided by the top 10 online retailers in the United States for 2020 (Figure 2.4). The data provide several takeaways. (i) The fulfillment machine is dominant; in a remarkable statistic, we find that after two decades of online shopping one company still accounts for close to 40 percent of all online sales. (ii) A few brick-and-mortar retailers are putting up a good fight and have successfully pivoted their growth strategy to online retail, and are making significant capital and talent investments to build a fulfillment machine. (iii) The new era pure online retailers are growing fast and starting to enter the top 10. In 2018, we saw only Wayfair, the online furniture innovator, break the top 10 but others such as Etsy and Chewy are growing fast. (iv) Manufacturers or brand owners are building out their Omni channel supply and see fast online growth, both LBrands and Nike are in the top 25.

Percent of Total Online Sales 2020

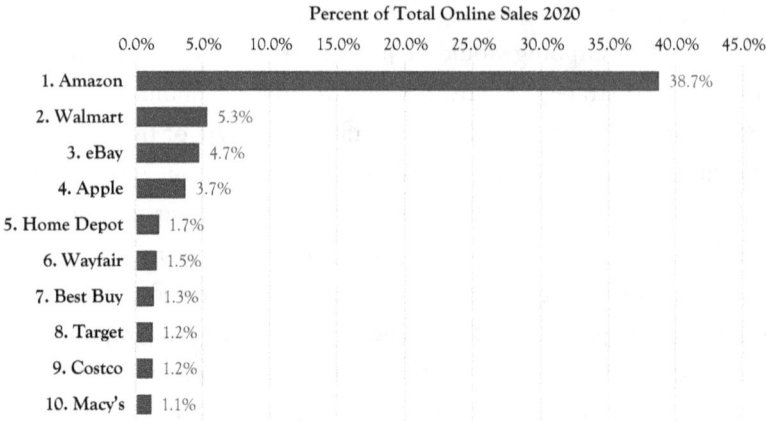

Figure 2.4 Top 10 U.S. companies' online product sales

Source: eMarketer, February 2020

Four Phases of Online Retail Fulfillment

Starting from 1995 and continuing through today, four phases in the evolution of online retail are identifiable (Figure 2.5). Here, we are less concerned with the sell- or consumer side of online retail, and more on the delivery or fulfillment side. In each phase, the innovations and transitions in the fulfillment machine are distinguishable.

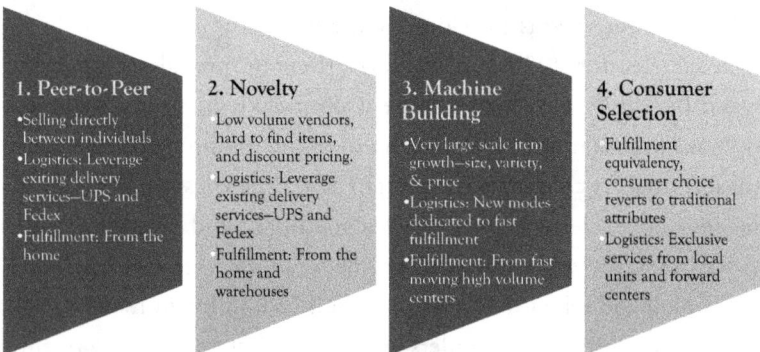

1. Peer-to-Peer	2. Novelty	3. Machine Building	4. Consumer Selection
•Selling directly between individuals •Logistics: Leverage exiting delivery services—UPS and Fedex •Fulfillment: From the home	Low volume vendors, hard to find items, and discount pricing. Logistics: Leverage existing delivery services—UPS and Fedex Fulfillment: From the home and warehouses	•Very large scale item growth–size, variety, & price •Logistics: New modes dedicated to fast fulfillment •Fulfillment: From fast moving high volume centers	Fulfillment equivalency, consumer choice reverts to traditional attributes Logistics: Exclusive services from local units and forward centers

Figure 2.5 Four phases of online retail fulfillment

Peer-to-Peer (1995 to 1998): The first significant online retailer is eBay, but it did not offer a curated catalog from which buyers could select merchandise. Legend has it that founder Pierre Omidyar created eBay to sell a collection of Pez candy dispensers. In the process, he created a peer-to-peer retail platform or a direct buyer-to-seller network. This innovation has been critical to the growth of e-commerce and is the principle on which many online retailers operate even today. Some key features of the peer-to-peer phase are as follows: (i) The retailer maintained no inventory, rather inventory was distributed throughout the buyer–seller network, it was an inventory blockchain long before Bitcoin. (ii) Product pricing was elastic, and a key function of the retailer was to match buyers and sellers and negotiate a price consensus, it was an online NYSE trading floor. (iii) Buyers and sellers were unknown to each other, and consequently, the transactional certainty was low. The retailer served as a guarantor or arbitrator and would resolve any product delivery or payment issue. This was a critical catalyst for the early growth of online retail.

There were a few fulfillment innovations during this phase. Transaction volumes were relatively small and offered no economies of scale. Buyers were in no hurry and speed was not essential. Most sellers were shipping products from their homes, and the existing parcel delivery infrastructure was sufficient. The one exception was Dell, which recognized early on the online shopping shift and effectively transitioned its mail-order fulfillment process for online orders.

Novelty (1999 to 2002): Profitability in-store retail is a function of scale, and this has been a key driver in the successful growth of big-box retail. A key store metric was revenues per square foot, and products with low or scattered demand were usually taken off the shelves. This constraint disappeared in online retailing, the world was your market, and products with scattered demand could be aggregated to a single fulfillment center. The original motivation for Amazon was to sell those low-volume books that were not available at Borders or Barnes & Noble. Innovation was on steroids and several start-up companies were created, many of these focused on some novelty product category. Overstock, Razorfish, Home-Grocer, Webvan, Zappos, and Pets are just some of the names.

Online sales were increasing rapidly during this phase, but the lack of a fulfillment machine meant costs were rising quickly. Unfortunately, the innovation did not cross over to the delivery side and the fulfillment strategy was simply to use traditional mail-order style warehouses. Investor capital was used to subsidize fulfillment costs, and for many of the online retailers, this solution was not sustainable. Financial challenges would force many of the start-ups to either close or be acquired. One of the prophecies of online retail was prices would be lower, and this phase proved it to be incorrect. The savings from not having physical stores were quickly absorbed by fulfillment costs. Convenience rather than price emerged as the key motivator of online shopping. Online retailers needed a low-cost fulfillment machine to grow and sustain the business. The process had already started at Amazon and its first two fulfillment centers were built in 1997.[9]

Machine Building (2003 to 2012): By 2003, online retail was on a secular growth trend and Amazon had over $5 billion in annual sales. The customer pivot function was sensitive to four factors: (i) Availability, (ii) selection, (iii) delivery speed, and (iv) reliability, all four were improving progressively and buyers were pivoting from physical stores to online stores. This was the golden period of fast fulfillment, the need was clearly defined, performance targets were specified, and the technology was available. I don't know whether the big box store retailers were aware of what was evolving, or they simply chose to ignore what was happening, but during this decade Amazon was earnestly and quietly building the fulfillment machine. Teams of brilliant innovators were designing and building order processing systems, fulfillment warehouses, transportation modes, and vendor partnerships—all of which were not modifications of existing infrastructure, but new designs focused exclusively on the online customer. There was a very large-scale expansion in the number of available items, and paradigm #6—The warehouse is the store—was becoming a reality. Online customers were excited and demanding more choices, and paradigm #5—Variety multiplication—the fulfillment machine had to build speed, size, and intelligence simultaneously.

By the end of this decade, Amazon would operate over 80 fast-moving high-volume fulfillment centers in the United States, with more than 75 million square feet of warehouse space. An additional 120 centers would operate in the rest of the world. The machine was constantly evolving, and the fulfillment centers would be labeled as generation 1, 2, 3, and so on. The innovation never stops and the eighth generation was introduced in 2014 and the ninth generation is currently being built.[21] During the same period, Walmart also expanded its online business, but orders were fulfilled from either store inventory or its general merchandise distribution centers. Walmart would open its first 100 percent online order fulfillment center in 2013, but it has been investing heavily in building out its fulfilment machine and in 2020 there are 25 such facilities.[22]

Consumer Selection (2013 to 2022): In 2013, online sales were close to 6 percent of U.S. retail sales and growing at a rate of 1 percent. In this current phase, not all the sales growth is from pivoting customers, a good portion of it is coming from an expanding selection of items. Consumer buying experts will tell you that that ease of search, ordering convenience, and price efficiency are changing the why and how we buy things. The fulfillment machine had made this transition seem easy and seamless. The expanding selection was driven by many small- to medium-sized product manufacturers and distributors setting up online stores. Paradigm #8—Supply Chain Subscription—let them focus on product innovation and let the machine builders take care of the fulfillment side of the business. Consider Jumia the largest online retailer in Africa, which is close to a pure fulfillment machine with 90 percent of its sales coming from third-party sellers. The fulfilled by paradigm is rapidly enabled by the machine. Both Amazon and Alibaba let small vendors sell and fulfill their online orders through their warehouses. Additionally, large manufacturers could bypass brick-and-mortar retailers. Price democracy was prevalent, and consumers gravitated to the lowest price. Margin redistribution was occurring rapidly.

During this phase, the fulfillment machine would sort of hit a speed limit, two-hour delivery. By 2016, it was offering two-hour delivery service for selected products in several U.S. cities. By 2018, Amazon would offer free same-day delivery for over three million items on qualifying orders over $35. Several crowdsourced delivery companies would also offer a similar service in partnership with large retailers; in this case, orders were fulfilled from store inventory. Fulfillment time equivalency, between online and physical store purchases, would have been achieved. Equivalency implied the inherent advantage of a physical store would be greatly diminished, and the fulfillment machine war between Amazon and Walmart would accelerate. In May 2019, Amazon announced plans to invest another $1 billion to expand the number of products with free one-day shipping. A few days later, Walmart announced next-day delivery on a wide range of general merchandise. Interestingly, we see the physical store retailers developing an alternate fulfillment machine, the strategy would be to use store-located or forward-positioned inventory. Buy online and pick up from stores becomes the retail mantra of physical retail chains. In the end, it will be speed and costs that will determine the winner.

Successful Machine Building

We all want to build an innovative machine that then creates an efficient business and commercially successful business. Later in Chapter 5, we will discuss different types of innovation and how they differentiate businesses. In an Internet-driven world, the business will design-build one or more disruptive innovations and these will drive the business to success. I summarize four traits a machine building team must acquire to ensure success. For each trait, I identify questions the team should ask itself before starting their machine building project. The answers will determine whether the team is ready.

Prerequisite: College courses frequently have prerequisites; these ensure that a student is well prepared for the course and reduces the risk of failure. Most machines are a complex manifestation of one or more ideas, and integrate several hardware and software components. This inherent complexity can quickly bog down an innovative idea. Why? Lack of contextual knowledge and experience. Successful innovation teams must meet the prerequisites: process knowledge, performance pivots, customer excitement, and technology trends, what is the competition, and likely capital and resources needs. A key role of venture capitalists is to check whether the team has the prerequisites, and if needed add people to close the gap.

> *The prefrontal cortex develops the ability to better communicate with other parts of the brain so that all areas of the brain can be included in complex processes such as planning and problem solving. The term that psychologists use for this sort of neurological maturity is an executive function. Executive function is simply the ability to see ahead and plan effectively, to connect actions to possible consequences, to see the probabilities of risk and reward.*
>
> —Rick Kalgaard, in Late Bloomers[23]

Executive function is a critical prerequisite for machine building; it separates the winners from the losers. Business machines involve many dynamic trends that can quickly deflate a great idea. The inability to see and operationalize the risk–reward relationship in the idea execution plan is a frequent cause of failure.

Questions to ask—What are the critical to success prerequisites for idea execution? Are these prerequisites sufficiently met by one or more members of the team? Do we have enough executive function ability in the team?

Timeliness: An innovative idea can be too early, too late, or just in time. Many of the early players in online retail did not survive because they were too early. Why? There was insufficient sales volume to sustain the business or the supporting technology and infrastructure were still being developed. Likewise, Walmart and Macy's are innovating too late, building new fulfillment machines to catch-up with Amazon.

> *Why did independent sellers do so much better selling on Amazon than they did on eBay? Of great importance are Fulfillment by Amazon and the Prime membership program. In combination, these two programs meaningfully improved the customer experience of buying from independent sellers. With the success of these two programs now so well established, it's difficult for most people to fully appreciate today just how radical those two offerings were at the time we launched them. We invested in both programs at significant financial risk and after much internal debate.*
>
> —Jeff Bezos, 2018 Amazon Shareholder Letter[18]

Timeliness is often not binary, rather an innovative idea or business machine is more likely to progressively meet customer needs. As Jeff Bezos describes in his letter to shareholders, the fulfillment machine, the third-party seller community, and the world of online customers all evolved in parallel. Classical economic analysis seeks that instant of timeliness, making it impossible to justify a radical idea with a delayed breakeven point. We all wonder why the plug-in electric vehicle industry was led by Tesla and not one of the large automobile companies with big budgets and deep talent.

Questions to ask—Yes, customers will pivot to the new machine, but are they ready to do it when you are ready? What are the machine-building milestones that relate capability with customer needs? What is the likelihood, and what can we do to reduce the uncertainty, that customer needs and wants will materialize?

Technology Enablers: The evolution of online retail was driven, maybe even pulled, by several technologies (Figure 2.6) that powered how we, and where we, connected with the Internet. None of these were sudden developments and their introduction and availability were widely advertised. Successful machine builders had the innate ability to utilize not only proven technologies but nascent technologies in their designs and solutions. They also had the prerequisites and futuristic insight to project how the technology enablers could be exploited to disrupt a business process, value chain, or entire industries.

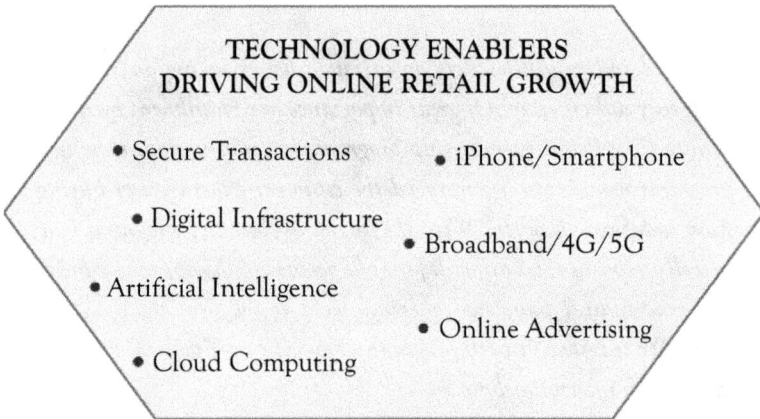

TECHNOLOGY ENABLERS DRIVING ONLINE RETAIL GROWTH

- Secure Transactions
- iPhone/Smartphone
- Digital Infrastructure
- Broadband/4G/5G
- Artificial Intelligence
- Online Advertising
- Cloud Computing

Figure 2.6 Online retail technology enablers

When you are coming up with product ideas such as the iPod, do you try to solve a problem? There are different approaches—sometimes things can irritate you, so you become aware of a problem, which is a very pragmatic approach and the least challenging. What is more difficult is when you are intrigued by an opportunity. That, I think, really exercises the skills of a designer. It's not a problem you're aware of, nobody has articulated a need. But you start asking questions, what if we do this, combine it with that, would that be useful? This creates opportunities that could replace entire categories of device, rather than

tactically responding to an individual problem. That's the real chal-lenge, and that's what is exciting. We don't do focus groups—that is the job of the designer. It's unfair to ask people who don't have a sense of the opportunities of tomorrow from the context of today to design
— Sir Jonathon Ives, Chief Design Officer at Apple[24]

While it may seem many online retailing innovations were accidental, the reality is that many innovators saw, planned, and executed their strat-egies in anticipation of these technologies. The value of these technologies is often not obvious to the final users. Forward-looking innovators, such as the designers at Apple, imagined how existing and upcoming technol-ogies would enable new business machines that added exciting value for customers and employees.

Questions to ask—What technologies and infrastructure do you need to support the market release of the machine and are they readily avail-able? What value opportunities will the machine create from the current and future technology enablers?

Long View: It is often mistakenly assumed that a Eureka moment occurs when you have an instant revelation, idea, or success. Rather, it usually denotes the culmination of long ideation, development, and ana-lytical process. The machine-building highway is littered with ideas that ran out of capital, talent, and customers. There was no eureka moment for these innovators. When management, investors, or the builders them-selves have a short view then the build process is handicapped from the get-go. The basic premise that increased levels of resources will result in faster project completion and success is not universally true. Sure, if you are constructing a residential tower or building a bridge, this assumption holds. But many business machine ideas are dependent on external evolu-tions that are outside the builder's control.

I think what Mr. Buffett realized in 1969 is that being a long-term investor with short-dated capital is just ultimately going to lead to a bad outcome at some point in time.
— Bill Ackman, CEO Pershing Square Capital, commenting on Warren Buffett's transition from managing a hedge fund to running a publicly-traded company—April 2019, 13-D Active-Passive Investor Summit[25]

Ackman's comments hold true in building the fulfillment machine. Paradigm #1—online shopping, provided a natural impetus for quick revenue growth, allowing many early online retailing innovators to succeed easily. In many cases, their backers (venture capitalists) were holding short-dated capital, and investments were directed to immediate and visible success. Little-to-no innovation talent or investment capital was directed to fulfillment; the assumption was that it's a commodity service provided by the brown truck guys. In stark contrast, Amazon starts building the fulfillment machine within a few years of its start. Later, many naysayers accused Amazon of subsiding delivery costs with investment capital! The instructive take way from a review of the online retailing evolution: *machine building requires a long-term view supported by long-term capital and acceptance of short-term deficits.*

Questions to ask—What is the time series value profile of the idea, that is, revenue and profitability projections? How long is long, when will investors, management, and/or the team lose patience or when will we run out of capital? How short is long, when will an innovative idea just become another idea?

I am always intrigued by the profiles of serial entrepreneurs or serial innovators. How is it that the same person is involved in multiple business successes, while so many other smart, and possibly smarter people, have failed to design-build their single idea? I suspect these serial geniuses were gifted with the foresight to plan for the four traits. They would put together a good team, build the four traits, and then gestate the idea successfully through an innovation process.

Chapter Summary

- Reviews how data and technology were used by several successful innovator-led companies to facilitate and validate the paradigm shifts listed in Chapter 1.
- Investigates the growth of Amazon with an in-depth analysis of GMV product sales and the third-party seller ratio. The importance of fulfillment as a subscription is highlighted and the enormous value to small sellers becomes apparent.

- Building and operating the fulfillment machine are expensive, and the capital investments require a long-term view. Analysis of Amazon fulfillment costs reveals that the fulfillment cost to GMV product sales ratio decreased from a high of 12 percent (2000) to 6 percent (2009) but has been increasing since and was back to 11 percent (2018). The point of use delivery and free shipping paradigms cost money, and businesses need to be ready for big investments as the start machine building.
- The innovations and transitions in the four phases of fulfillment machine evolution are identified and discussed.
- Four team traits for successful machine building are proposed. For each trait, prerequisite self-check questions are presented.

CHAPTER 3

Speed—The Necessary Condition

Explains why speed is the dominant process flow objective, and why fast fulfillment is the key to success in online retail. The dominance of Amazon is driven by an early and total business obsession with process speed. Models the relationship between fulfillment time and the point where customers pivot to online buying. Analyze fulfillment friction and speed bumps and differentiate fulfillment machines based on frequency and immediacy.

Four-day shipping, Two-day shipping, Next day delivery, or Same day delivery*—it's all about speed! How fast do you want it? What will it cost you? Amazon's key strategy for linear growth does not seem to be driven by price or quality, but rather on delivery speed. Why has speed outranked conventional marketing goals and become a necessary condition for online retail success? First, a quick primer on necessary and sufficient conditions. If a sufficient condition is met, then the desired outcome is certain. A high-quality, well-priced, and uniquely branded kitchen utensil on Williams & Sonoma has met the sufficiency condition, and sales success is guaranteed. Conversely, if a necessary condition is not met then we can be certain that the desired outcome will not be met. Without high-quality sales service, a luxury car brand is not going to be successful. Satisfying the necessary condition is not a guarantee of success, but without it, you are just not competitive.

For centuries, shoppers have gone to the store, market, or mall to select, pick, and pay for the product they wanted. The consumer received instant gratification whether they needed it or not. Online retail could not provide instant gratification, and this was the wide moat that protected brick-and-mortar retail, at least that was the conventional wisdom. The oft-repeated cliché—*The Internet is a disruptor*—worries all business executives. Transactional functions and service businesses are most likely to be disrupted and this is self-evident from the plethora of successful new companies in old service business lines. Physical businesses, however, usually involve a core human or machine activity that provides a moat that is more difficult to disrupt. But the moat is not so wide that an innovative disruptor cannot breach it. When innovative disruptions are successful, they commonly follow one of four performance themes: (i) *Time Efficiency*—Activities are done faster or quicker, (ii) *Cost Efficiency*—Fewer or cheaper resources are used, (iii) *Quality Enhancement*—Products satisfy higher levels of customer wants, or (iv) *Provider Expansion*—A larger number of providers entering the market increasing availability and competition. The effect of the disruptor always results in an order of magnitude performance improvement. Long before the Internet, Jiffy Lube disrupted the automobile service industry, providing time-efficient oil changes that untethered consumers from dealerships and auto repair shops. More recently, Warby Parker and Zenni have disrupted the prescription eyeglass business through attractive cost efficiencies. Similarly, Norwegian and Spirit have redefined air travel into a series of itemizable options that are tracked through an online à la carte menu. They have achieved cost efficiency by disaggregating the passenger profile so that everyone uses and pays for exactly what they want. Finally, Airbnb and Uber have disrupted two legacy businesses, hospitality, and taxis, both of which are dependent on capital-intensive physical assets. Through an exponential increase in the number of providers, they radically changed the competitive landscape.

When companies innovate it is important to identify the necessary conditions early on, else you run the risk of a great idea being unsuccessful. Likewise, if the plan is to disrupt an existing business you need to identify the disruption theme. Start-ups frequently identify a disruptor and then pursue it passionately. But not all startups succeed, sometimes because the disruption is not strong enough and sometimes it's because a necessary condition is not satisfied, and together these protect the mature entrenched business. Speed is directly connected to three of the fast fulfillment paradigm shifts: point-of-use delivery, free shipping, and the warehouse is the store. My conclusion is that delivery speed is a necessary condition for online retail, and I make the case in this chapter. Who is the fastest of them all? It's Amazon and that's a key reason why it has attracted so many monogamous shoppers and accounts for 40 percent+ of all U.S. online retail sales.

Convenience Versus Waiting for Delivery

Why do people shop online instead of going to the store? Well, there are many reasons and many studies have come up with ranked lists. A KPMG global survey[26] of online shoppers identifies the top five online (positive) shopping reasons as (i) *Ability to shop anytime*, (ii) *Ability to compare prices*, (iii) *Better prices online*, (iv) *Save time*, and (v) *Not going to the store*. In summary, its convenience that drives consumers to the Web, and if you did an informal survey of friends and family you would come to the same conclusion. The same KPMG study also identifies the top five reasons why shoppers prefer to shop at a store (negative): (i) *See or touch the item*, (ii) *Try on the item*, (iii) *Web image different from reality*, (iv) *Delivery takes too long*, and (v) *High shipping costs*. The first three are inconveniences and detract from the convenience of online shopping. Reasons (iv) and (v) are delivery side issues and both are directly related to fast fulfillment. Slower fulfillment leads to longer customer waiting times, which detracts from the convenience of online shopping. If the delay is sufficiently long, it will completely negate the convenience advantage. All retailers believe their online fulfillment times are fast enough since there is no hard number to compare it with. Consider that Walmart.com introduced free two-day shipping for online orders only in January 2017, a full decade after Amazon.[27] Let's define the *online convenience (OC) coefficient* as the combined effect of the five positive and five negative reasons. When the coefficient is one, customers are strongly attracted to online shopping, conversely when it's zero the attraction is very weak. The OC coefficient will vary by product category and regional markets, but a good marketing survey can reliably estimate the coefficient.

To guess estimate what the delayed gratification or fulfillment time threshold is, I often pose the following question to a fulfillment engineering class: You have the option to buy an iPhone case online or in-store, all variables (price, brand, style, etc.) are the same, then what is the delivery waiting time at which online shopping is no longer an option? The results of this anecdotal survey are shown in Figure 3.1. If the best a retailer can offer is two-day delivery, then they have already lost 24 percent of the market. If a brick-and-mortar retailer provides a seven-day delivery with free shipping they would have no customers, even if they ramped up to four-day delivery, they would still be attractive to only 32 percent of the market.

DELIVERY WAITING TIME	RESPONSES
Next Day (1 Day)	6%
2 Days	18%
3 to 4 Days	44%
5 to 7 Days	32%

Figure 3.1 What is the maximum acceptable fulfillment time?

The convenience of online shopping is counter-balanced by the waiting time delay. When the fulfillment process is slow then the convenience of online shopping is easily lost, this is the relationship we used to build the case for speed or fast fulfillment. Several academic surveys have found that speed or timeliness is a critical performance metric for online shoppers.[28, 29]

Pivoting: In-Store to Online

The study of consumer behavior is an important subject in marketing science and a vast knowledge base exists. Many of these behavior models, though, are challenged by the fast and furious influence of social network marketing and online reviews. The online placement of products has severely disrupted traditional consumer behavior to the point that many customers have completely abandoned their store shopping habits. The study of online shopping is a new facet of consumer behavior, and a wide variety of innovative sell-side tools have been adopted by online retailers. The growth of online retail, though, is driven mainly by consumers switching from a store to an online purchase. Marketers call this channel switching, but a key question is not easily answered: Under what conditions will a customer pivot to online shopping? As the OC coefficient approaches 1, the probability of switching will also approach 1.

Knowing the pivot is critical to business success. Humans are comfortable doing the same thing if it meets their needs and satisfies their expectations. That's why consumer behavior is a science, the behavior is predictable and can be modeled. The behavior is only going to change if there is some compelling reason, for example: meets new needs, meets the needs more efficiently or economically, or increases their satisfaction. Pivot identification is a two-step process. Step 1 is to identify the *Pivot Factor*—something that influences customer behavior or choice. Step 2 is to identify the *Pivot Transfer Function*—a mathematical relationship that defines the pivot probability at various levels of the pivot factor.

Certainly, there are multiple pivot factors in the store to online purchase transition. The proposition here is that fast fulfillment is a critical and necessary pivot factor. What is the basis of this proposition? Many big-box retailers have embraced Omni channel retailing and launched online stores. While they have grown their online sales, the growth rates are nowhere close to that of Amazon. Comparing the online initiatives of these retailers to Amazon, we find that fast fulfillment is an area with a stark difference in invested capital. This leads me to infer that faster fulfillment is a pivoting factor in the online purchase transition.

For Step 2, we hypothesize that the shorter the fulfillment time the higher the likelihood a customer will switch from a physical store purchase to online, assuming equivalent pricing and quality. Fulfillment time represents delayed consumption that can be modeled by a discounted utility function.[30] The discount factor is inversely related to the OC coefficient and measures the consumer's delay inconvenience, such that a larger discount implies more inconvenience, and the consumer may choose a different retail option. The probability of pivoting can then be described by a nonlinear decreasing function of time[31] as illustrated in Figure 3.2. For same-day delivery, this probability is maximized, and this will be less than one since a portion of customers will always demand immediate fulfillment. For an online retailer to be successful, it must therefore offer delivery times close to same-day delivery. This is reflected in Amazon's progressively shorter fulfillment time targets: two-day, next day, and now same-day. Depending on the nature of the product and the associated consumer behavior, the waiting time disadvantage could be steep or shallow. For products with a steep disadvantage curve, such as grocery items, fulfillment must be within a day to ensure retail success.

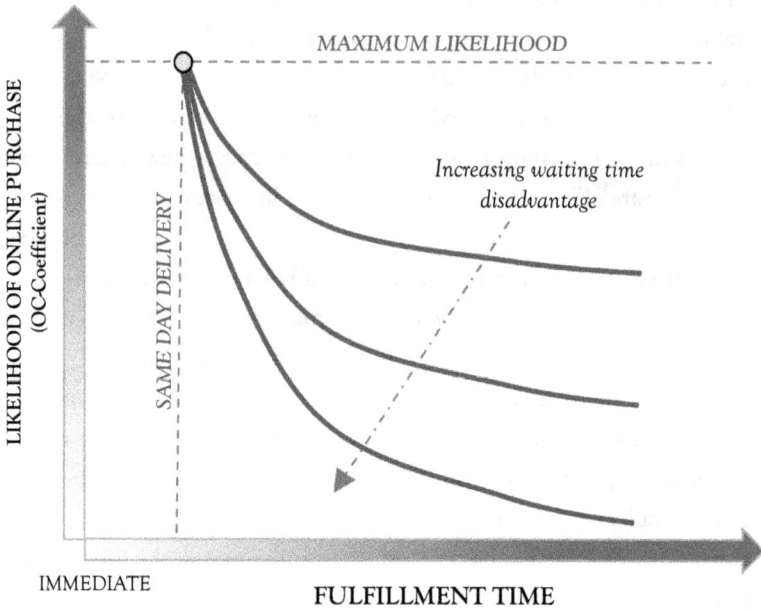

Figure 3.2 Fulfillment time and the probability of pivoting[32]

Many disruptors are using speed to motivate customer pivoting from legacy companies to new upstarts. Consider the mortgage business, which has seen several disruptive companies aggressively grow their business through fast fulfillment.

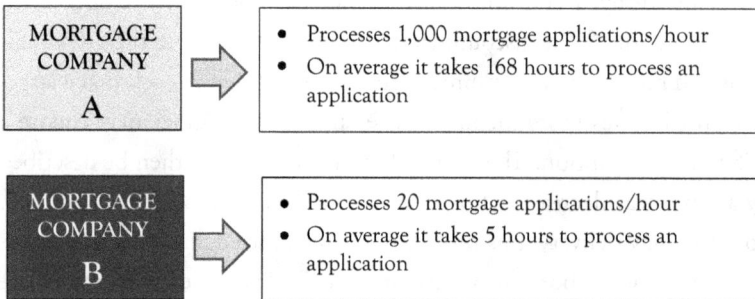

Figure 3.3 Company B is disrupting company A through fast fulfillment

Consider the case of two providers (Figure 3.3), the legacy company A appears, at first glance, to be having an efficient approval process. But the innovative company B, with a much lower application rate, is the fast fulfillment machine. If a faster approval is important to customers, then very quickly they will start pivoting to B. Identifying the correct speed metric is critical in machine building.

Fulfillment Friction and Speed Bumps

Higher process speeds are the critical fast fulfillment challenge. Process mapping is a great tool, when done correctly it tells you what is right and what is wrong in the process. Too often managers know what is right and are busy making the right even better. But what is wrong is often the roadblock that slows down fulfillment speed. Process mapping identifies what is wrong, and this provides disruptive innovators with the seed for accelerating the process. So, let us process map (Figure 3.4) what happens after a customer clicks <SUBMIT ORDER> on a retailer's website.

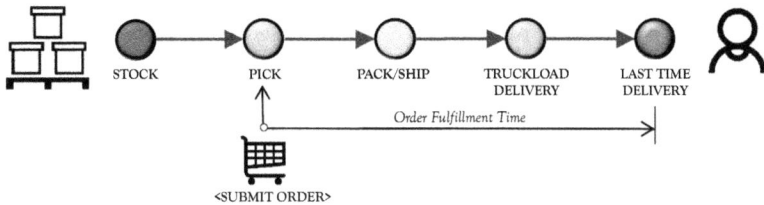

Figure 3.4 Order fulfillment process map

Where and how these functions are executed is what differentiates retailers. Traditional retailers have designed their online fulfillment logistics, around existing stores and warehouses. New and pure online retailers each do fulfillment in their unique ways. In all variations, though, the process is initiated by the receipt of a customer order. Most online retailers will only accept orders if there is a fillable inventory so there is rarely an order stock out. To fulfill a customer's order, the product must be stocked somewhere. The somewhere could be an artist's garage, a retail store, a warehouse, a distribution center, or a fulfillment center.

Process maps can be used to effectively identify wrongs or opportunities, it's just how you look at things. So, we take a positive view and seek out redesign opportunities to improve process speed. There are two classes of such opportunities:

Friction (F)—Slows down the process flow by the insertion of decisions, activities, or uncertainties, which impede the throughput efficiency. Four sources of friction—*Seek lubrication solutions to reduce friction.*

> *Skill Inefficiency:* Workers/Machines not trained or optimized
> *Data Search:* Data needed to complete activity not readily available
> *Process Design:* Requires many steps or lengthy activities
> *Time Waste:* Unnecessary or redundant steps and activities

Speed Bump (SB)—Temporarily stops the process flow by creating a queue or holding stage. The delay time is typically a function of one or more internal or external factors. Four causes of speed bumps—*Seek structural solutions to flatten out the bumps.*

> *Resource Short:* Queue formation due to fully utilized resources
> *Decision Optimize:* Process control delays, waiting for assignment
> *Batch Process:* Processing occurs at fixed intervals or quantities
> *Low Priority:* Waiting for resource attention

Once a customer clicks <SUBMIT ORDER>, then their only concern is fulfillment. How do they measure fulfillment performance? The three top priority metrics are delivery speed, product quality, and delivery reliability. When the products are already known to the customer, then quality is predetermined, and delivery is the only issue. Table 3.1 identifies a range of friction and speedbump causes that would slow down order delivery.

How to generate a similar table for your business. First, bring together a team of people with real, not just a high-altitude view, operational process knowledge. Then a great tool is the *Process Speed Analyzer (PS-Analyzer).* This tool provokes a team of employees to investigate the process and list all friction and speed bump causes. The list then triggers innovation ideas for making the process faster. Finally, the team decides whether to Fix-It: Reengineer the process or Design-Build-It: Build a fresh

Table 3.1 Order fulfillment friction and speed bump causes

No.	Slow cause	Type	Source of slow down
1	Warehouse picker/stocker/robot aisle congestion (F)	Friction	□ Skill Inefficiency □ Data Search □ Process Design ■ Time Waste
2	Long order picking routes (F)	Friction	□ Skill Inefficiency □ Data Search ■ Process Design ■ Time Waste
3	Unknown inventory stocking location (SB)	Friction	□ Skill Inefficiency ■ Data Search □ Process Design □ Time Waste
4	Order is waiting to be processed or picked (SB)	Speed Bump	■ Batch Process ■ Low Priority □ Resource Short □ Decision Optimize
5	Slow mechanized or automated picking (F)	Friction	□ Skill Inefficiency □ Data Search ■ Process Design □ Time Waste
6	Inline unpacking of bulk items (F)	Friction	□ Skill Inefficiency □ Data Search □ Process Design ■ Time Waste
7	Low order accumulation rate (SB)	Speed Bump	■ Batch Process □ Low Priority □ Resource Short □ Decision Optimize
8	Single stocking location (F)	Friction	□ Skill Inefficiency □ Data Search ■ Process Design □ Time Waste
9	Batch co-ordination of delivery players (SB)	Speed Bump	■ Batch Process □ Low Priority □ Resource Short □ Decision Optimize
10	Search and reorder of delivery packages (SB)	Speed Bump	□ Batch Process □ Low Priority □ Resource Short ■ Decision Optimize
11	Store picker processes orders slowly (F)	Friction	■ Skill Inefficiency □ Data Search □ Process Design □ Time Waste
12	Order arrival volatility queue (SB)	Speed Bump	■ Batch Process □ Low Priority □ Resource Short □ Decision Optimize
13	Item consolidation into single order package (SB)	Speed Bump	■ Batch Process □ Low Priority □ Resource Short □ Decision Optimize

new process. Details on how to apply the PS-Analyzer tool are provided in the Appendix.

The PS-Analyzer facilitates digital innovations that leverage the Internet. The Internet enables the *virtual permeation* of the customer throughout a company's physical operations. What does this mean? Status reports and online tracking data provide customers with real-time operational insights into a company's process flows. It's as if they were right there in the manufacturing plant or distribution warehouse, and they can see your strengths and weaknesses. The online customer expects virtual permeation, it's smart in the smartphone, and retailers who block this permeation are likely to see a surge of negative reviews. A fast fulfillment machine cannot hide process frictions or speed bumps. Several days of "Our team is working diligently on your order" messages are easily trumped by the alert "Your order has shipped from our warehouse" arriving a few hours after <SUBMIT ORDER>. The implications are that a slow fulfillment process is obvious to the customer, and they can even tell where the slowdown is.

Who Is Fastest of Them All?

If speed is critical to success in online retailing, then we should expect that Amazon provides faster delivery than all other online retailers. Hard data analytics is the best way to confirm any hypothesis and is more reliable than expert opinions or qualitative surveys. While most online shoppers will tell you, Amazon is the fastest of them all, we could not find any hard data to support this perception. To investigate this question, a team of researchers at the New Jersey Institute of Technology surveyed the fulfillment time for 1,000 different products.[32] For each product, identical orders were placed on Amazon and the online store of a competing brick-and-mortar retailer, including Walmart, Best Buy, Home Depot, Staples, and Barnes & Noble.

The results (Figure 3.5) are stunning, and the speed dominance of Amazon is self-evident, no advanced analytics were needed to confirm who is fastest. Next day delivery is the gold standard of online retail and the pivoting point where consumers are most likely to switch from a brick-and-mortar option to an online option. The study found that Amazon delivered 43 percent of all orders within a day, but for the competing retailers, only 9 percent of orders achieved this standard. The fulfillment time differences may explain why many large and historically successful retailers have struggled to match Amazon's online sales growth. The

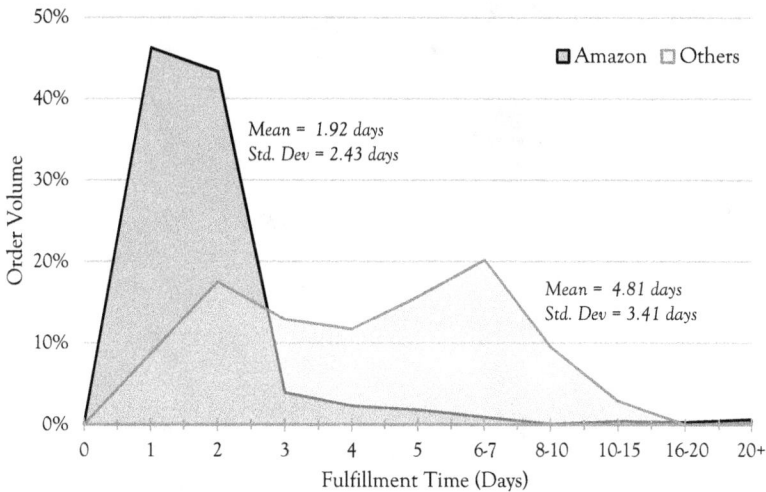

50%

40%

30%

20%

10%

0%

Order Volume

☐ Amazon ☐ Others

Mean = 1.92 days
Std. Dev = 2.43 days

Mean = 4.81 days
Std. Dev = 3.41 days

0   1   2   3   4   5   6-7   8-10   10-15   16-20   20+

Fulfillment Time (Days)

Figure 3.5 *Order fulfillment time of amazon and competitors*[32]

survey was done in 2017, and possibly the gaps are closing but they are wide enough that even the most agile and capital-rich retailers will find it a challenge.

This is a wake-up-call performance metric, and it confirms that fulfillment times are shorter than the pivot time for many customers. The shift from brick-and-mortar to online retail is permanent and secular. Every online retailer should track and benchmark their order fulfillment times in a daily report. A 2015 survey found that 65 percent of online buyers want next day delivery and 24 percent said same-day delivery was important[33], these numbers are only going to increase.

Immediacy and Shopping Frequency

The pivoting fulfillment speed is not the same for all products and we are not suggesting that retailers target next day or same-day delivery for all their product categories. That would be an operational overkill and an economic burden. Two dimensions are in play when trying to identify the target fulfillment speed:

Shopping Frequency—The rate at which an individual customer shops for this product category. The highest frequency products are shopped

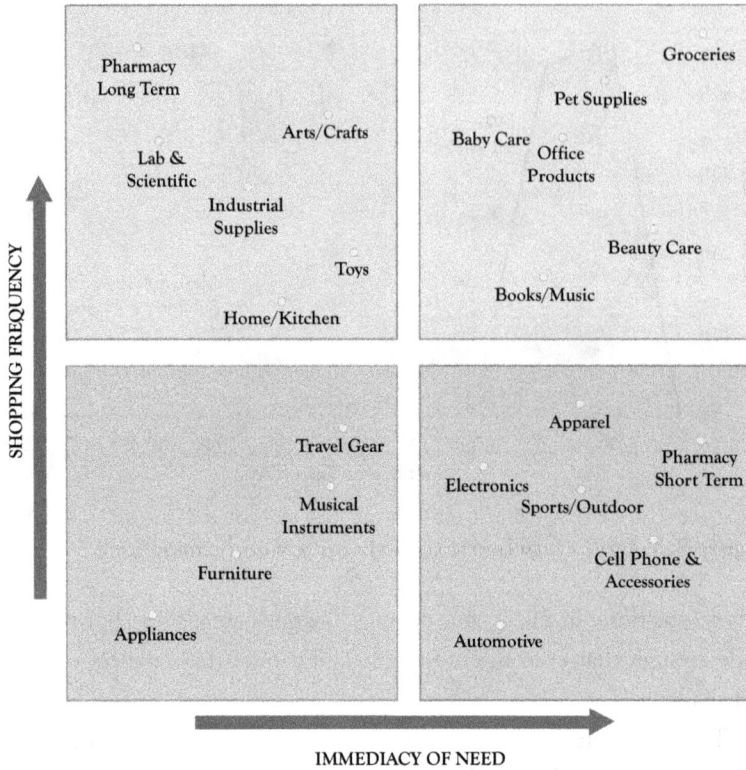

Figure 3.6 Products belong to four online order quadrants

weekly (e.g., groceries), while the lowest frequency products are shopped once every few years (e.g., appliances).

Immediacy—The need or excitement of using the product either now or in the future. The greatest immediacy is when the need is within the same day and decreases as the need is further in the future possibly one or two weeks from now.

Both dimensions are existential to the retailer and dictated by consumer behavior. Products can be categorized into four quadrants (Figure 3.6) as they relate to the two online consumer dimensions. Online sales data for 2017 indicate that the most popular product categories are in quadrants A and B. These are also the quadrants with higher levels of immediacy, and it is not surprising that customers are going to pivot to the retailer with faster fulfillment. Quadrant A includes logistically aggressive products, and these require frequent shipments at the fastest fulfillment speeds. Quadrant D includes logistically passive products and customers order products in long intervals, and are willing to wait long periods for fulfillment. A fulfillment machine delivering quadrant A product is going to be inherently more complex, requiring significant capital investment and the implementation of advanced technologies and operational control methods. Conversely, quadrant D is much simpler and likely not much different from traditional distribution center-based fulfillment. Ikea offers a wide selection of furniture items in its online catalog, and delivery is efficiently completed from its existing logistics operations. The lower level of immediacy implies a higher time pivot that is easily satisfied.

Amazon has fewer offerings in quadrant D, possibly because their fulfillment machine does not provide a competitive advantage in this category. Retailers in quadrant D are more likely to succeed in an online channel, given that both the capital investments and immediacy levels are much lower. Wayfair is the online pioneer in furniture sales[34] and in 2019 accounted for a third of all online furniture sales in the United States.[35] Evolving from a basket of independent retailers, they have cleverly deployed a strategy of combining sell-side innovations with the existing logistics capabilities of furniture suppliers. The longer furniture delivery pivot times were easily satisfied with a little redesign and some investment in these capabilities. To further enhance these capabilities and achieve even faster fulfillment speeds, they launched the CastleGate fulfillment network, allowing suppliers to forward-position their inventory. Quadrant A is the current battlefield in online retail and many players are proactively responding to the fulfillment challenge. The reality, though, is that the weak and undercapitalized players are not going to make it.

The interesting case of prescription medications—Large-scale mail-order pharmacies started in 1980 and Medco was an earlier pioneer, and today is merged into Express Scripts. A core function of these pharmacies is to fill prescriptions, usually long-term or maintenance medications, a quadrant C item. From their onset, the performance driver for these pharmacies was labor and retail space cost savings plus higher dispensing accuracy. Subsequently, pharmacy benefits management became a key driver, and the cost savings came from bulk buying of drugs. Express Scripts operates four pharmacy fulfillment facilities across the United States and each of these fills over 70,000 prescriptions a day. The facilities are highly automated and typically employ less than 400 people. Fulfillment time was never a key metric and the facilities are not explicitly designed with this objective in mind. Today, the industry standard is three to five days for online refills and five to eight days for online renewals.

Certainly, filling and checking a bottle of pills manifests additional risks and complexities, but it is not unreasonable to ask why it cannot be the next-day or two-day delivery. One survey of Medicare patients found that 60 percent of respondents were not fast enough to deliver medications when they needed them right away. In 2016, mail-order pharmacies dispensed only 10 percent of all 30-day equivalent prescriptions in the United States,[36] and in 2015, the number actually declined.[37] Why is it not 50 percent or even 20 percent, I would argue it's because of slow and unreliable fulfillment speed. The interesting part of prescription medications—will an innovative player such as Amazon promise next-day delivery and disrupt the pivoting transfer function? It was bound to happen, and Amazon acquired Pillpack in 2018. One expert predicts that fast fulfillment will disrupt the pharmacy industry and identifies convenience, customer experience, distribution capabilities, and cost efficiencies as the disruption drivers.[38] On a much smaller scale, the startup pharmacy Capsule claims their "fulfillment process is smarter, safer, and nicer." Using a clever inventory positioning strategy and smart analytics, it provides same-day prescription delivery in a few cities.

The even more interesting case of groceries—One of the most enigmatic questions in online retail is: Why did Amazon buy Whole Foods? The pundits have postulated many theories, but the bold move is neither unique nor unusual. In 1988, at the peak of its growth cycle, Walmart also entered the grocery business by opening its hypermarket or super Walmart stores. In 2017, groceries accounted for half of Walmart's U.S. sales. Groceries are at the extreme corner of quadrant A, and the supply chain logistics are the most complex, perishable products, touch-and-feel product selection, and items that are easily damaged during transport. Complicating matters further are the generally low gross margins that characterize the grocery business. The fulfillment costs have to be borne by the grocery chain, service is not a sufficient condition and cost-effective speed is the challenge.

Groceries are the most opportunistic case for online retail. A high frequency activity that has become a chore for millions, it not only has a high convenience coefficient but also the shortest pivot times. Multiple retailers have risen to the challenge and several fulfillment innovations are being deployed.[39] Uber-style designs—freelance shoppers pick and deliver—leverages existing grocery stores requiring no new physical infrastructure only a digital infrastructure (Instacart and Shipt). Grocery store centric design—employee pickers package orders from mini fulfillment centers within the store and/or store shelves, customer delivery via company fleet or Buy Online Pickup in Store (BOPS)—requiring some new physical infrastructure (Peapod, Kroger-ClickList, ShopRite from Home, and Walmart Grocery Delivery). Fulfillment center design—employee pickers pick and prepare packages from warehouse facilities, customer delivery via company fleet or delivery service—requiring considerable new physical infrastructure (Amazon Prime Pantry, FreshDirect, and BlueApron). Each of these has an underlying delivery cost that initially is being underwritten by investment capital. In the final shakeout, the players with the best speed and cost will win. The more interesting part of groceries is that there may be a hybrid solution, busy customers dislike the hassle of grocery shopping but do enjoy the occasional exploration of new and interesting grocery products. Possibly the cocktail of Whole Foods, Amazon Go, and Amazon Pantry is the utopic martini that satisfies all.

Speed Is Amazon's Stealth Weapon

When brick-and-mortar retailers were building their online channels, fulfillment speed was not a priority design objective. Why was that? Online was recognized as a growing channel, and convenience was correctly identified as the primary driver of that growth. Fulfillment speed was not seen as a pivoting enabler or a necessary condition. This, I argue, became Amazon's stealth weapon. Silently they had operationalized the paradigm shifts into a fast fulfillment machine that tilted the pivoting transfer function in their favor. The argument is easily confirmed by comparing

Amazon's fulfillment infrastructure capital investments with that of all other retailers. Till recently, the fulfillment investments of brick-and-mortar retailers were quite limited, and the default option was to pursue a store-based or S-Fulfillment strategy. In contrast, since 2003, Amazon has been focused on speed and this is evident in the operational design of their fulfillment centers and delivery network. The result, when customers were ready to pivot, they pivoted to Amazon 70 percent of the time.

What has been Walmart's response to the need for speed? Only since 2016 has Walmart accelerated its fulfillment infrastructure investment, possibly figuring out the stealth effects of speed on the pivoting transfer function. To their credit, they are putting up a good fight and building up innovation talent at their San Bruno eCommerce facility. Furthermore, using a technology industry strategy, they have been acquiring startups to rapidly build a fast fulfillment machine. Bonobos for apparel fulfillment, Jet.com for fulfillment center operations and online inventory management, and Parcel for their last-mile delivery machine optimized for urban settings. The infusion of Jet.com methods and talent through Walmart's e-commerce operations has been a huge positive.[40] The acquisition strategy is working and should be a model for all other brick-and-mortar retailers. The caveat, acquisition costs are high, and you must abdicate innovation to the acquirees. From its initial missteps, though, Walmart has learned quickly and its teams are highly focused on fast fulfillment. During the pandemic of 2020, their fast fulfillment machine worked wonderfully and Walmart was able to meet the speed and variety needs of a locked down population.

The necessity of fast fulfillment has few exceptions and all retailers, whether Omni channel or purely online, need to be aware of the potential customer loss if they are not fast enough. In March 2018, an iconic retailer that had nurtured generations of Toys R Us kids declared bankruptcy. It had a well-known retail brand, stores that were a fun place to visit, and an inventory of good products, but these did not provide a wide enough moat to keep the online T-Rex at bay. Yes, Toy R Us had a crippling debt burden, but the consensus among the CNBC (Consumer News and Business Channel) experts was unanimous, the slayer was Amazon. They were right, Toys R Us had no online fulfillment strategy and certainly lacked the capital to build a quadrant C machine. In the Darwinian evolution of online retail, the fastest will survive and many early movers couldn't survive simply because they were too slow to overcome the pivot point. The good news is that the strong brick-and-mortar retailers (Walmart, Best Buy, Staples, and Home Depot) are innovating and putting up a good fight against the online infidels. The bad news is that the weak (Macy's, Target) lack the technological, intellectual, and investment capital to innovate a fast fulfillment machine. Later in Chapters 10 and 11, a three-team sequential plan to build a fast fulfillment machine is presented.

Chapter Summary

- Innovative disruptors use the Internet to drain the wide moats, and their strategies pursue four performance themes: (i) Time Efficiency, (ii) Cost Efficiency, (iii) Quality Enhancement, and (iv) Provider Expansion.
- Fulfillment speed and time are introduced as the critical parameter in customer pivoting from in-store to online. Survey data confirm this trend, and we explain why it's Amazon's stealth weapon.
- Process Speed Analyzer (PS-Analyzer) is presented as an effective tool to investigate the fulfillment process and list all friction and speed bump causes. Fulfillment process maps describe what happens after <SUBMIT ORDER>.
- Four product quadrants defined by immediacy and shopping frequency are introduced. Retailers can use these quadrants to determine the optimal fulfillment speed and allocated innovation capital.

CHAPTER 4

Mathematics of Fast Fulfillment

Probability theory explains why old designs cannot achieve fast fulfillment. Design facilities that are mathematically configured to respond quickly to the highly uncertain online demand behavior. Mathematical transfer functions describe the physics or the cause–effect interrelationships of the process. Discover how intelligence-driven design and control can accelerate fulfillment speed.

Mathematical modeling and statistical analysis are a necessary condition for success in the digital economy. Neither of these methods are newly minted and are relatively ancient in the world of management science. Then why the sudden surge in their relevance and popularity? There are many reasons, but two key reasons are, first, the economics and availability of computing power and, second, the ability to immediately advise and execute decisions at the lowest level of control. This makes it possible to build and implement large-scale data-driven analytical models. Realigning business operations to execute the optimal decisions prescribed by these models, then justifies the investment and ensures profitability. The development and application of such models are easiest in industries where there are few physical transactions. A prime example is the financial industry, which has been a pioneer in the use of math-driven models. Consider the growing popularity of Robo-advisers, possibly the most disruptive trend in wealth management. One research article[41] projects a 30-fold increase in Robo-advised assets. Why? The researchers found that mathematical model-driven Robo-advised services could be delivered at much lower costs in comparison with human advisers while generating approximately the same investments return as traditional advisers.

Physical transactions that move a product or move a person require physical resources and, typically, execute at a relatively slower rate. This makes it inherently more difficult to optimize and manage every decision instantly. Technology savvy retailers such as Walmart and Macy's have for many years used mathematical models to control their supply chains, but these are limited in the level of decision control. Probably the most aggressive user of math models has been Zara, and their highly successful fast fashion supply chains are based on high-resolution math models[42]. Fulfillment is a hardcore physical operation and not amenable to high resolution or microcontrol. But to efficiently fulfill millions of packages from millions of stocking locations, there is no choice but microcontrol. The early builders of fast fulfillment machines recognized this and it's apparent in their designs. Our research found that Amazon fulfillment centers are mathematically modeled down to the smallest level of detail. I propose that this is driven by the early adoption of the ROC principle in operations design and control.

ROC principle—Every physical transaction can be Recorded, Optimized, and Controlled—Data-driven algorithms can then decide the what, where, who, and when of every physical transaction.

The Internet and associated technologies make ROC a reality on an unprecedented scale. Every physical transaction business with high flow volumes is being disrupted by the ROC principle. Healthcare, retail, transportation, and construction are just some examples.

Decisions are made either by "finding optimum (computer modeled) solutions for a simplified world (problem)" or by "finding satisfactory (human) solutions for a more realistic world (problem)"
                    —Herbert Simon, Nobel Prize Lecture[43]

Advances in computing technology, and particularly cloud services, have brought the simplified problem closer to the real-world problem. Optimum solutions are now more achievable and necessary than ever before. Furthermore, computerized decision making can be instant and readily integrated into a ROC principle-based process. Math-modeled automatic decision processes are a disruptive necessity in building a fast fulfillment machine.

To process millions of orders every day and deliver them the very next day anywhere in the United States requires a highly engineered and capital-intensive solution—the fulfillment machine. In this chapter, we introduce the basic math of fast fulfillment, and in the following chapters show how it is implemented in building the physical fulfillment machine. Along the way, we explain why old warehouse designs cannot achieve fast fulfillment.

Pickers and Picking

Fast fulfillment warehouses are unique to online retail,[44] with operations occurring in quick succession when an order arrives. Let's look first at the immediate change to the supply chain when customers stop going to the store and start ordering online. When an activity is transferred from the store mode to the online mode, what tasks are immediately transferred from the customer to the retailer's employees? In fulfillment, the obvious answer is picking. In traditional retail, when a customer walked into the store, they picked the item they wanted from the thousands of items stocked in the store. In online retail, the fulfillment center now must do this task, and picking items from stocking locations becomes a core job or activity. The net outcome, a new high-growth low-paying job category was created in the U.S. labor market. The generic job title is *warehouse order picker*, or in Amazonian terms a *fulfillment associate*. You may wonder, what do pickers and picking have to do with the mathematics of fast fulfillment? Picking provides an excellent example of how mathematics and the ROC principle were used by Amazon to design-build an innovative process with no friction or speed bumps.

There are several subclassifications associated with the fulfillment associate position; the four most common ones are:[45]

- *Stocker:* Transfer items from full totes to bin locations as per stocking list
- *Picker:* Transfer items from bins to tote as per picking list
- *Exploder:* Breakup bulk loads into a tote of mixed SKU items
- *Consolidator:* Pack items from multiple totes as per customer order

These jobs are almost exclusively computer directed, and the Amazon job description (Table 4.1) clearly states the employee responsibility is to follow instructions from a web interface. Like most warehouse jobs, there are also significant physical demands. Using mathematics-driven decision models, Amazon first reconfigured the way items were stocked in the warehouse, and second, controlled the movement of fulfillment associates to match the arrival of customer orders.

Table 4.1 Job Description—Amazon fulfillment associate

Job Responsibilities:	Physical Demands:
• Adhere to strict safety and quality standards • Regular attendance and punctuality • *Train in using web interface tools* • *Receive product using a web interface* • Process outbound shipments (pick product, print packing slip and shipping labels, load outbound product to carrier) using the web interface in a limited area • Analyze and determine the root cause of issues • Perform needed cycle counts and/or • Relocate product virtually and physically • In the absence of leadership be able to be self-directed	• Lift and move up to 49 lbs • Lift, bend, and reach above the head • Kneel, squat, and walk for long periods • Engage in full manual dexterity in both hands and wrists • Workaround moving mechanical parts • Noise level varies • Continuous reading or writing

While pickers are not highly paid, they are the largest operational cost of a fulfillment center. Glassdoor estimates the average annual salary of a fulfillment associate at Amazon is $24,000. A typical fulfillment center will have 1,500 associates for an annual payroll of $36 million. This is money spent to do tasks that previously the customer was doing. Certainly, the online retailer saves on the costs of the store associate who stocks the shelves, but this may not be as big as we expect. Fulfillment centers also employ stockers who prepare shelves for picking. An efficient fulfillment center is designed to leverage automation, facility layout, and intelligent algorithms to minimize the number of pickers required to achieve fast fulfillment. Fast fulfillment using an inefficient machine requires a lot more pickers and the costs will ultimately kill the business. In response to Amazon, many brick-and-mortar retailers are advertising two-day delivery. I worry that they don't have an efficient machine and the economics are desperate.

A legacy asset, infrastructure, or system is often not easily, or more likely impossible to reengineer for micro modeling and control. *A common and fatal flaw made by those vested in a successful legacy operation is the assumption that reengineering is the solution.* My advice is that you analytically confirm your assumption once, twice, and thrice before proceeding. Let's investigate the case of a Buy Online Fulfill from Store or BOFS strategy. Whether in a conventional warehouse, a grocery store, or any retail store for that matter, items are stocked in a logical and organized manner. You walk into the Walmart, it is linearly laid out in racks and designed to enhance your shopping experience. You need to pick up exactly 15 items, know the store layout very well and move fast, it will still take you about eight minutes to collect the items. So, if there was a trained order picker working a 10-hour shift, they would only be able to process 75 orders/day, assuming the average order is for 15 items. To process 1,000 orders/day you would need 14 pickers, and to process 10,000 orders/day you would have 140 pickers. These pickers would be running around the store, crashing into customers, and transforming the store into a hybrid store warehouse. If the order size drops to just two items, efficiency is going to decline rapidly, and the costs would increase quickly. It's going to be slow fulfillment and not scalable.

Natural Law Models and Artificial Intelligence

The news media and technology pundits are all abuzz about artificial intelligence (AI) and machine learning. Few of us understand what these phrases mean, but we all know and accept that in the near future they will be critical to the performance excellence and competitive advantage of any company. An elementary 101 definition of AI is "the capability of a machine to imitate intelligent human behavior." An AI machine uses this intelligence to make decisions. The academic view is that AI will be used to make big and complex decisions. But from a business view, AI could be used to make not-so-complex decisions and make them frequently and immediately. A brief article in Forbes[46] provides an informative drill-down of the many AI definitions and speculates on how AI will become more commonplace in business. Highlighting the importance of AI to business, Forbes states that "without AI, Amazon couldn't grow its business, improve its customer experience and selection, and optimize its logistic speed and quality." The thoughts of the Forbes article can be extended into a two-part AI definition as it relates to business processes: *Strong-AI*—hardcore neural modeling with deep machine learning, and *Lite-AI*—get systems to work smartly without necessarily replicating human reasoning. I do not claim to know the advanced AI methods that drive Amazon's fulfillment machine, but certainly, their broad hiring of AI talent and data-driven decision-making experts in their logistics operations confirm the importance of AI.

In the absence of any serious AI expertise in your team or organization, Lite-AI is a more doable option. It can be implemented as a combination of process flowcharting, mathematical modeling, and statistical analysis. In all AI approaches, there is an underlying model that is specifically built for the series of decisions that accompany a process. This model describes the physics, or the cause–effect interrelationships, of the process or system being controlled. In the world of flying, this is called the natural law model and forms the basis of the autopilot that flies a plane with no human intervention. Natural law specifies what is going to happen with certainty. You run a promotional pricing program with an expected demand of 60 to 80 units/day and have a supply process of 62 units/day. The probability you will be unable to fulfill all the orders is 100 percent. You start a biker-based restaurant delivery service with a 50-minute guarantee. It takes the restaurant at least 30 minutes to prepare the order and the farthest points in the delivery area are a 40-minute ride apart. Again, it is a certainty that many orders will miss the service guarantee. Good management, a motivated workforce, or even a forgiving customer base cannot change the natural laws behind your processes and any innovation must model the laws. A natural law model will consist of several submodels, and in engineering, we call these transfer functions. *Google dictionary definition of a transfer function—a mathematical function relating the output or response of a system to the input or stimulus.* In engineering control systems, these functions are exact, but in an AI analysis, we can model them as approximations. A transfer function blends the certainty and uncertainty of the business process and provides the building blocks of Lite-AI.

The people who built the fulfillment machines at Amazon and other companies were mathematical innovators who constructed transfer function models and integrated them with the natural laws of fast fulfillment. Affordable access to computing power enabled the implementation of these models in physical facilities. Almost every decision was data-driven in real time, and their customer promises became a certainty. Going forward, all machine builders must embrace the ROC principle and must assume that every decision in the process is controllable and optimizable. This will allow you to abandon simple machine designs and progress to more complex designs with many more variables. To start building a Lite-AI model, the team needs to investigate and identify the following components of the transfer function in the context of a specific fulfillment activity.

- *Performance Metric*—The outcome you are focused on achieving, or literally, the performance target or goal. It is critical to ensure that the right goal is identified, else you will be efficiently progressing in the wrong direction. Brick-and-mortar retailers building online retail channels, until very recently, never identified fulfillment as a goal. No amount of analysis would have prepared them for the fulfillment machine that just sailed past them.
- *Process Variables (Dependent Inputs)*—Physical and digital attributes of the process that are changing or changeable. These inputs are known determinants of the performance metric, which implies that as they change the process performance changes. Variables should be described at the functional level with as much precision as possible. For example, the daily arrival rate of applications at a mortgage processor would be a process input. A more precise input would be the arrival rate of simple and complex applications.
- *Decisions or Controllable Variables*—Decisions could be either stationary (design) or dynamic (operational) in nature.

Stationary decisions are made occasionally and have a much lower frequency, while dynamic decisions are often real time and have a higher frequency. In a traditional warehouse, the stocking location of an item is fixed and hence a stationary decision. When an order arrives for an item, then we must decide when to pick and fulfill that order. The operational decision is should it be processed first, wait in a first-come first-served queue, or prescribed using some prioritization model. Take a disruptive approach to identify the decisions. Often, we assume something is fixed or cannot be changed, challenge this assumption, and designs with faster speeds will become possible.

• *Performance Transfer Relationships*—This is the guts of the analysis and comprises the intelligence driving the AI solution. The intelligence team projects the steady-state effect of each input on the performance target, this could be either positive or negative. For example, as the order arrival rate at the restaurant increases, then the order wait time will increase. On the other hand, if the restaurant increases the inventory of already prepared menu items, then the fulfillment time will decrease. The effect is measured by the likely percentage increase in the performance metric for a unit/category change if all other variables are fixed.

In the toolbox, you will find the Lite-AI Builder, this can be used to support your efforts to design-build innovative processes with transfer function driven decision making. The main steps in the Lite-AI Builder are: (1) Identify the performance metrics and process variables. Classify the variables as uncontrollable, design decisions, or operational decisions; (2) Describe an approximate performance transfer relationship, by estimating the effect coefficient of each input and the underlying math; (3) Use the model to create a data-driven decision control and optimization model.

Sketched in Figure 4.1 is the performance transfer relationship for creating order picklists in a fulfillment warehouse, and the target performance metric is fulfillment time. Four input variables and three decision variables associated with the activity are identified. The wavy lines are intentional, the relationships individually and in combination are not fixed, but the general trend is known. For each variable, the steady-state effect on fulfillment time is estimated. As the number of pending orders increases, the queue time increases and the fulfillment time increases. Conversely, as the staffing level increases, there are more pickers, and the fulfillment time decreases. Order consolidation is a design decision in that there may be several options, and at certain times of the day, a different method is used. The sketch provides the team with an immediate view of the math behind the decision problem.

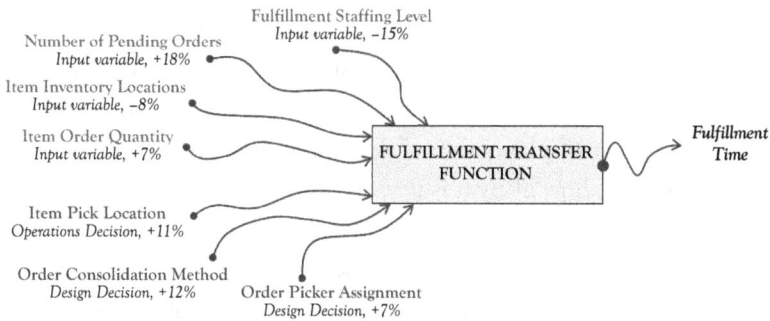

Figure 4.1 Transfer relationship for creating order picklists

Two of the decision variables are operational, which means they are made continuously, possibly hundreds of times a day. These decisions are made in three ways: (i) Human or staff responsibility, (ii) computer-made fixed rule if X do Y, and (iii) data-driven intelligent algorithms. Fulfillment systems involve fast amounts of data and a rapid flow of orders, this implies that options (i) and (ii) are going to make acceptable and even maybe good decisions, but certainly not excellent or optimal decisions. Using the transfer function sketch, development can now build a rule-based or AI-based model to make decisions at every instance. The goal would be to construct a model that prescribes decisions that consistently generate good performance across the spectrum of uncertainty.

For many successful legacy companies, their Enterprise Resource Planning (ERP) systems have become a competitive disadvantage. Why? These ERP systems are very efficient in the storage and retrieval of transactional data and are efficient facilitators of decision-making options

(i) and (ii). But these ERP systems are often too big to turn in the face of fast-flowing data and a swarm of decision problems, and the iceberg of data just slashes through them. Lite-AI models may not be compatible with the business's current IT systems and this is a challenge in fast fulfillment machine building.

Pick Probability the Underlying Math

We already know that in a fast fulfillment process, picking is a high volume and high-cost activity. Analyzing the fast fulfillment transfer function, we conclude that the longer distances a picker needs to walk and the more trips they must make, the longer the fulfillment time. What this means is that the overall warehouse design and the associated decision variables must both, minimize the picker travel distance and also maximize the number of picks per trip. An online store gets N orders in the next 15 minutes, how likely it is that all items in all N orders are stocked within a 20-feet zone. The design decision then is: How should we assign inventory stocking locations so that these ultra-efficient picklists are possible? We quickly discover that the underlying math of the fulfillment transfer relationship is described by probability theory.

Probability explains the likelihood an event or condition will occur in the future. These probabilities can be described in increasing levels of complexity. What's the likelihood we will get an order for 20 purple shirts today? What is the likelihood there is enough inventory in warehouse-A to fulfill this order? Let's call these simple probabilities. Continuous data gathering coupled with statistical analysis, though, makes it possible to answer more complex probability questions. What is the probability we will get an order for 20 purple shirts and 15 green shorts from zip code 07102 between 9 a.m. and 12 noon today? You may wonder why we need to know these complex probabilities. Or what decisions can we make with this expanded intelligence? When Walmart was building its formidable retail supply chain in the 1970s and 1980s, these complex probabilities were irrelevant. The natural law models governing their system had no use for this intelligence. Their intelligence requirements were the monthly data for purple shirts in the Edison, New Jersey store. But a fulfillment machine is looking to achieve high speed, and this requires precise predictions about what may happen in the future. The complex probabilities allow the machine to position itself for the range of likely outcomes.

So how do we use probability theory to design a fulfillment machine? Fast fulfillment requires that an incoming customer order be immediately picked. If picked within the next hour, it can be packaged and shipped with the next few hours. How quickly an item gets picked is a function of how closely it's stocked to an available picker. If the item is stocked in only one location, then we must wait until the picker in that location is free. If several ordered items are waiting for the same picker to be free, then a queue will form and fulfillment will become slower. An Amazon style fast fulfillment machine is designed to stock and disperse items throughout the warehouse.[47] The advantage is that an ordered item is stocked within the immediate proximity of several pickers. An item's proximity to each picker can be described by a probability model, which is a function of the warehouse stocking policy. Amazon understands this problem very well and applies probability theory to all design and operations decisions.

To explain the mathematics of fast fulfillment, consider the simple case of a warehouse with four pickers. Each picker has immediate access to a different corner of the warehouse. The pickers are very busy, and analytics tells us that at any point in time only one of the pickers is available for an immediate pick. The warehouse is organized into racks, and each item can be stocked in one or more locations. Let's consider the transfer function decision variable: stocking layout and the number of stocking locations. Selecting different decisions, we evaluate two different warehouse designs and discover what probability theory tells us about fulfillment speed.

Warehouse #1—Layout design with 16 locations
Racks are arranged to provide 16 stocking locations, and aisles are designed to give each picker fast fulfillment access to four locations (Figure 4.2). For example, the first picker can fulfill any item stocked in locations A, B, C, and D. The number of noncontiguous locations where an item can be stocked is an input design decision. If an item is stocked in A and B, then it's a single contiguous stocking location. Alternatively, if it's stocked in A, G, and L then that would be three noncontiguous locations. Let's

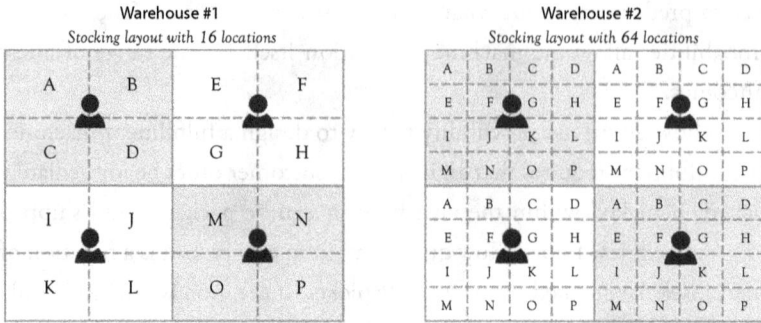

Figure 4.2 Order picking warehouse—Two rack designs

calculate the fast pick probability for a specific item when the next picker is available (Table 4.2). We will assume each location can stock only one item, further, the warehouse limits the number of noncontiguous storage locations for an item.

Table 4.2 Order picking warehouse—Fast fulfillment probability

#1 Stocking layout with 16 locations				#2 Stocking layout with 64 locations			
Items stocked	Number of noncontiguous locations			Items stocked	Number of noncontiguous locations		
	1	2	4		1	2	4
1	1	1	1	1	1	1	1
2	1/2	1	1	2	1/2	1	1
4	1/2	3/4	1	4	1/2	1	1
8	3/8	1/2		8	1/2	3/4	1
16	1/4			16	3/8	5/8	1

When only one item is stocked in the warehouse, then it is in all 16 locations and the fast pick probability is 100 percent. If the decision is to limit storage to one noncontiguous location, then the probability drops with an increasing number of items. For two and four items, it's 50 percent while for 16 items it is 25 percent. How do we increase the fast pick probabilities? One option is to increase the limit on locations. If the decision is to increase to four locations, then for both two and four items stocking the probability jumps to 100 percent.

Warehouse #2—Layout design with 64 locations

A second option to increasing the probabilities is to make a design decision and change the stocking layout. By making each location smaller, the total number of storage locations in the warehouse can be increased (Figure 4.2). In warehouse #2, the racks are redesigned to provide 64 stocking locations, and aisles are designed to give each picker fast fulfillment access to 16 locations. What is the effect of these changes? All the fast fulfillment probabilities increase. When each item can be stocked in four location blocks, then the math shows us that all 16 items have a 100 percent fast pick probability (Table 4.2).

Scaled-up examples

A scale-up of the previous examples shows how design decisions can affect the efficiency of large fulfillment warehouses. Warehouse #3 has the same physical layout as #2, but the design decision is to allow up to 16 stocking locations for each item. The analysis shows that this decision has no performance impact for up to 64 items stocked (Table 4.3). Since the warehouse has only 64 locations, the pick probability for 64 items is bounded at 25 percent. The solution, the team needs to control additional design decisions to increase the fast pick probability beyond this bound.

Table 4.3 Order picking warehouse #3—Fast fulfillment probability

Warehouse #3 Stocking layout with 64 locations					
Items stocked	Number of noncontiguous locations				
	1	2	4	8	16
4	50%	100%	100%	100%	100%
8	50%	75%	100%	100%	100%
32	25%	50%	50%	50%	50%
64	25%	25%	25%	25%	25%

For warehouse #4, two additional variables are changed; first, the stocking layout is redesigned to provide 6,400 smaller capacity stocking locations. Second, the number of pickers is increased to 16, and each picker has fast fulfillment access to 400 locations. To put the underlying math of warehouse #4 to test, the number of stocked items is increased to as many as 1,600.

Table 4.4 Order picking warehouse #4—Fast fulfillment probability

Warehouse #4 Stocking layout with 6,400 locations and 16 pickers					
Items stocked	**Number of noncontiguous locations**				
	1	**2**	**4**	**8**	**16**
64	25%	38%	50%	75%	100%
200	13%	25%	38%	63%	100%
400	13%	19%	31%	56%	100%
800	10%	16%	29%	54%	54%
1600	8%	14%	27%	27%	27%
Each location can stock two different items					
1600	10%	16%	29%	54%	60%

The design decision changes have a dramatic effect on the pick probability (Table 4.4). For up to 400 stocked items and 16 locations, warehouse #4 has a 100 percent fast fulfillment probability. As the warehouse gets busier and more items are stocked, the probability does drop. But the transfer functions provide the design team with operational intelligence to meet the target performance. With eight storage blocks, it is possible to maintain a greater than 50 percent fulfillment probability for up to 800 items. For 1,600 items, the probability is bounded at 27 percent and a new design decision is made. The stocking policy is changed such that two different items can be stocked in the same location. The warehouse is transformed once again, and with 16 storage blocks, a 60 percent probability is achieved for 1,600 items.

Warehouse #4 is structurally and operationally more complex. IT systems will need to keep track of a lot more data and process a lot more instant decisions. When you scale up to 200,000 items and a million locations, the complexity is enormous, but the math still holds, and fast fulfillment is achievable. A traditional warehouse or store just cannot be reconfigured to achieve the same probabilities, and fast fulfillment is not going to be economically or operationally feasible.

Intelligence-Driven Design and Control

Speed is the pivoting enabler in fulfillment, but just a physical redesign is unlikely to achieve the pivot threshold. Intelligence-driven digital innovations are the key to accelerating the process. For a high-volume retailer cataloging tens of thousands of items, speed can quickly become sluggish and orders delayed. Fast fulfillment cannot be achieved through a casual design project, it requires an intelligence-driven project. Any physical operation is a series of transactions involving the movement of goods, processing of orders, and transfer of payments. These transactions could be macro or micro. A store receives 100 units of product and 60 units are then stocked in the designated shelf location, this is a classical macrotransaction. The store manager then uses her market intelligence to move 20 units in front of aisle 6 for the weekend, this would be a microtransaction. Macrotransactions are regularly tracked by enterprise systems and are the core functionality needed to operate a business. Technology, today, increasingly permits managers and systems designers to track and control microtransactions. Zara is a great example of a company that has used microtransactions to build what the New York Times describes as a "mind-spinningly supersonic" supply chain.[48] Store managers provide daily micro feedback on what shoppers like, dislike, or are looking for. This microdata from thousands of stores enter the transfer function models, which then generate product make and supply decisions.

To build a fast fulfillment machine, the team needs to ask which microtransactions are not being recorded. What microtransactions can we create? What microdecisions can we and should we make? Understanding the underlying math coupled with technology provides the platform for intelligence-driven design and control. Every movement in a fulfillment machine is tracked, multiply that with the millions of orders flowing through and you get an estimate of the number of microtransaction and microdecisions made every hour. You just can't make that many decisions in such a short time and optimize a performance metric without a mathematical model. The old principle of keeping it simple is an innovation roadblock. Rather, ask the question why is it so simple?

Chapter Summary

- Mathematical models are a necessary condition for fulfillment success and the ROC principle (Recorded, Optimized, and Controlled) should be applied to every operation. This will generate the needed modeling data.
- Picking is the primary activity transferred from the customer to the retailer and pickers are the largest operational cost of a fulfillment center. Economical fast fulfillment requires innovative warehouse designs that efficiently use the pickers.
- Designers must have an intimate view of the fulfillment operations and understand the natural law models that govern the operations. This knowledge should be used to define transfer function relationships, build optimization models, and integrate artificial intelligence.
- Because of the high degree of uncertainty, probability models are needed to design and analyze the operations. This chapter illustrated how a similar analysis was used to arrange stocking policy in Amazon's fast fulfillment machine.

CHAPTER 5

Innovative Differentiators

The physical Internet-of-Things is driving the development of inno-vative fulfillment machines. Discover how inventive, functional, and process innovations are being developed by the disruptors to create customer value. Use the uncertainty ideation worksheet to push the probability frontier and weaponize the innovation machine. Does your business have an innovation lookout team? Learn how to avoid the Nash equilibrium.

The steam engine, the internal combustion engine, the electric motor, in the evolution of machinery there has always been an inno-vation principle at the core. That core principle is what differentiates the before and after and makes possible the huge productivity gains that follow. In the past, the core innovation was often a mechanical or elec-trical feature. In contemporary times, though, it is more likely to be a redesign of the physical process (hard innovation) the introduction of new information technology-driven decision and control methods (soft innovation), or a combination of both (physio-digital innovation). If you are looking to reinvent or design a new process or system, first model the underlying mathematics, and second identify the hard/soft innovation principles that operationalize your idea. If done correctly, and you are somewhat lucky, your idea will blossom into one of the four disruption performance themes: time efficiency, cost efficiency, quality enhance-ment, and provider expansion.

The fulfillment machine developed by Amazon and others was not accidental or the result of good luck. It was the result of a focused effort to develop a machine that integrated the Internet and other associated tech-nologies. The machine was not built in response to knowing customer wants, rather the machine transformed customer needs, expectations, and dreams. In this chapter, we explore how innovators built this extraordinary machine.

The Physical Internet of Things

We are all familiar with the digital Internet and frequently interact with it through a browser or apps on our laptops or cell phones. The digital Internet has expanded into the Internet of Things (IoT), which Wikipedia describes as the network of physical devices, vehicles, home appliances, and other items embedded with electronics, software, sensors, and actuators, enabling these devices to connect and exchange data and remotely trigger actions. The Nest thermostat, SimpliSafe security monitor, and Ring Doorbell found today in millions of homes are all examples of IoT devices. A few years ago, researchers at <u>Georgia Tech</u>[49] introduced the concept of the physical Internet. So, what is the physical Internet? It is a "global logistics system founded on physical, digital, and operational interconnectivity through encapsulation, interfaces, and protocol." The outcome, it improved by an order of magnitude, the speed by which physical objects are moved through the supply network. Today, the physical Internet is a key enabler of disruptive innovations. The easiest and most effective innovation pathway is to design-build systems that integrate the Internet into your physical flows.

In Chapter 3, we process mapped what happens when a customer clicks <SUBMIT ORDER>, and then identified speed bumps and friction, which slowed down the process. In online retail, the physical Internet starts with that <SUBMIT ORDER> click and ends with the package delivered text. At the center of this process is a *Fulfillment Center—a facility where a digital or online customer order is converted into a physical delivery package.* The physical Internet-driven fulfillment machine is growing rapidly and replacing the large supply chain network, which forms the backbone of the U.S. retail economy. The sell side of online retail does not involve any product movement and is built almost completely on the digital Internet. When retailers adopt Shopify or BigCommerce to create their online stores, they are essentially building their digital Internet infrastructure. The delivery side is the fulfillment machine (Figure 5.1), which includes the physical facilities, transportation equipment, and information technologies needed to move product through the stocking, picking, shipping, and delivery steps.

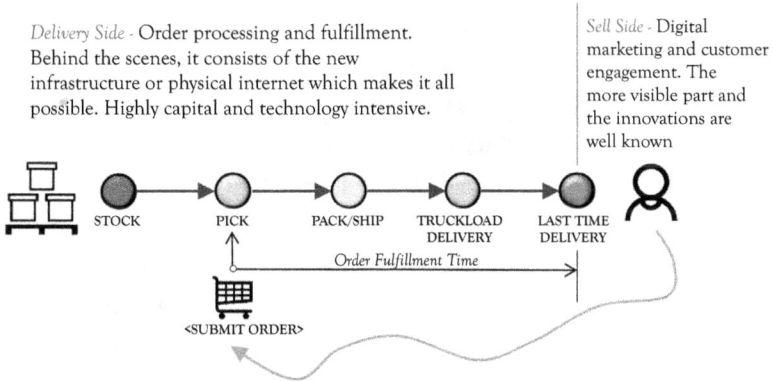

Delivery Side - Order processing and fulfillment. Behind the scenes, it consists of the new infrastructure or physical internet which makes it all possible. Highly capital and technology intensive.

Sell Side - Digital marketing and customer engagement. The more visible part and the innovations are well known

STOCK   PICK   PACK/SHIP   TRUCKLOAD DELIVERY   LAST TIME DELIVERY

Order Fulfillment Time

<SUBMIT ORDER>

Figure 5.1 *Sell side and delivery side of online retail*

It is important to distinguish between a regular physical process and one designed to operate as the physical Internet. A brick-and-mortar retailer may opt to make minor modifications and use their existing stores to satisfy their online business. This would not be an example of the physical Internet, why? The physical Internet must leverage data and communication technology to match the speed, variety, and information accessibility of the digital Internet. None of these capabilities can be achieved simply by fulfilling orders from store shelves. The physical Internet must be designed specifically for the online economy, and I suspect in most businesses the ideal design is radically different from the regular customer comes to the store design. One reason why many large and established companies are being outsmarted by start-ups in the online economy could be traced to a poor or nonexistent physical Internet component. A necessary condition for companies to succeed in the online economy is excellence in both the digital and physical Internet components of their business infrastructure.

Let's consider some examples. A restaurant offers online ordering through GrubHub or UberEats and promises high quality and fast delivery. They assume their existing food preparation processes are good enough for the online business and make little-to-no investment on the physical side. Quality and delivery are both compromised, and the online business sees no growth. Today, few restaurants operate purely in the online delivery model, but it's only a matter of time that innovators will enter this space. Here's another example. Prescription fulfillment is one of the largest industries in the United States and more than four billion prescriptions are filled every year. Several big retailers and mail-order pharmacies have adapted their operations for the online economy. But PillPack a start-up pharmacy disruptor built a physical Internet process that sorts and packs your medications by the dose and then delivers it to your door. In 2018, Amazon acquired PillPack, and on that day the three largest U.S. pharmacies (Walgreens Boots Alliance, CVSHealth, and Rite Aid) together lost 10 percent of their market cap. In response, one of the CEO's commented "the pharmacy world is much more complex than the delivery of certain pills packages," while another CEO said, "We already have the capabilities that PillPack is offering and we have the scale in the business ... we have not seen a large shift of patients that are looking for their medications to be delivered."[50] The orthogonal differences between a physical Internet fulfillment business and a regular delivery business were not obvious to these CEOs. The customer loves the digital Internet and expects or rather demands that the physical business behind the digital wall is equally versatile, making it a necessary condition for success.

Fulfillment—Design Choices

Innovations are most valuable when they are differentiated and disruptive. The base process or platform selected to design-build the machine will limit or expand the innovation boundaries. An online retailer has several different base process options when building their fulfillment machine and the associated operations. The most common options are listed here:

- *Buy Online Pickup in Store (BOPS)*—Picked from store inventory and customer pickup from a store counter.
- *Buy Online Fulfill from Store (BOFS)*—Picked from store inventory and then packed and delivered to the customer. Multiple delivery options: (i) Store vehicle, (ii) National service, (iii) Local parcel delivery, and (iv) Uber delivery.

- *Ship to Store (STS)*—Picked from distribution center inventory and shipped to store as part of scheduled replenishment. Customer pickup from a store counter.
- *Fulfill from Distribution Center (FDC)*—Picked from distribution center inventory and then packed and delivered to the customer by national package service (UPS, FedEx, etc.)
- *Fulfill from Seller/Manufacturer Warehouse (FSM)*—Picked from warehouse inventory and then packed and delivered to the customer by national service (UPS, FedEx, etc.)
- *Order Processed at Fulfillment Center (OFC)*—Picked from FC inventory and then packed and delivered to the customer by national service (UPS, FedEx, etc.) plus forward delivery by retailer fleet.
- *Fulfillment by Amazon/Third Party (FTP)*—Fulfillment through a subscription service, one of the Chapter 1 paradigms. The manufacturer or distributor ships the product to a third-party warehouse and transfers all fulfillment functions to the party.

The first three are S-Fulfillment strategies, in that the retail store (S) is an integral part of the fulfillment process.[51] For a brick-and-mortar retailer, this is a cost-effective and attractive design choice and several have leveraged this strategy.[52] The S-Fulfillment strategies provide an immediate and low-capital solution, but both time and cost efficiency are very likely compromised. If a large pool of pickers is employed at the store you may get a quick pick but will incur high labor costs. Additionally, the logistics costs of moving inventory to the store and stocking it on shelves provide no added value to an online customer. I argue that S-Fulfillment is not sustainable and only a temporary defensive strategy. Then why are so many retailers adopting it? Because when they do a SWOT (strength-weakness-opportunity-threats) analysis, their existing store network appears in the strength quadrant, and the logical inference is that stores provide a competitive advantage relative to a pure online retailer. This is one of the traps of a SWOT analysis, a strength becomes a diversion in the face of disruptive forces. A purely online retailer is not vested in any legacy strengths and unconstrained innovation is readily pursued.

Amazon should be having trouble sleeping at night, I mean, seriously. Amazon same-store sales in the U.S. are now single-digit. Target and Walmart, these big retailers have learned how to leverage their stores' inventory (S-Fulfillment Strategy) to create a better shopping experience. That's where customers are going right now.
                    —Former J.C. Penney CEO Ron Johnson[53]

The previous quote illustrates how easily one can dismiss the innovative differentiators, and even go so far as to assume the innovative champion has been vanquished.

The last three designs, FSM, OFC, and FAM are the base process for most pure online retailers. These are O-Fulfillment strategies, in that they are designed exclusively for processing online (O) orders. OFC describes Amazon's fulfillment machine, while FSM describes a strategy followed by many small and large online retailers including Etsy and Alibaba. Pop-up retailers with no in-house distribution machine, are growing by pursuing an FAM process.

Let's Get Innovative—Swimming in the Shark Tank

Management 101 teaches us that strategic and operational objectives must be perfectly aligned for a company to achieve its business goals. A key strategic objective for any retailer, today, is building an online sales channel. In Chapter 4, we learned that fulfillment time is what motivates customers to switch from brick-and-mortar to online shopping. This implies companies must pursue operational objectives that increase speed through a range of supply chain and logistics innovations. Innovation is orthogonally different from progress or improvement, and one must avoid falling into the "innovative because it is better than before" trap. Here are some definitions to highlight the difference:

Dictionary Definition: Something new or a change made to an existing product, idea, or field.[54]

Experts Definition: Executing an idea that addresses a specific challenge and achieves value for both the company and customer. Where the added value is a huge leap from the present to the future, in that it embraces new concepts and technologies.[55]

The first definition is quite general and almost any incremental change would qualify as innovative. Many retailers, including those that were among the most innovative in the past, implemented what they thought were innovative ideas in response to online retail, only to discover later that they were not. The second definition is from an innovation expert,[55] who surveyed several other experts. The consensus view was there must be a specific challenge that is overcome, and this results in an additional value for either the customer or the company. I have added the second sentence to the expert's definition. The additional value must be an order of magnitude different from the present design or choice. Furthermore, it must integrate new processes and technologies that provide customers with unexpected value.

We all want to get innovative and be part of team innovation, or better still, be presenting our innovations on the popular CNBC show Shark Tank.[56] Successful products or services are usually a combination of several innovations, and the innovators are knowledgeable of the enabling technologies and razor-focused on the customer value or utility. The fast fulfillment machine is no exception, it is an amazing collection of cohesively integrated innovations. In this chapter, we identify several of these innovations, but first, let's understand the three different types of innovation (Figure 5.2). This understanding allows innovators to pursue an effective and efficient strategy that increases the likelihood of success.

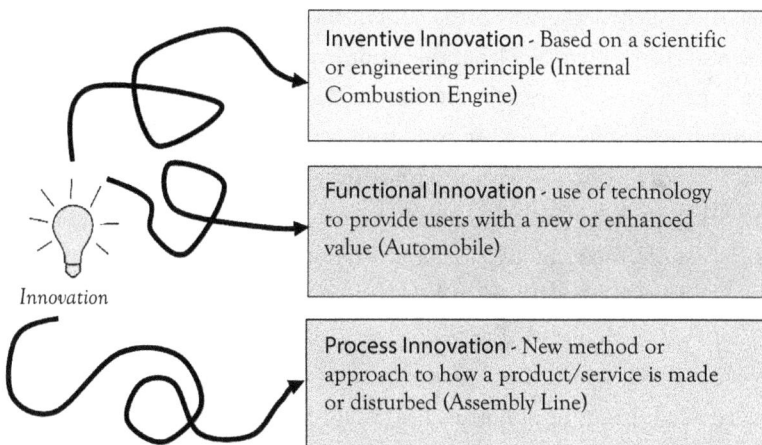

Inventive Innovation - Based on a scientific or engineering principle (Internal Combustion Engine)

Functional Innovation - use of technology to provide users with a new or enhanced value (Automobile)

Innovation

Process Innovation - New method or approach to how a product/service is made or disturbed (Assembly Line)

Figure 5.2 Three innovation-driven value creators

There are three types of innovation-driven value creators. The first, inventive innovation, is Edisonian and typically originates from a scientific or engineering principle. This type of innovation is the intellectual property of the inventor and is often protected by patents or licenses. Many fantastic products are the result of inventive innovations, and a recent example is Keurig the coffee pod machine. One of the innovators was a graduate of my university, and he explained their challenge was to invent the machine that automated the French press coffee-making process. In their case, as in many others, the end goal or target product was clearly defined, and the market value was obvious to the innovation team. The further the end goal is from the current capability, the higher the value creation potential. In the extreme case, it would be a moonshot project. To achieve the end goal, the development team will design a series of inventive innovations that progressively overcome the challenges. It is rarely a single Eureka moment!

Most of us, though, are unlikely to be involved in inventive innovations. Functional and process innovations are more commonplace in a business environment. Functional innovation is a highly valuable activity with potentially immediate benefits. The trick is to identify one or more existing technologies and then apply them to an unmet customer need. If successful, the result will generate new or undiscovered value.

When discussing innovation, start-ups, or venture capital investing, the two words most frequently mentioned are *disintermediation and disruption.* These two words imply that the delivered product or service is not necessarily new or novel, but rather the process by which it is made or distributed. We label this as process innovation, and frequently the innovator will leverage existing technology to either reduce costs, improve user efficiencies, or minimize setup time and effort. It starts with identifying an opportunity to disrupt the current process and then the design-build of an innovative solution. The Internet is the growth hormone of process innovation, and when mixed with cloud computing the opportunities are 10-fold. Almost every existing product/service can be radically redesigned. Every company should position an *Innovation Lookout Team,* whose job is to constantly scan the horizon, looking for unexpected threats or opportunities. Why? Experts tell us that innovative ideas rarely come from those vested in the current product. In the case of

Internet-enabled process innovation, it almost always originates from the outside. Usually, the threats will come from companies that are not on your top-10 competitor list. The innovation lookout team scans the universe of start-ups, researching, and learning from the disintermediators and disruptors. Later in Chapter 11, we discuss the purpose and activities of the lookout team.

The IoT provides numerous examples of product and service process innovations. There is a common theme in these applications. It is physio-digital process innovation—the integration of digital control and cloud computing into the physical devices and associated activities that constitute a product or service process. This integration opens a wide range of opportunities that previously would have been impossible. Let us look at a few physio-digital process innovation examples, all of which originated from start-ups:

- *SimpliSafe*—Traditional home security systems require a high upfront cost, a contractor to estimate and install the system, minimal expansion flexibility, and limited to no remote access. The SimpliSafe system overcomes all these drawbacks. The innovative differentiators include a network of wireless sensors, peel and place sensors, an intelligent and attractive table-top base station, and multiple user controllable functions. A similar innovator is Ring, they disrupted the doorbell! They deserve the Oscar for the least likely to be innovated product.
- *Nest*—Traditional home thermostats (now called nonsmart thermostats) have very basic functionality, only monitor room temperature, a decades old user interface, and an unattractive aesthetic design. The Nest smart learning thermostat launched in 2011 changed the role of the home thermostat. The innovative differentiators include an intelligent module that learned user heating and cooling patterns, an attractive user interface, multiple input data (outside temperature, inside humidity), and WiFi-enabled communication. Honeywell, the leading manufacturer of residential thermostats, launched its competing Lyric product three years later. An *Innovation*

Lookout Team would have alerted them much earlier, possibly getting to market much earlier.

- **Uber**—The taxi business is old, established, and regulated. In every taxi ride, there are two participants, the taxi driver, and the passenger, and both have a long list of what's wrong with the current system. Let's just make a short wish list of passenger wants: short and informed ride availability time, proforma trip cost, anytime anywhere service, and a safe and secure ride. Uber, Lyft, Didi Chuxing (China), and Ola Cabs (India) are ride-sharing companies that fulfill all of these wants. The innovative differentiators include an open pool of drivers, intelligent matching of drivers to riders, real-time arrival times, and demand surge-based ride pricing. It's a fulfillment machine that satisfies rider needs immediately and today is an integral part of the millennial lifestyle. What is the disruptive impact? The declining price of New York City taxi medallion prices is self-explanatory (Figure 5.3).

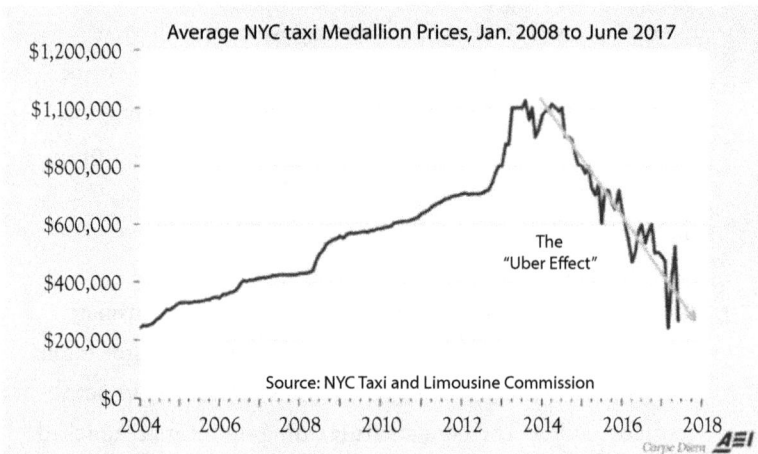

Figure 5.3 New York City taxi medallion prices

Source: Mark Perry at the American Enterprise Institute[57]

Innovations typically start with an idea and then grow from there. But not all ideas are innovative, so you need to do an innovation test. Answer three questions to do a rapid innovation check: What is the unmet challenge being solved? What is the novel value generated? What is the enabling technology? If all three answers pass your benchmark or threshold, you have a winner. How do you get yourself and other colleagues into the innovation mode? As a first step, you should watch at least three episodes of the *CNBC show Shark Tank*.[56] You need to be a swimmer before you can swim with the sharks. Learn from both the innovative entrepreneurs and the sharks.

Six Innovative Differentiators

The previous chapter modeled the fast fulfillment transfer function and we discovered how probability models are being used by the disruptors to describe the input/output relationships that drive performance. How has Amazon used this knowledge to design a fast fulfillment machine? Our research team has been investigating this question and has identified at least six innovative differentiators (IDs) that distinguish their fulfillment operations from that of all other online retailers.[47] Each of these IDs started as an idea, which then collectively grew into the Amazon fulfillment machine. Together the IDs comprise the physical Internet and network of optimized transfer functions that lets an Amazon fulfillment center pick and ship, thousands of online orders every day, within a few hours of <SUBMIT ORDER>.

Go to YouTube and watch a video on Amazon's warehouse operations.[58, 59] This will provide you with an "in the belly of the beast" view of a fulfillment machine. You will likely come away with two visual takeaways. First, it does not seem like a well-organized warehouse. Rather, it more closely resembles a mega-size lost and found department, stuff is just randomly stocked anywhere and everywhere. Second, a sea of yellow totes is moving quickly and deliberately through the warehouse in a fully automated flow. The fast fulfillment IDs we list as follows are fully integrated with what you would have seen in the YouTube videos. All eight fast fulfillment paradigms are affected by these IDs.

- *ID #1—Immediate Fulfillment Objective*—Management 101 teaches us that strategic goals and operational objectives must be perfectly aligned. Fulfillment time, we know from Chapter 1, is a key parameter in the transfer function, which describes customer switching from brick-and-mortar to online retail. Traditional warehousing objectives include higher space utilization and lower labor costs. Sure, the warehouse plans to ship orders as quickly as possible, but it's a secondary objective. The approach is "we will do our best to ship your order as soon as possible." In a fast fulfillment machine, the objectives are inversed, and fulfillment time is the primary objective resulting in that perfect strategic-operational alignment. We found that every physical and digital component is deliberately and purposefully designed to shorten fulfillment time.

Legend has it that the first customer order at Amazon.com arrived on April 3, 1995, and the item ordered was the book *Fluid Concepts and Creative Analogies*. An unconfirmed blogger notes: "The really funny behind-the-scenes part is that the book wasn't on hand when ordered, so rather than disappoint his first customer, Jeff Bezos had to buy and pick up the book from a local bricks-and-mortar bookstore." If true, it tells us that fast fulfillment was objective one on day one.

- *ID #2—Very Large Number of Small Volume Stocking Locations*—The entire warehouse is organized into small storage spaces or bins as opposed to large bulk holding spaces. These bins could be as small as 8" by 8" by 8" deep. There are two common design formats: Stationary Racks—Library style metal bin racks organized into aisles, which are dimensionally optimized for operations efficiency and ergonomics. Moving Racks—Four-sided lightweight bin pods, optimized for easy transport by Kiva robots.[60] Strikingly, common warehousing items such as forklift trucks, wooden pallets, cardboard boxes, and high bay racks are missing from the stocking areas. More than two-thirds of a million square feet warehouse is often set up as a fast pick facility. All stocked items have been stripped of their bulk packaging and ready for immediate fulfillment.

- *ID #3—Explosive Storage Policy*—In my research of Amazon's fulfillment centers, the two IDs that confounded me the most were #3 and #4. It was *what the heck is going on here* moment.

How could these be efficiency catalysts, it just did not make sense. They had completely disrupted the principles of good warehousing practice. After my team investigated the effects on the transfer function and fulfillment probability, though, it all made sense. In a typical warehouse, items are stocked in bulk at a specific location. The organizational benefits are obvious, pickers know exactly where the item is located, multiple orders for the same items can be aggregated and picked at the same time, bulk items are moved efficiently, and cubic space utilization is high. In explosive storage, the incoming bulk is immediately broken into lots of a few units. These exploded lots are then dispersed to bins throughout the warehouse with almost no restriction. The net result, the same item is stored in small quantities in multiple bins simultaneously.

Every time a new bulk quantity for an item is received, the bin assignments are different, implying the inventory storage profile for an item is never the same. It's like every time you walk into the grocery store, the Tide detergent is stocked in a different place. What are the memory implications? Nobody knows where any item is stocked! What are the process productivity implications? Expend a lot of labor time to explode the bulk into lots and convey the lots to all these distant locations?

- *ID #4—Bins with Commingled Items*—This is a radical, if not a crazy, differentiator. Every bin in the warehouse stocks several different items simultaneously. Furthermore, there is no plan or arrangement by which items are stocked in a bin. Figure 5.4 shows a snapshot view of racks in an Amazon fulfillment center, it like the kitchen pantry in many of our homes. Items are just randomly stuffed in the bins. See the Soft Scrub bleach next to the Kellogs Mini-Wheats or the M&Ms next to the string of Mini Lights? Look inside the bins, there is stuff in the back that is not even visible to the picker. I never imagined I would see a million square feet warehouse organized in a sea of randomly stuffed bins. What are the process productivity implications? The picker needs to visually identify each item correctly, else the process slows down. The stocker has no constraints when stuffing a bin, so gets the job done fast and increases space utilization.

Figure 5.4 View of stocked inventory in an amazon fulfillment center

- *ID #5—Short Picking Routes with Single Unit Picks*—We know from Chapter 3 that speed is the necessary condition, while Chapter 4 identified pickers and picking as the core activity. Order picking efficiency is a key decision in warehouse operations, and the picklist decision problem is focused primarily on travel time minimization. In a fulfillment warehouse, most orders are for only a few units and in most cases for only a single unit. A picklist, therefore, retrieves several different items within a short pick zone. This is made possible by the explosive storage policy and beehive storage.
- *ID#6—High Transaction Volumes and Total Digital Control*—The explosive storage and the series of single unit picking actions result in a much higher rate of store/pick movements per unit shipment, and the number of data transactions is also much larger. There is a high level of digital activity control in

the fulfillment warehouse with little decision making being done at the worker level. Almost all movements are modeled and instructed by a central controller. Both stockers and pickers have only short-term visibility, possibly less than 15 minutes, of their next actions.

Many retailers have chosen to build their online order fulfillment facilities by adapting traditional warehousing approaches in combination with current information technologies. Whether this will provide the needed fulfillment speed remains to be seen.[61]

Pushing the Probability Frontier

Innovative differentiators are often of the physio-digital type, and they disrupt the fulfillment process focus by eliminating speed bumps and friction. All businesses experience uncertainty, and the first step in responding to uncertainty is converting it into a probability. A closer look at the Amazon IDs reveals that several of them operationalize the underlying math and associated probabilities of the fast fulfillment transfer function. This allows them to excel in two of the disruption performance metrics, time, and cost efficiency. The FSB analysis in Chapter 3 identified where and how friction and speed bumps slow down the machine. A major source of friction and/or speed bumps is uncertainty—basically, we don't know precisely the what, when, and how of future events. Since the fast fulfillment transfer function inputs are uncertain, the performance outcomes are unpredictable. To consistently achieve high performance, the machine needs to get smart about uncertainty and react immediately to the variance.

In retailing the most common uncertainty is demand, and this reverberates through the supply chain. Specifically, we don't know how many purple shirts we will sell today at the Mall of America store. Will an online order include both a purple shirt and yellow leggings? Can the order be shipped within 24 hours? Speed is a necessary condition for a fulfillment machine, but speed is highly sensitive to uncertainty. Online retail experiences a range of uncertainties all of which adversely affect the fulfillment cost and time efficiency. Machine designers must be fully aware of all the uncertainties. Many retailers have built an online channel with almost no research or understanding of the system uncertainties. Consequently, the resulting designs are often inadequate and likely to underperform.

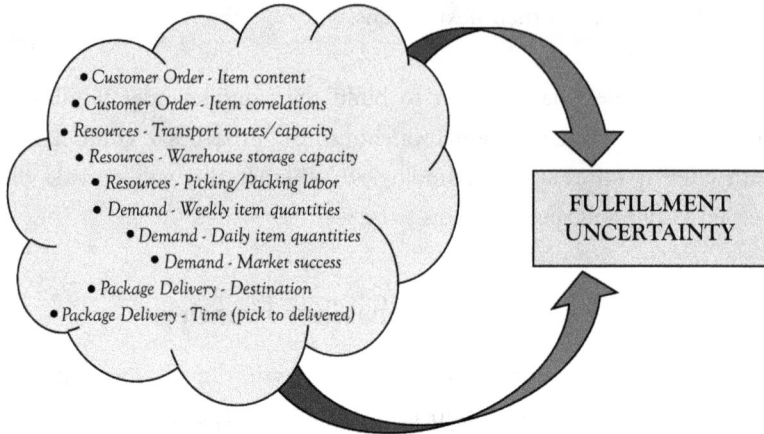

Figure 5.5 Uncertainties effecting order fulfillment time

Figure 5.5 identifies the cloud of uncertainties that overhangs fulfillment performance. A key step in any system design project is to identify and quantify the associated uncertainties. Skip this step, and you are ignoring half the available data and hoping for the best-case scenario. There is a reason why data analytics is a hot subject, it mobilizes event and activity knowledge into robust decision making. Once you do the investigative diligence and have a list of uncertainties that affect your fulfillment process, what next? A key challenge for managers is how to build a system or fulfillment process that responds positively to the uncertainties. There are three general strategies:

1. *Manage the uncertainty*—How? Implement programs or initiatives to dampen the uncertainty. For instance, promotional pricing can be used to normalize sales for a slow-moving item. The retailer offers only a one-week delivery option, ensuring that fulfillment uncertainty is hidden from the customer.

2. *Build a quick response system*—How? Two-part solution, first, create an early warning system that detects a shift. Second, build a response process that is activated and optimizes operations for the detected shift. A hospital emergency room uses analytics to set up

a system that reliably predicts a short-term surge in patient arrivals. From a previously formed roster of nurses, the hospital calls in nurses ensuring care quality is maintained. Zara, famously, built the super-efficient fast-fashion retailer Zara. Demand for fashion products is notoriously uncertain. Zara built both a store-based alert system for popular products and backed it with a network of quick response manufacturing facilities.

3. *Use probability theory to compensate for the uncertainty*—How? Design an uncertainty compensator that effectively neutralizes any speed bumps or process friction created by the uncertainty.

The first is a good strategy but is old school and provides no competitive advantage today. The second works well if you can build a speedy supply chain but is susceptible to uncertainty in the uncertainty. For example, Home Depot will position inventory at the regional warehouses to respond to historical demand uncertainty across stores in the region. But market shifts lead to demand certainty across regions instead, the supply chain then scrambles to reposition the inventory.

The third strategy operationalizes physio-digital innovation into a disruptive advantage. Modern computational methods and decision support capability make this strategy feasible, profitable, and competitive. The science of studying uncertainty is probability theory and we start teaching it in high school. Almost all business organizations use it in some way or the other. The underlying science of many futuristic technologies, including Artificial Intelligence, BlockChain, and Machine Learning is probability theory. Probability theory is a core knowledge in investment analysis and has been successfully used by hedge funds to reap millions of dollars in profits. Correctly forecasting future events and hedging against the outcomes is a lucrative skill. Where did Jeff Bezos work before he started Amazon? It was the fast-growing quantitative hedge fund D.E. Shaw.

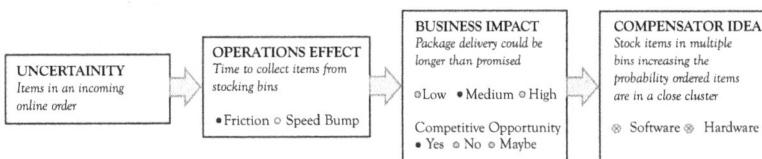

UNCERTAINITY Items in an incoming online order	OPERATIONS EFFECT Time to collect items from stocking bins • Friction ○ Speed Bump	BUSINESS IMPACT Package delivery could be longer than promised ○ Low • Medium ○ High Competitive Opportunity • Yes ○ No ○ Maybe	COMPENSATOR IDEA Stock items in multiple bins increasing the probability ordered items are in a close cluster ⊗ Software ⊗ Hardware

Figure 5.6 Linking uncertainty to a compensator idea

The *Uncertainty Ideation Worksheet* links uncertainty to a compensator idea (Figure 5.6), and lets you integrate probability into the machine building innovation process.

1. First, list the uncertainties that affect your business, followed by quantitative analysis to generate the associated probabilities. This provides an effective seed for the physio-digital innovation process.
2. Second, for each uncertainty identify how it is affecting the business operations. Relates the effects to identifiable friction or speed bumps.
3. Project these effects on the overall impact on the performance goals of the business. The team should identify the impact level, low to high. If an effective response to the uncertainty could lead to a competitive opportunity that should also be highlighted.
4. The ideation worksheet culminates with the generation of compensator ideas.

Compensator Idea: A solution to counter the effect of the uncertainty and consequently mitigate or possibly eliminate the business impact. The solution may or may not directly minimize uncertainty. The solution may involve the design and build of equipment or facilities (hardware) or operational control systems (software).

The end goal of the uncertainty ideation worksheet is to flush out the compensator idea in enough detail, such that the idea is sustainable, and the team can move forward. There are many ways to generate ideas and there is no sure winner way, but here is a possible way. In one of the rare in-depth presentations by an Apple product development engineer[62], the concept of paired design meetings was introduced, a process in which innovators iteratively go through two complementary meetings:

- *Brainstorm meeting*—Leave your hang-ups at the door and go crazy in developing various approaches to solving a specific problem. This meeting involves free thinking with no constraints.
- *Production meeting*—The absolute opposite of the brainstorm meeting, where the aim is to put structure around the crazy ideas and define how to, why, and underlying math.

This is a great approach that drives creativity and infuses discipline. One may flippantly question the utility, but *Hey! It worked for Apple.*

A review of the Amazon IDs demonstrates and validates the application of probability theory in fast fulfillment. The most obvious examples are ID#2 and ID#3. Both IDs would appear crazy to someone vested in traditional supply chain and distribution operations. But the innovators understood information technology allows the fulfillment center to track inventory for every single item in explosive detail. The decision space was expanded 100-fold and required computer control of all operational transactions.

Here is a pizza fulfillment example to confirm the role of probability models in an uncertain environment. Chipotle invented the fast-casual restaurant concept, and since then several innovators have launched similar restaurants with a different food focus. Pizza is a notoriously uncertain business. If the pizzeria offers 10 toppings, the possible combinations are boundless. New York City has many great pizzerias, and they manage uncertainty by aggregating demand to present four to five fresh pie choices. An arriving customer makes a limited option choice for immediate fulfillment. If you are not finicky about your pizza then Sbarro is a good choice, a dozen premade pies are displayed, and freshness is in the eye of the beholder. Visit a Blaze pizzeria[63], enjoy the pizza, and observe the order fulfillment process. There are no slices only thin-style personal pies, which are immediately made on a tortilla press. Your unique set of high-quality toppings are sequentially added, and the pie is rapidly baked in a specialized oven. Probability models control the topping supply inventory ensuring freshness at the ingredient and final product levels. The innovators converted uncertainty into a business opportunity.

Avoid the Nash Equilibrium

Game theory and the Nash equilibrium were famously introduced to all of us by the movie *A Beautiful Mind*. Nobel laureate John Forbes Nash[64] proposed an equilibrium theory that provides a mathematical explanation of the best decisions for a pair of rational competitive players. Widely used in economics, the Nash equilibrium is applied in business marketing to make quantity and pricing decisions in a duopoly. A Nash equilibrium occurs if neither player gains by changing their current strategy, given the other player continues their current strategy. What this means is that the business is not motivated to change its current policy if nothing changes. This equilibrium or status quo can also be used to explain why established companies often do not pursue an obvious innovation strategy or design. For a disruptor, on the other hand, the Nash equilibrium provides an opportunity.

Most existing businesses operate in a competitive environment and they perceive innovation as a competitive strategy as opposed to an opportunity. Let us consider a zero-sum game between two companies A and B, which manufacture the same product and are the dominant market players. They perceive the market sized as fixed, and the objective of the game is simply to steal market share from the other player. Designers at both companies have ideas for an innovative radical new design to replace the current design. Like most innovations, the new design will require significant capital and resource investments.

The payoff matrix is shown in Table 5.1, if either company decides to pursue the new design while assuming the other player does not, then they gain a negative payoff. Why? Considering the capital investment to develop and launch the new design plus the initial loss in market share, a short view will show a net loss. Since neither company has a motivation to pursue the new design, we have a Nash equilibrium, and innovation is

Table 5.1 Zero-sum game between two companies

Player strategy		Company-B	
		Radical new design	Old design
Company-A	Radical new design	0/0	−1/1
	Old design	1/-1	0/0

nipped in the bud. Established companies are thus more inclined to pursue incremental design improvements, where the payoff matrix is more favorable to an economic justification. Now consider a disruptive third player D with zero market share. D is motivated to pursue the innovative new design since any market share gain increases D's payoff. All D needs is capital investments from risk embracing long view financiers. Step in venture capitalists, who are the magic ingredient in disruptive innovation, and they finance D to innovate and build a great company. What happens next? Once D starts growing, the payoff matrix for A and B changes, and then in a follower strategy, they must pursue the new design. Alternatively, either A or B acquires D.

I have no scientific evidence to support this hypothesis, but there is a ton of anecdotal evidence. Venture capitalists use a similar analysis to evaluate the disruptive utility of new ideas. Why was the Dollar Shave Club not an innovation of the large razor companies? Why was the suction loss-free Dyson vacuum cleaner not invented at Hoover? Why did Walmart wait for so many years before making online retail a number one strategy? Why was the high-quality fast casual restaurant concept innovated by Chipotle and not McDonalds? Every time an innovation is sidetracked, ask the question: *Is it a Nash equilibrium trap?*

Chapter Summary

- The chapter explores how innovators built the fulfillment machine and integrated the Internet and associated technologies to achieve speed.
- The fulfillment center is defined and the delivery side activities after <SUBMIT ORDER> are introduced.
- The seven base process options to design-build the fulfillment machine are presented. These are categorized as S-Fulfillment and O-Fulfillment strategies.
- Introduces three innovation-driven value creators and shows how to avoid the "innovative because it is better than before" trap. Introduces the role of the Innovation lookout team.
- The six innovative differentiators (IDs) that distinguish the fast fulfillment operations of Amazon are presented.

The chapter describes how the IDs enable the physical Internet and network of optimized transfer functions driving the machine.

- Explains how the Amazon IDs operationalize the underlying math and associated probabilities of the fast fulfillment transfer function.
- Introduces the Uncertainty Ideation Worksheet, which facilitates the integration of probability into the machine building innovation process.

CHAPTER 6

Last Mile Fulfillment

Every address has unique delivery options, design the process to keep products flowing constantly and with continuous tracking. Understand last mile parcel delivery and the channel options. The effect of density, proximity, and randomness on the delivery transfer function. Discover how crowdsourced delivery is being used as an efficient fast fulfillment option.

The biggest challenge in fast fulfillment is last mile delivery—how do you ship a $10 variety pack of pocket squares to any address in the United States in less than 48 hours with free shipping?—Over several decades, industry giants FedEx and UPS have developed a fantastic parcel delivery machine. FedEx founder Fred Smith's[65] package transfer hub in Memphis, Tennessee, is a legendary innovation in the world of delivery logistics. The fast-flowing transfer hub paved the way for an efficient parcel delivery network that covered the entire United States. Then why is last mile fulfillment a challenge? First, the existing systems were fast but they were not fast enough, and speed we already know, is a necessary condition for success in online retailing. FedEx and UPS were designed and optimized for three- to seven-day parcel delivery, not the next day. Yes, you could send a next day delivery letter, but not a 20-lb. vacuum cleaner. Second, their cost structure was too high for online retail. Remember all those TV commercials with an endnote announcing shipping and handling charges, in effect doubling the cost of an item. The free shipping paradigm requires a last mile fulfillment process that can deliver a $10 item at a nominal cost in three, two, or even one day.

Amazon eases the pain of drudgery—getting the stuff you need, just clicking. Their formula: an unparalleled investment in last mile infrastructure, made possible by an irrationally generous lender—retail investors. The story is coupled with execution that rivaled D-Day

—Scott Galloway[66]

Imagine a future world in which there are no stores, and every item we buy or want is delivered to our home or office. Maybe you are skeptical of this hypothetical exercise. Make a list of things you can buy at a Walmart store, but are not available at Amazon.com or some other online retailer. Agreed it's not an empty list, but it is very likely a shortlist. Imagine further that all the items you buy are delivered to your doorstep. Accomplishing this futuristic delivery scenario will require a 10-fold, if not more, increase in the last mile delivery infrastructure. Both Amazon and Walmart are directly investing in the buildout of this expanding infrastructure. Consider that Amazon's 2018 capital expenditures on fulfillment assets exceeded $13 billion,[19] a good portion of which was directed to last mile delivery. Many innovators are also entering the business, and new channels, conveniences, and delivery modes are being proposed, seeded, and built. We are nearing the end of Fast Fulfillment 1.0 and 2020 was the starting point of a transition to Fast Fulfillment 2.0. What are the implications for business? The first two paradigms, online shopping, and point-of-use delivery will continue to grow, and traditional distribution and retail channels will continue to be capacity- and speed challenged. *Every consumer products company must have a fast fulfillment plan for the 100 percent Online Retail vision.* Regardless of whether you make cookies, toothpaste, laptops, or a chest of drawers, you need to be planning now. Our task here is to help you prepare for this future world. ***Fact:*** U.S. online sales were 14.3 percent of total retail sales in 2018, up from 6.4 percent in 2010.[15]

Parcel Delivery—The Numbers

The Internet progressively reduced the need for postal mail (nonparcel), and in the last 10 years, the average household has probably seen a 50 percent reduction in the number of postal mail items received. Many had projected that the U.S. Postal Service (USPS) would be significantly downsized, and daily mail delivery would be a thing of the past. None of this has happened and the USPS is busier than ever before. Why? Parabolic growth in parcel delivery. In 2018, the USPS delivered about six billion parcels, almost double the number from a decade ago. The USPS relationship with Amazon is critical to the finances of the USPS, and a few years ago it added Sunday delivery exclusively for Amazon. This relationship was often a focal point in the Trump-Bezos war of words.[67] When the smoke clears, though, it's all about last mile delivery, without which the fast fulfillment machine goes nowhere, and the point-of-use delivery paradigm fails. The USPS operates the largest last mile delivery infrastructure in the United States, and it delivered 2.8 billion pieces in 2017 for retailers including Amazon.[68]

For an online retailer, last mile delivery is expensive even in a regular fulfillment mode. Accelerate too fast fulfillment, add the free shipping paradigm, and you have the biggest logistical challenge of online retailing. Promising next day or even two-day parcel delivery to any address in the United States is a remarkable achievement. Expand this globally and the challenge grows multiple-fold. The good news is that innovators all over the world, including the United States, India, and China are designing and implementing last mile solutions. Pitney Bowes monitors global parcel shipping volumes and estimates 87 billion parcels were shipped in 2018 in just 13 countries.[69] The volume is projected to rise to 200 billion by 2025, or 2,300 deliveries every second, or 22 parcels per person per year. Last mile delivery is the wide moat that protects brick-and-mortar retail, but it's shrinking faster than many retailers realize.

An A.T.Kearney study[70] provides an insightful snapshot view of last mile fulfillment and its cost share (Figure 6.1). Fulfillments costs account for 16 cents of every dollar spent on online shopping, of which about 9 cents is parcel delivery. Half of all UPS parcel deliveries are related to online order fulfillment, accounting for a $17 billion revenue stream. The data is a tale of opportunities and portends a basket of innovations yet to come. Why? The three legacy players (USPS, FedEx, and UPS) account for more than 70 percent of all last mile deliveries, but their logistic designs were not built for the online retailing world. The free shipping paradigm dictates a relatively smaller profit margin for online retail parcels, and the legacy players are not highly motivated to upgrade or innovate a low margin business. The two smaller slices in the market share pie are where future innovation is likely to occur.

E-commerce sales and fulfillment costs

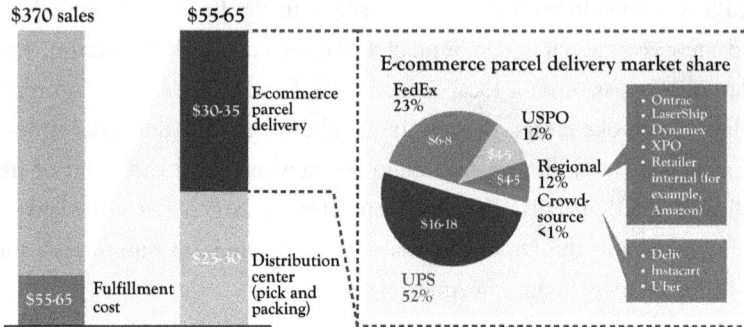

Figure 6.1 U.S. online fulfillment costs

Source: A.T. Kearney70

Last Mile—Some Definitions

In any analysis, it is always important to state and understand definitions. It is not uncommon for teams to be meeting for hours or even days before they realize that a basic or core element is defined differently by two or more team members. Last mile delivery is no exception, does it involve just the last mile? We all know the answer is no, so let's introduce some definitions.

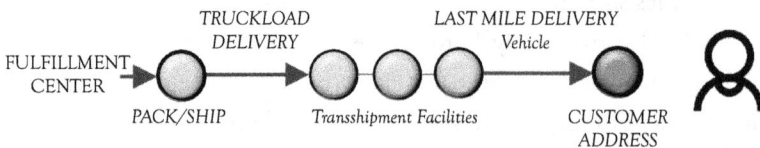

Figure 6.2 Online order delivery sequence

The delivery sequence (Figure 6.2) starts when a customer order is packed and shipped from the fulfillment center. The goal of the fulfillment machine is to transport the parcel in the shortest time and lowest cost to a given customer address. There are several ways this can happen, some traditional, some new, and some still in the innovation stage.

- *Delivery Vehicles:* Used to transport product from the fulfillment center to the customer address. Each parcel will travel in or more such vehicles and in almost all cases there will be multiple parcels in the vehicle. The most ubiquitous delivery vehicle is the brown UPS truck driving around your neighborhood, while a futuristic vehicle is a drone hovering above your house. The flow capacity of the fulfillment machine is a function of the number, size, and type of vehicles deployed.

- *Transshipment Facilities:* When more than one vehicle is involved in the order transport, then at some point the parcel is transferred between vehicles. These transfers are done at a transshipment facility, and every USPS post office is an example facility. Likewise, every FedEx and UPS delivery hub is also a transshipment facility. The U.S. distribution network has thousands of transshipment facilities and Walmart cross-dock warehouses, seen along many interstates, are just one example. But these facilities are designed and built for brick-and-mortar retail and cannot readily service the online retail market.

- *Last Mile Delivery:* Refers to the final transport step in the parcel delivery sequence that is the scheduling, loading, transit, and unloading of the vehicle that visits the customer address. Examples are the postman delivering the box of pocket squares you ordered from Etsy, the Fresh Direct truck delivering groceries or the furniture delivery from a Wayfair partner. An extended definition of last mile delivery could include all the transport steps between the fulfillment center and customer address.

- *Sequenced Vehicle:* Usually, the last mile delivery vehicle carrying many parcels will load them in random order. A sequenced vehicle is loaded for delivery efficiency and vehicle volume utilization. The goal is to minimize the parcel search time at each stop. In the optimal case, a sequenced vehicle would arrange parcels to match the delivery sequence. Parcel sequencing is most effective in the last mile step but could be done even earlier starting from the moment they are packed in a fulfillment warehouse. The operational goal: A fulfillment center should prepare a sequenced trailer for a defined delivery area, a group of collocated zip codes, or a single or partial zip code.

The Delivery Channels

Every address has unique delivery features, and a retailer must select or design the delivery channel to match those features. Consider an address in a small town on a rural route with less than one parcel delivery per month for the entire route. Now consider an address in a 40-story San Francisco condo building, with 30 parcel deliveries per day. The optimal fast fulfillment channel is different for these two cases, and a retailer should have multiple channels in-place to maximize cost and time efficiency. Investigating the last mile delivery methods of online retailers, we find there are seven different channel designs. Each of these starts from the final inventory location where the item is positioned for customer delivery.

1. *National Parcel Service:* Retailer prepares parcel(s) and informs a third-party logistics carrier (e.g., FedEx, UPS, and USPS), which then picks up packages from retailer warehouse. Carrier processes parcel through its distribution system, and typically no other service provider is involved. This is the default or traditional delivery channel, representing the greatest portion of the delivery pie shown earlier in Figure 6.1.

2. *Sequenced Trailer + Parcel Service:* Fulfillment center loads trailer in delivery sequence and transports to local transshipment point. Loading data shared with parcel service, which then executes customer address delivery.

3. *Sequenced Trailer + Retailer Vehicle + Dense Addresses:* Fulfillment center loads trailer in partitioned sequence and transports to local transshipment point. Each partition represents a dense address and there is no sequencing within partitions. Retailer vehicles are prepositioned and make bulk delivery to dense or multiunit addresses. An apartment complex or condo building are examples of dense addresses. Possibly the highest cost efficiency delivery channel.

4. *Sequenced Trailer + Retailer Vehicle + Lockers + Customer Pickup:* Fulfillment center loads trailer in partitioned sequence and transports to local transshipment point. The retailer operates self-service locker kiosks. Retailer vehicles transfer parcels to kiosks and load lockers. The customer is alerted and provided a pickup window. Not a pure delivery channel and requires customer pickup. Lockers are located to minimize pickup effort. University bookstores, 7–11 convenience stores, and office buildings are some examples.

5. *Local Dedicated Parcel Service:* Fulfillment center or retail store is located within the delivery zone. The fleet of dedicated delivery vehicles pick up and deliver parcels to customer addresses. Delivery vehicles could be retailer owned or third-party service. The fast-growing start-up delivery service, Parcel, was recently acquired by Walmart. A special case is where delivery occurs at an intermediate point, frequently referred to as pickup boxes or click and pick points.

6. *Local Shared Parcel Service (Milk Run Model):* Fulfillment center or retail store is located within the delivery zone. Demand is insufficient to justify a dedicated fleet of delivery vehicles. Parcel service serves multiple fulfillment centers and creates a milk run delivery route from daily order data. This channel is essential to small retailers, who can pool resources to succeed in the online economy.

7. *Crowdsourced On-Demand Local Parcel Service (Uber Model):* Fulfillment center or retail store is located within the delivery zone. Parcels are delivered exclusively by independent service providers who are accessed on an as-needed basis. There are no commitments on either side. Uber-style apps make delivery matches when each parcel is ready. The channel is ideal for small retailers and markets where online orders are limited and the delivery addresses are sparse.

An investigation of the last mile delivery transfer function reveals three factors that significantly affect delivery performance:

(i) The density of the customer addresses or the average distance between sequential delivery locations;

(ii) The proximity of the fulfillment center to the customer address, or the distance the parcel must travel; and

(iii) The randomness of the arriving batch of parcels, or the time and effort needed to sequence the parcels.

Delivery channels are differentiated by their unique values for each of these factors, and a fast fulfillment machine will apply the optimal delivery channel in each case. National parcel service (#1) is the easiest channel to implement and till recently the only choice available to many retailers. Even today, a start-up online retailer is limited to this channel, this includes independent sellers who market their products through retailers such as Etsy. Chapter 3 introduced shopping frequency and immediacy as key dimensions in determining the target fulfillment speed. Both dimensions are also determinants of delivery channel selection.

A common delivery chain will involve three vehicles and two transshipment facilities. Ideally, the last vehicle should have the parcels indexed or arranged in the delivery sequence. Fulfillment speed will be a function of where in the chain parcels are sequenced. As shown in Figure 6.3, the best case is where sequencing starts at the fulfillment center and then parcels are progressively partitioned at each step. Channel designs #2 to #4 all involve a sequenced trailer departing from the fulfillment center, so let's explore why this is advantageous. The delivery person spends no time searching for the parcel, and the hold time is minimized at each delivery point. Parcels commonly depart the fulfillment center in a random order, the first transshipment point partitions the parcel by regional delivery addresses, while the second transshipment sorts or indexes the parcels into a delivery sequence. Each transshipment point generates friction in the fulfillment process, and we need to speed them up. What is the solution? First, reduce or eliminate the need for sortation, and second, perform sortation at the most efficient point. Total digital control (or ID#6) is the solution enabler.

Amazon provides tours of selected fulfillment centers and these all end at the trailer loading section. There you see no pallets, only parcels spinning around in a conveyor. Hidden algorithms and robotic arms partition and sequence the parcels into dozens of waiting trailers. Your neighbor's box of Bose headphones is right behind your six-pack of Nike socks. Both of you placed the online order within a couple of hours of each other, the physio-digital innovators leveraged that information for parcel flow control. The trailer assigned to your region backs up for loading at

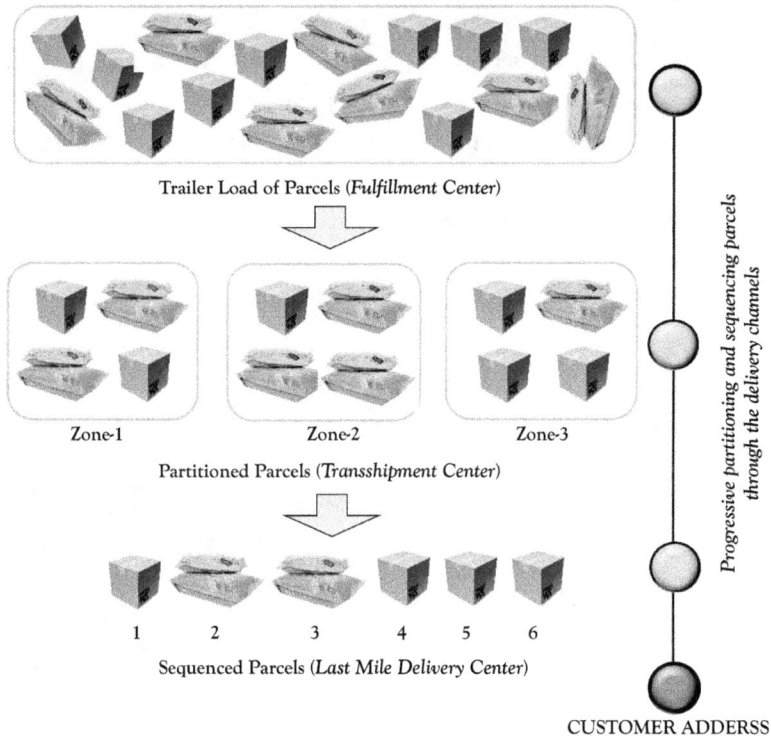

Figure 6.3 Sequencing and partitioning of parcels through the delivery sequence

2 p.m., both orders are released for picking at 11 a.m., packed and spinning in the loading dock by 1:45 p.m., side-by-side and ready to be loaded at 2:15 p.m., and on the road by 4 p.m. For this to be possible, the last mile delivery sequence (e.g., postal delivery route) of all addresses must be known by the parcel flow control algorithms. An example of extreme physio-digital innovation.

Amazon has progressively grown its fulfillment capacity using channels #2 to #4, though, channel #2 is critically dependent on its USPS partnership. Condo and apartment buildings with their high address density provide the highest fulfillment efficiency, and channel #3 is tailored for this market. Conversely, channel #4 is suited for less dense locations. Machine designers must isolate a market with unique transfer function attributes, if the segment is sufficiently large, design a solution for that market. The time and cost efficiency gains are the lowest hanging fruit in the system.

Quadrant-A products, those with frequent shipments and faster ful-fillment needs, are best served by fulfillment centers located close to the customer address. Groceries, office supplies, and beauty care are all quad-rant-A products. Of these groceries are a huge market and the holy grail of fast fulfillment. Why? Many items per order implying higher picking cost and time, selling ultra-low profit margin products, and short ful-fillment times of three to four hours. At first glance, it's a money los-ing proposition, but many players including Amazon are building out delivery systems. In channels #5 to #7, the fulfillment center serves only addresses within a defined geography. Channel #5 and #6 are different only in whether the parcel delivery service is shared or dedicated.

- Parcel is a 24/7 operation that delivers packages in scheduled two-hour windows.
- Use technology to automate parcel flow and provide clients/customers with live updates throughout the delivery process.
- From a warehouse in Brooklyn, Parcel receives packages destined for customers throughout New York City. 
- Using routing algorithms, a fleet of leased trucks, and a professional, employee-based workforce, they're able to quickly sort and load packages for delivery routes.
- Acquired by Walmart in 2017

    "Delivery is one of the most important elements for today's online shoppers, as demands for speed, flexibility, and reliability continue to grow. That's why my team spends a lot of time thinking about ways we can make deliveries faster and more convenient for customers." - *Nate Faust, Senior VP, Walmart U.S. eCommerce Supply Chain*[17]

Figure 6.4 Parcel—A last mile delivery company

The Store is The Fulfillment Center: The most aggressive brick-and-mortar retailers, led by Walmart, are using an S-Strategy or BOFS model to grow their online business. In effect, they have converted the store into a fulfillment center. The key advantage is that there are no transshipments and last mile delivery occurs directly from the store. A second advantage is the ability to offer same-day delivery. Channels # 5 and #6 are integral to this strategy and in 2017 acquired last mile delivery innovator, Parcel,[71] which is described in Figure 6.4. A special case of channels # 5 and #6 is when the customer picks up the order from the store or BOPS. Amazon is also pursuing a similar strategy with the acquisition of Whole Foods. The efficiency question is: Are these channels economically sustainable for

Quadrant-B, C, and D products. My inference is no, and the good news is that forward-thinking retailers, Walmart and Macy's, are progressively building a fast fulfillment machine.

Crowdsourced Delivery

We hear it all the time—*It's a gig economy*—don't buy it, don't own, just rent it on an as needed basis. Uber, Lyft, Ola, and Didi, these ride-hailing innovators demonstrated and confirmed that you can create a billion-dollar service industry by crowdsourcing. Amazon has invested billions of dollars and terabytes of knowledge to build their fast fulfillment infrastructure, they have it all, planes trains, and automobiles. The legacy retailers, other than possibly Walmart, don't have the resources to match this infrastructure and are looking for low capital assets and resource lite solutions. Is crowdsourcing the answer? Maybe. To investigate this question, let's first understand the role of crowdsourcing in parcel delivery. There are three participants (Figure 6.5) in the delivery sequence, as follows:

Figure 6.5 Three participants in crowdsourced delivery

- *A Pool of Nonprofessional Drivers:* Willing to provide parcel delivery services with their own vehicles. Parcel size is limited by vehicle size, and driver chooses their own work schedule. The base premise of crowdsourcing is that such a pool exists.
- *Online Retailer:* Fulfilling online orders from inventory stocked in either local stores or warehouses.
- *Delivery Service Aggregator:* The last mile delivery company. Creates and operates a software platform to connect retailer parcels with the pool of drivers and track the delivery process. Deliv, Shipt, and Instacart are all examples of companies that aggregate a pool of drivers.

Separating the physical parts of the delivery process from the aggregator allows tech-savvy innovators with little knowledge of transportation or retailing to enter the business. There are several start-up delivery service aggregator companies, all of them are growing, but most operate in a limited service area. The largest companies are Instacart, Postmates, Deliv, Roadie, UberEats, and DoorDash. For a brick-and-mortar retailer, the delivery service companies in combination with a BOFS strategy provides an immediate response to the Amazon challenge. As you explore your innovative ideas, it is important not to get romantic and think you can walk on water. Make no mistake, there are several operational challenges in the crowdsourced delivery channel.

At least two leading delivery companies, UberRUSH and Shyp, shut down in 2018. A transfer function analysis (Figure 6.6) reveals the challenges that may have precipitated the shutdowns. There are six critical input factors, three from the customer demand side and three from the driver supply side. Each can be described by a probability function, which then predicts the on-time delivery performance.

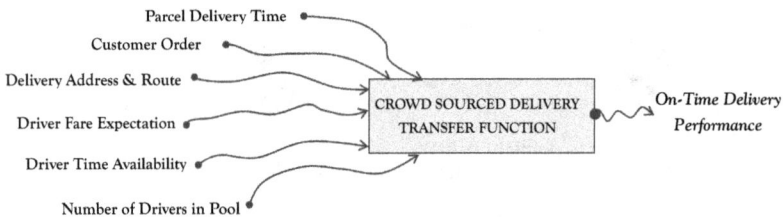

Figure 6.6 Crowdsourced delivery—transfer function analysis

The first potential transfer function speed bump occurs when the likelihood of customer-order volumes is much greater than the pool of available drivers. A necessary condition for crowdsourcing models is that the supply (number of drivers in the pool) must be greater than or equal to customer demand (customer order volumes). But cannot be a lot greater, else driver fare expectations are not met and the supply shrinks. The operational performance of a crowdsourcing delivery business is therefore closely related to population density. In sparsely populated areas, not only are both order volumes and the number of drivers low, there is likely to be a shorter overlap between delivery time windows and driver time availability, which generates a second speed bump. The transfer function analysis shows that the biggest challenge is driver fare expectation. Paradigm #4, free shipping, pressures the model and last mile delivery needs a very low per parcel cost to succeed. This is evident in the food delivery business, where many restaurant owners are finding that fulfillment costs are eating into their margins.[72]

Crowdsourced delivery has worked best in the restaurant food delivery fulfillment business. Walk around Manhattan at dinner time and you will see bikers/drivers from GrubHub, UberEATS, and DoorDash busily serving customer orders. But that business is not covered by the free shipping paradigm, and customers are either explicitly and/or implicitly paying for delivery. An UberEats order from McDonalds has a price hike of $0.50 on the in-store menu price of $9.49, plus a delivery fee of $1.49. If we assume UberEats has negotiated a supply price of $8.99, then the true delivery charge of $2.49 is split between the driver and UberEats (Figure 6.7). Restaurant delivery is also less uncertain, the order arrival and delivery windows are predefined, and daily volumes are steady and more accurately predicted. Even then, a quick scan of customer reviews will show that delivery times are a common cause of negative customer reviews. The free shipping paradigm will inevitably progress in restaurant food delivery fulfillment, and this will be achieved through innovations that lead to more cost-efficient deliveries. Doordash already offers Dash-Pass, an annual subscription with no delivery fees, while PFChangs has negotiated preferential contracts with delivery services that allow it to absorb the fee and offer free delivery.

Modeling the Delivery Process

Network flow models describe the movement of products or services from a source to a destination. Open any textbook on Management Science and you will find a chapter on network flow optimization. Large airlines move millions of passengers every day, and they use network flow models to develop flight schedules and route capacities. Coupling those models with real-time customer demand, they can dynamically adjust ticket prices to maximize revenues. Following his failed investment in U.S. Air, Warren Buffet described *airlines as a commodity business where it was impossible to be a lot smarter than your dumbest competitor.*[73] Well, times have changed; the airlines learned their lessons and are now a lot smarter and savvy mathematicians. Mr. Buffet was quick to see the transition, and in 2019 he was the largest investor in not one but four of the largest U.S. airlines.

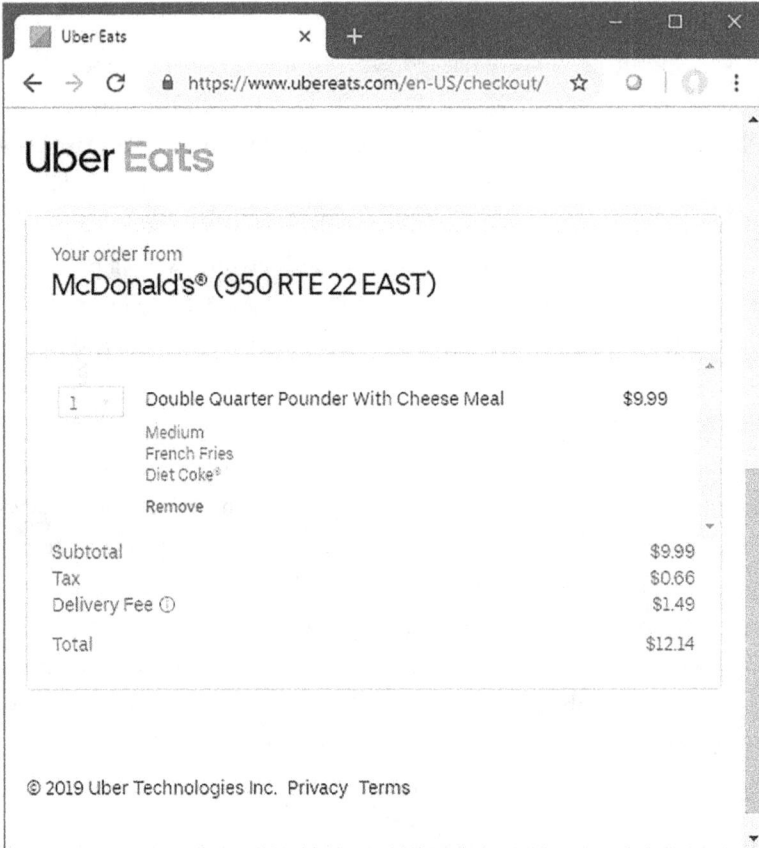

Figure 6.7 UberEats delivery fee—free shipping paradigm coming soon

The point-of-use delivery paradigm completely changes the network flow structure (Figure 6.8) and jeopardizes all existing supply chains and distribution channels. Traditionally, product manufacturers have built a distribution relationship with the retailer and a marketing relationship with customers. This strategy has worked amazingly well and great brands have been created. The fulfillment machine disrupts this relationship, it connects the manufacturer directly to the customer. Remember the supply chain subscription paradigm, it allows small, new, and less resourceful manufacturers to build delivery channels quickly. Fast fulfillment requires the development of dynamic network flow models that direct and track flows through the chain down to the last mile. A retailer with a static approach to its online delivery channels is soon going to face an airline like commodity pricing squeeze.

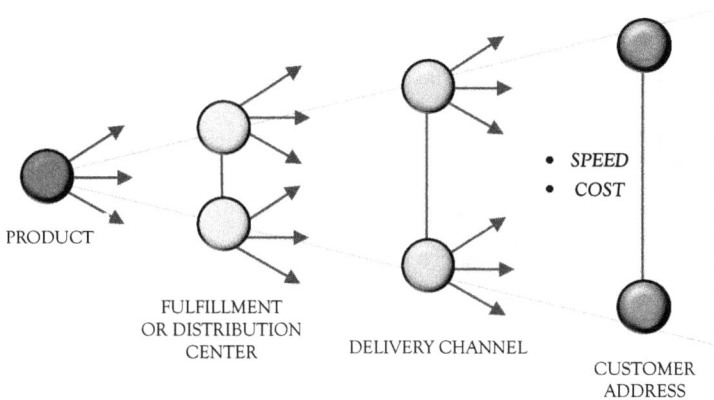

PRODUCT

FULFILLMENT
OR DISTRIBUTION
CENTER

DELIVERY CHANNEL

- SPEED
- COST

CUSTOMER
ADDRESS

Figure 6.8 Product fulfillment—a diverging network model

Chapter Summary

- Last mile delivery is the biggest logistical challenge in fast fulfillment. The need for speed and the free shipping paradigm make last mile a significant fulfillment cost component and ultimately a key determinant of profitability. The explosion in parcel volume through the delivery infrastructure is highlighted.
- Last mile delivery and its components are defined explicitly in the context of the overall fulfillment process.
- There are seven different last mile delivery channel designs. Each of these starts from the inventory location where the item is positioned for customer delivery and ends with the

customer. Three factors affect delivery performance: address density, proximity of the fulfillment center, and randomness of the arriving batch of parcels.

- Crowdsourced delivery is presented, and its role as a low capital asset and resource lite solution is highlighted. There are three crowdsourced participants, and together they define six critical inputs to the last mile delivery transfer function.

CHAPTER 7

Humans and Automation

Physio-Digital innovations that accelerate process speed must leverage automation which is smartly blended with humans. Use the automation challenge analysis to drill down on automation opportunities— situation attributes, machine capability, performance boost, and constraints. Discover the three classes of automation focus—Alpha or productivity, Sigma or intelligence, and Gamma or societal.

The Star Wars vision of fulfillment sees smart programs selecting wines to match your taste and mood; mobile robots picking bottles from shelves and packing them into boxes; self-driving trucks transporting boxes to a transshipment center; delivery drones flying to your house and remotely unlocking the front door; so that when you come home that evening, a case of fine California wines is waiting for you in the foyer. I dream, I hope, and fully believe that this will become a reality. But it's not going to be tomorrow or anytime soon. Not because of technological barriers or economic constraints, Wine.com already exists, but the delivery is not fast enough. Humans are amazing, their cognitive abilities, sensory sophistication, and instincts let them respond to every unique customer add in some automation and you can have both high service and high efficiency.

Retails supply chains, like many businesses, employ many workers and labor costs are a key determinant of profitability. Company executives, managers, and engineers are constantly exploring opportunities to reduce labor costs by introducing more automation in their business operations. The exploration projects range from simple one-person initiatives to large multiteam capital-intensive projects. Historically, the goal of an automation project has been to replace a human worker with an automatic machine. Net result: lower costs and higher productivity. Today, though, automation is more broadly defined, extending into the decision-making domain and includes those magical words, artificial intelligence (AI) and machine learning. A fulfillment machine can be partitioned into several automation blocks each of which has a specific operational objective. These automation blocks need to be closely integrated with human employees, both at the physical level and information sharing level. To ensure successful integration, a necessary first step is an investigation into the associated human to machine automation challenges. Next, you need to determine what is being automated and how it will be automated.

The Human to Machine Challenge

An automation project focuses on a presented situation and then develops a machine, or automation solution, which response by executing a programmed task. In some cases, the project is relatively straightforward, and an engineering team can quickly design and develop a solution. Visit any factory and you will see many successful automation machines: shampoo bottle filling machines; toothpaste tube cap screwing machine; or welding robots on an automobile assembly line. Similar examples can also be found in the services industry: Robo-advisers managing client accounts at a brokerage house; credit application review programs at a credit card company; or an automated claims processor at an insurance company. The programming or coding aspects of these projects is not the challenge, it's the transfer function that relates the input variables to task execution.

Once an automation idea is described, the next activity is an Automation Challenge Analysis (AC-Analysis). The AC-Analysis identifies specific challenges in transitioning actions and decisions from humans to an automatic machine. Why is this important? Under- or overestimating the challenges can start you on a path of low performance or conversely missed opportunities. Automating the fulfillment machine requires ideas that integrate the capabilities of both humans and machines. People often assume Amazon fulfillment centers are fully automated, but are then surprised to learn that a typical fulfillment center has more than 1,500 employees.[8] High speed is attained by using human workers in complex tasks that would slow down an automatic machine. Kiva robots move racks quickly in a fulfillment center but picking is almost always done by human operators. Automation tasks must be analyzed for feasibility before starting the project.

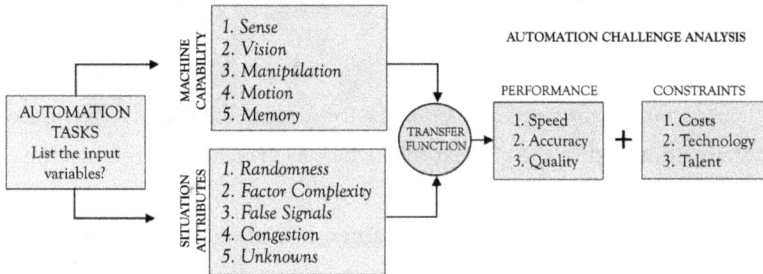

Figure 7.1 *Automation challenge analysis logical flow*

Automation Challenge Analysis (AC-Analysis): OK, so you have an automation idea, what next? First, be sure to define what is being automated, and then explore the building blocks of the automation solution. The automation challenge analysis will logically identify the needed capabilities and performance opportunities (Figure 7.1). Successful projects start with this foresight and allocate resources and seek solution builders accordingly. Underestimate the automation challenges and the project will struggle to succeed. Underestimate the performance opportunities and you are likely to do nothing and risk a disruptor passing you by.

An automation problem is characterized by several input variables or factors that determine the difficulty by which the task can be automated. The first step is to identify and describe the generalized tasks or process which will be automated, and then list the input variables that will be processed by the automation program to execute a specific task. In a fixed automation program, there are no input variables, the machine just keeps repeating the same task.

Product Flow Example
General Task: Pick up a box from the storage rack
Input Factors: 1. Box Size 2. Box Color 3. Box Shape
Specific Task: Pick up a medium-sized blue box from the rack.
Service Flow Example
General Task: Assign an available car to a ride request

Input Factors: 1. Car Location 2. Ride Start Point 3. Ride End Point
Specific Task: From the set of 10 cars located closest to the ride starting point, assign an available car to a ride request to maximize probability driver will accept end point.

Situation Attributes: Each input factor is described by five attributes that are evaluated in the context of the task as presented to the machine.

- Complexity—Possible input values, including shades of gray in each factor. How many different colors plus variations of the same basic color (blue, dark blue, and light blue)?
- Randomness—Uncertainty in the combination of factors presented in each automation event. How many different sizes on the rack and their physical arrangement?
- Congestion—The problem scale in each automation event, as measured by the number of presented entities. How many boxes are on the rack and how closely are they located?
- False Signals—Error is reading or receiving an input variable, possibly due to environmental errors. Likelihood box color or size is misread due to lighting conditions.
- Unknowns—Factors or situations not considered in the design. The box is damaged, or there are no medium-sized green boxes.

Machine Capability: To complete a task with given situation attributes, the required machine capability is specified in five requirements.

- Sense—Ability to identify the presence of an entity and/or its attributes. How many boxes are on the shelf?
- Vision—Ability to capture and digitize a picture of the situation or analog data. Where the boxes located and what is the positional arrangement of each box?
- Motion—Ability to move entities or objects from one point to another. Pickup and move a box from the shelf to the cart.
- Manipulation—Ability to change the position or arrangement of an entity. Rotate a box to change its position or orientation.

- Memory—Ability to immediately access data about past events or transactions. What boxes were placed and removed from this rack in the past 30 days?

Performance: Business success requires the task to be completed at a target level of performance, measured in three dimensions. Speed—The task completion rate; Accuracy—Percent of tasks completed correctly; and Quality—Relative to a human benchmark the output quality.

Constraints: Business justification of the automation investment is evaluated in three measures: Costs—The capital cost to build and implement the automation solution; Technology—Availability and feasibility risk of the underlying automation technology; and Talent—Availability and sustainability of the talent pool to support the automation effort.

Automation challenges are determined by how easy or difficult it is to build a transfer function that achieves the target performance within the constraints. The more complex or unique the situation attributes the greater the capability requirements and lower the probability of success. Solution builders have developed automation machines that facilitate efficient transfer functions in a wide range of industry groups. Looking back, we find examples such as Hobart (food processing) and Fanuc Robotics (automobile manufacturing). Looking forward, we see multiple examples in the digital economy. Cloud-based companies Twilio (customer messaging), ServiceNow (enterprise workflow automaton), and Veeva (pharma research operations) are the new digital flow automation innovators. Fast fulfillment requires companies to constantly explore automation ideas, it is integral to the physio-digital innovation shift.

What Is Being Automated?

The Amazon fulfillment machine is an orchestrated blend of human activities combined with a series of automation activities. To build this machine, teams of innovators would have focused on groups of activities that provided the greatest opportunity for increasing speed. A key prerequisite in designing these speed innovations is answering three basic questions.

- What is being automated? Identify activity boundaries.
- Will automation be significantly faster and smarter than humans?
- What is the projected increase in fulfillment speed?

The first question can be a trap, broad, and ever-changing boundaries can result in an unending project. To avoid this trap, the Apple design process step of paired brainstorming and production meetings, discussed in Chapter 5, can be very effective. The answer to what is being automated question will be one of three types:

Task → Machine: A specific task with easily defined start and points. Examples: Transfer items from racks to packaging stations; Transfer blood glucose reading data from patch to app. The project output is an automation machine that completes only this task.

Process → System: A sequence of tasks that together constitute a process. Examples: Last mile delivery of orders from restaurant to customer address; Credit card application approval for a new customer. The project outcome is a systems automation solution with multiple components and transfer points.

Decision → Control: A decision point where an evaluation is made based on situation attributes or data. At the task level, a single decision could be made, while at the process level we can expect a plurality of decision points. Examples: Assigning last mile delivery orders to a delivery driver; determining the length of credit history data needed for a specific customer. The project outcome is an algorithmic solution that integrates with the machine or systems automation solution.

The next two questions are gate questions in that they justify the project. If the projections are for benefits that do not radically affect the process or speed, then the project is unlikely to be a success.

Automation—Alpha, Sigma, and Gamma

The next is how to automate, or what is the focus of the automation machine. Looking back at successful automation projects across industries and looking forward to the transformative power of new technologies, I identify three classes of automation focus. These are differentiated by increasing levels of intelligence and motion complexity. Intelligence is a complex subject combining both logical inference and deeply mathematical transfer functions. The Googles and Amazons of the world are herding the leading intelligence experts to their ultra-innovation labs. But no worries, evolving technologies will allow us all to integrate intelligence into our automation projects. So, let's start with an elementary approach and divide intelligence into types: reactionary and analytical. Humans are constantly displaying reactionary intelligence; we see or sense a situation and execute a reactionary action. Driving on the highway, we see a car 20 feet ahead and apply the brakes. A warehouse worker recognizes the square green box on the shelf and picks it up. Analytical intelligence, on the other hand, involves reasoning and inference, implying the inputs are uncertain and semantic. Several different decision strategies are possible, and the result is performance differentiated, which means there are good and bad decisions. A self-driving vehicle or a stock trading algorithm are examples of automated analytical intelligence.

Alpha Automation: Productivity Focus—Automates a specific task or process such that a human worker is partly or fully replaced. May include sensory and vision automation.

Performance Value—Human productivity declines when activities are repetitive (boring!) or when they are physically demanding (fatiguing!). By automating these activities, we first, eliminate the boring and fatiguing effects, and second, achieve a significant increase in the activity speed. Higher accuracy and quality levels are also achievable.

Situation Uncertainty—Best suited for repetitive and predictable tasks, with little variance between sequential cycles. All cycle variations are known, and the machine is programmed to identify the current condition and execute the corresponding automation cycle. Where randomness and/or congestion can be digitized, then higher machine memory capabilities can improve performance.

Sigma Automation: Intelligence Focus—Automates a specific task or process including intelligent decision analysis, such that a human worker is partly or fully replaced. Intelligence is embedded in computer-coded algorithms that may access both repository and real-time data.

Performance Value—Many physically simple tasks include a reactionary intelligence component and thus require human workers. It is easy to find such tasks across both the industrial and service sectors of the economy. Examples include janitorial services such as floor cleaning, quality control inspectors on an assembly line, and train drivers on a commuter railway. Sigma automation could potentially release a large workforce from these job functions while achieving significantly higher activity speeds and quality. Roomba from iRobot has already accomplished this and eliminated this time-consuming chore for millions of households. To reduce store headcount, Walmart is placing a fleet of intelligent floor scrubbers, developed by Brain Corp, in all its U.S. stores. High-end sigma automation integrates analytical intelligence, allowing for the replacement of higher wage employees.

Situation Uncertainty—Well suited for repetitive tasks with high factor variance between sequential cycles. Intelligence algorithms respond to randomness and factor variations, maintain performance across a range of situational scenarios. AI algorithms can process high factor complexity and identify false signals.

Gamma Automation: Societal Focus—Replicates the motions and cognitive behavior of humans or animals. Machines have a humanoid structure, are often equipped with mobility, and can work in teams and alongside humans. This is the Avatar robot, remember the amplified mobility exoskeleton warrior on the battlefields of Pandora in the epic movie that was gamma automation at its best.

Performance Value—The number of workers is a key indicator of the maximum productive output organization, company, or country. Gamma automation machines may not necessarily be more productive than a human, but they can increase the implied worker count leading to higher net output. The societal impacts can be significant. Imagine a fleet of senior care nursing robots, home painting robots, and first responder robots.

Situation Uncertainty—Gamma machines are mobile and could experience a wide range of terrain profiles. Factor complexity is usually severe and advanced AI, machine learning, and motion control systems are a prerequisite. Working collaboratively with humans will generate very high levels of randomness, requiring analytical reasoning with big data inference algorithms.

Could We—Should We—Must We Do It?

At the end of the day, any automation project must add value or enhance performance. While the fulfillment machine was being developed, were the brick-and-mortar retailers asleep at the wheel? No, they were comforted by the wide moat of fulfillment speed and cost. We have already identified the paradigm shifts that drained this moat. One of the stealth tools in that shift was automation, it facilitated faster speeds and lower costs.

> *If a window of opportunity appears, don't pull down the shades.*
> —Tom Peters, Best-selling Author of In Search of Excellence

Disruptors have an inherent advantage in building an automated solution, they have no existing assets and hence are not replacing a human, a store, or a legacy IT system. Businesses need to constantly survey new technologies and evaluate whether they provide a disruption opportunity. Investigate three questions, before you build or discard automation ideas.

Could We?—Technical Feasibility: Given the situation attributes can a capable machine be readily acquired or built with the specified constraints. If there are technological barriers can they be overcome with a reasonable accumulation of talent?

Should We?—Business or Economic Value: Will automation significantly reduce the cost of the product/service or significantly add customer value. It's important to know the pivot point at which the answer is obvious. In Chapter 4, we noted that speed is a necessary condition and a pivoting determinant of online retail growth. The fulfillment machine integrates both alpha and sigma automation to achieve higher levels of speed.

Must We?—Moonshot Opportunity: Will automation allow us to do things in a way that is currently not possible. Not simply faster or cheaper but a new way of doing things, one which is likely to disrupt the current business model. Uber's driver–rider matching algorithm[74] is an example of moonshot automation. Without automation, instant matching would not have been possible and the business could not be built.

> *I have to fight for it like a dirty dog in the street. But you? You don't even have to try. She makes it so easy for you. You're just a fat kid sitting with his mouth open at the end of a chocolate assembly line. You disgust me.*
> — Everybody Loves Raymond.[75] In the famous sitcom, Raymond's bother complains about how easy it has been for Raymond to get their mother's love.

Very often we are looking for the proverbial *Low Hanging Fruit*—what can we automate easily with less capital and zero risks. Unfortunately, this is the approach that often stagnates us, we get happy with the easy bounty and become the kid in the chocolate factory. Disruptors are deliberately looking for *Canopy Blossoms* that grow on treetops, they are willing and ready to climb the vines, inhale the risk and exhale the success. The automation challenge analysis will help you make the case for your low hanging fruit, but more importantly, discover and pound the table for your canopy blossoms.

Amazon Fulfillment—Optimizing Automation

The fulfillment machine provides us with a great learning opportunity on how humans and automatic machines can be integrated for optimal performance. Amazon has progressively integrated a wide range of alpha and sigma automation initiatives in its fulfillment network. To be fair, these initiatives have benefited from unbounded capital budgets and a deep talent pool, a luxury that few companies have. But this was only possible because Amazon's leadership believed and pursued an automation strategy to build speed. In almost all cases, the Amazon team has set lower thresholds for technical feasibility and economic value, while aggressively seeking and building moonshot opportunities. Here are some canopy blossoms that Amazon has nurtured into competitive advantages.

Kiva Robots Moving Rack Pods

Order picking is a labor-intensive activity involving a series of walk–pick–walk tasks. Order pickers are often the largest labor cost component for a fulfillment center. Picking is a relatively easy task to automate when the items are organized in a fixed pattern. But with increased randomness and factor complexity, the technical feasibility of a picking operation quickly deteriorates. Recognizing the moonshot opportunity of picking automation, Amazon has set up a recurring robotics challenge to solve this problem. But the innovators also had a feasible idea, in a brilliant design they separated the walk from the pick. The warehouse was converted into thousands of lightweight rack pods that could quickly be lifted and moved by an army of Kiva platform robots. Today, Amazon has over 200,000 Kiva robots working alongside fulfillment associates. The picker is stationary, computers match pods to pickers, and robots move pods to and from pickers who spend all their productive time picking. It is sigma automation at its industrial best and the iconic image of an Amazon warehouse.[76]

Tracking the Exploded Inventory Across Millions of Locations

Traditional warehouses stock items in a known fixed location. In small areas, pickers can manually remember the stock locations, while in large warehouses enterprise IT systems track the locations. A key fulfillment machine innovator is explosive storage, which means an item is stocked in thousands of constantly changing locations. Multiply that across a million different items, and the memory requirements for quick picking need to be big and fast. Again, Amazon innovators leveraged available technologies in cloud computing and AI algorithms to fully automate the process of linking a customer order to a specific stocking bin. Very high fulfillment speeds became a reality.

Delivery Sequence Loading of Truck Trailers

In the last chapter, we identified the role of sequenced vehicles in the last mile delivery. In the optimal solution, trailers departing the fulfillment center should be sequenced. In a warehouse with hundreds of departing trailers and tens of thousands of parcels, sigma automation is the only solution to achieve scale. Sortation is a great example of alpha automation, what you do with a parcel is independent of what action was taken with parcels before and after it. Sequencing though is different and the actions are related, meaning the automation needs a parcel buffering component and could see performance deterioration with highly random parcel arrivals. Integrating algorithms that control the release of pick orders and packing queues, sigma automation minimizes randomness such that parcels arriving at the loading dock are already 60 percent sequenced.

These examples illustrate the practice of automation of automation. The processes are automatic but their settings need to be changed rapidly and optimally, and even that activity cannot be left to human input. Accompanying decision models should automatically reset the automatic process frequently.

Chapter Summary

- Retail supply chains employ many workers and fulfillment adds even more workers. Automation, including, automated decision making and artificial intelligence provides an opportunity to lower the labor costs and achieve higher productivity. It is a must pursue opportunity, else fulfillment costs can eat up all the profits.
- The Automation Challenge Analysis (AC-Analysis) tool is introduced. It identifies specific challenges in transitioning actions and decisions from humans to an automatic machine.

It identifies input variables that determine automation task difficulty and evaluates these in the context of situation attributes, and then estimates the required machine capability.

- Three classes of automation focus are introduced: Alpha, Sigma, and Gamma. These are differentiated by increasing levels of intelligence and motion complexity.
- Disruptive automation requires canopy blossom ideas not just low-hanging fruit projects.

CHAPTER 8

Brownian Organization

ERP driven streamlined flows are being replaced with Brownian process flows which dynamically adapt to the highly uncertain and highly temporal demand for products and services. Discover the Brownian catalysts—An Unbounded Selection, Crowdsourced Information, End of the normal distribution and Random is the new normal. The Brownian Multiplier to Idea process will facilitate the harvesting of digital and physical ideas to leverage uncertainty into a success.

Brownian Motion—The erratic random movement of microscopic particles in a fluid, as a result of continuous bombardment from molecules of the surrounding medium (Oxford Dictionary). Streamlined Motion—The organized and repetitive flow of fluid particles in a constrained environment with little-to-no uncertainty. It is obvious from these definitions, that a machine with streamlined flows is way more efficient than a Brownian motion machine, both in terms of cost and speed. Modern supply chains and industry have for decades been designed around the streamlined motion principle. Design and deliver a focused portfolio of products through a standardized process and you have a winner. The strategy has worked very well, starting from Industry 1.0 to 4.0, and companies with streamlined business process flows have grown and achieved great success. The building blocks of Enterprise Resource Planning or ERP systems are business process models that permeate streamlined and standardized operations throughout the firm. This chapter describes how Brownian process flows are evolving into the new normal, and explains why companies need to organize themselves to efficiently and rapidly respond to the varying demand trends in an online economy.

Brownian motion is not a common concept, so let's first understand the analogical relationship to business operations. Scientifically, it describes the random motion of particles suspended in a fluid. The two primary factors driving this motion are the kinetic energy of the particles and the collision with other particles. The motion was first described by the botanist Robert Brown, who observed it while studying the dispersion of pollen in water. The interpretation is that there is a very high degree of flow uncertainty in the fluid space and every instance or snapshot is different. The business analogy is that online customers have a wide variety of selections or choices, allowing them to exhibit their specific preferential idiosyncrasies. *The implication is that the demand for products and services is going to be highly uncertain, highly temporal, and more a function of current dynamics and less of historical trends.* Parcels in a fulfillment machine are like particles in fluid flow and if you have stable demand behavior, then you can build a wonderful, streamlined flow process. But online customers are not constrained into normal or constant behavior and every customer and every day is different. The fulfillment machine needs to anticipate the Brownian flow of parcels and create models that optimize these flows for each day. One difference between natural Brownian flows and a fulfillment machine flow is that parcels do not circulate endlessly. Each parcel has a definite start and end, and the flow time determines the speed performance. As we build transfer functions to control the flows, the parameters of each order or an aggregate of orders must link and prioritize the conflicting objectives so that the overall system objective is optimized.

Looking at the definitions of Brownian and Streamline motion, you see that the key differentiator is uncertainty. If you know what you are selling, where you are selling, and how many you are selling, then you have a deterministic flow process and you can streamline and optimize every aspect of it. Since product demand is inherently uncertain, a retailer will smartly attempt to minimize that uncertainty by managing the product portfolio, selecting optimal retail points of sale, and launching an array of marketing campaigns. The benefit of all this is a streamlined product delivery machine. Uncertainty mitigation, or what is more eloquently termed *risk management*, is not unique to retailing and is practiced in every industry. Henry Ford, the pioneer of streamlined efficient flow systems, very famously said "A customer can have a car painted any color he wants as long as it's black." What he meant was, optimize your product-mix offering so that a *majority of customers* are satisfied. Then design-build a fulfillment system to serve these customers and you have a winning solution. This is the *economies of scale mantra*, which has been the underlying productivity principle of modern industrialization. If everybody in the world ate the same cookie, engineers would design and build a highly efficient streamlined system to deliver those cookies to each of us at an unbelievable price.

The basic premise in designing a streamlined supply chain is the existence of an identifiable customer or demand majority, with a common or similar set of wants. The larger this majority the more valuable the supply chain and its associated processes. The keyword in Ford's explanation is the majority, and my argument is that since 2000 the majority has been disbanding and dispersing helter-skelter. In the 1960s, companies were generating products driven by inventive and functional innovation. They were effectively specifying or describing the customer wants, and there was a clear and dominant majority. By the 1980s, many retailers had built streamlined machines to efficiently transfer these products to the customer. Malls across the United States were dotted with these familiar retailing names. By the 1990s, the strongest retailers, such as Walmart and Best Buy, had continued to innovate the streamlined machine and had built formidable supply chains.

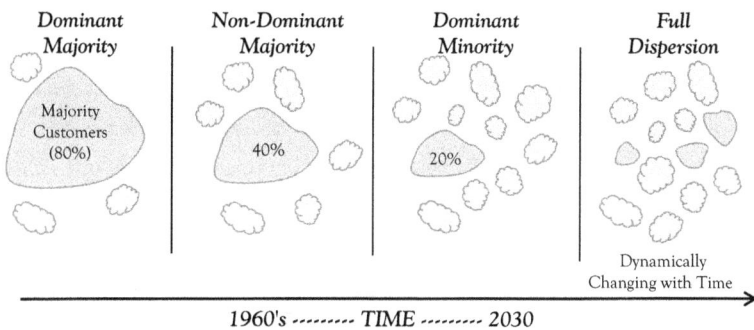

Figure 8.1 Dispersion in customer wants and demands

Brownian Catalysts

For a long time, most customers were satisfied with, or accepted the standardized catalog of products or services. Ten-day delivery with a hefty shipping charge was acceptable. The customer wants progressively expanded over time, and the majority started to differentiate and disperse (Figure 8.1). The majority shrank first to 40 percent, then to 20 percent, and then helter-skelter into full dispersion. The streamlined supply chain was sufficiently robust to accommodate the partial dispersions up to a 40 percent majority. Streamlined chains were able to increase product selection and distribute the product through multiple channels. But with further dispersion, these traditional chains struggled to fulfill demand and the disruptive innovators quickly moved in.

So, what has led to the Brownian dispersion of customer wants? Our research identifies four sequential catalysts that are driving customer demands. These catalysts are requiring companies to not just redesign but build completely new fulfillment machines to meet the behavior trends of the online customer.

1. *An Unbounded Selection*—You may have heard of the maker revolution but are not sure what it is or how it affects the product catalog. It's the ability of an individual or small company (start-up) to innovate and rapidly design-build a product or service. Makers cracked the economies of scale mantra and could produce new products in low volumes at a reasonable cost. Whether it was cookies, t-Shirts, or handbags, there were choices outside the grocery store and shopping mall. The majority cannot disperse if they do not have choices. The maker revolution provided these choices, and progressively eroded the economies of the scale mantra, giving customers a large selection of products and services.

2. *Crowdsourced Information*—Social media is an effective influencer and has become a dominant variable in the transfer process that determines consumer opinions, preferences, and ultimately a selection decision. The underlying information is crowdsourced, that is, it originates not from a few verified expert sources but a very large number of our peers. This information resides in blogs, online reviews, webzines, e-mails, Wikipedia, Facebook pages, the list is endless. This information is instantly available to all of us but is also constantly changing as the crowd adds new opinions. The effect of this information on consumer decisions is also unpredictable. Why? Each of us reads a small and different portion of the information,

since the information is usually in the form of opinions, we all draw different inferences, and finally we value each source differently. A group of us is convinced that mountain-grown Peruvian quinoa flavored with Kangaroo island honey is the best breakfast cereal in the world. TripAdvisor, Yelp, and Influencers (e.g., the Kardashian sisters) are all examples of companies and organizations that have successfully deployed the crowdsourced information model.

3. *End of the Normal Distribution*—The normal distribution is an excellent and effective descriptor of the majority. Create a streamlined machine that focuses on the mean ±1 sigma (standard deviation) population, and you have an efficient fulfillment machine. This is exactly what many great companies have done (Coca Cola, Ford, and Ikea). But as sigma becomes larger this becomes increasingly difficult. In the Internet age, customers are seeking a wider range of choices, options, and configurations. Sigma is becoming hyper large and the central tendency is crumbling. To be clear, it's not the end of the normal distribution, but the end of its widespread use to design and build products and the accompanying fulfillment machine. With a flattening out of the demand curve, the five-sigma customer has the same market importance as the one-sigma customer. The influencers, both individuals and blogs, are not only shifting demand away from the mean but they are also making them fickle, so they choose a different flavor every time they make a buy decision.

4. *Random is the New Normal*—The customer has many choices and the fulfillment machines make it readily and economically available. Consumer behavior kicks in and you make the selections you like best. Even further, you can make selections that are best suited for you: a 7.25 mg dosage of Lipitor or size 9.65 sneakers. With so many choices, customers have the freedom to keep changing the selection. Every Friday you visit the 87 Prime beer pub in your local downtown, you can choose to order your favorite or try a new craft beer every visit, in effect you are randomizing the demand. The Budweiser customers (the dominant majority of the past) are now a minority in the present. Crowdsourced information is an exogenous factor that promotes randomness, and companies are unlikely to effectively control and/or predict the behavior of this factor.

Proven Innovators

Some will argue that these catalysts are nothing new and are a constant in business. So how do we validate that these catalysts are radically changing customer demands such that traditional fulfillment systems cannot meet the expectations of online customers? The best way to prove this hypothesis is to look at some innovators who have already implemented Brownian flows.

- **Facebook—Advertising machine:** *Streamline flow*—Print or media advertisements are delivered to magazines and then bulk distributed to the audience. The primary differentiating variable is regional or market-specific content. Ads are aggregated or standardized for the majority, so everyone in New York City who reads the Wall Street Journal sees the same ad content. *Brownian flow*—Facebook delivers ads specifically to individuals, it's an advertising machine with billions of different delivery points. Ad flow is a function of many differentiating variables, possibly including, your ad click history, friends' network, likes, news history, and many others. The delivery algorithms are proprietary to Facebook and part of their AI-driven knowledge base. Every user is unique with a transient likelihood of clicking on a particular advertisement.
- **Uber—Taxi Service:** *Streamline flow*—Vehicles move on primary roads or wait at defined stands. These roads or arteries are aggregate pints that are closest to the majority of riders. Riders either walk to a primary road or a stand, then wait for a vehicle to initiate a ride. Vehicle availability is uncertain and waiting times can be short- or long based on location. *Brownian Flow*—Uber accepts the rider's current location as the start point for all rides, creating a large and random set of ride requests at any time. The current status and location of all drivers are tracked and known. Matching algorithms generate optimal assignments using multiple attributes. Algorithms are proprietary to Uber but most likely are designed to minimize both wait times for riders and idle times for drivers.

The system is highly transient and sensitive to the number of drivers. By using surge or dynamic pricing, Uber can incentivize drivers to enter the active pool and better achieve equilibrium in the flow process.

- **Amazon—Order Picking Warehouse:** *Streamline flow*— Items are organized in the warehouse in fixed locations and optimized by order frequency. Incoming orders are processed in a batch mode, or daily cycle, and orders are picked to minimize picker travel time and reduce warehouse labor costs. *Brownian Flow*—Amazon uses explosive storage and items are stored in multiple locations, and the locations are changing continuously. An infinite number of storage arrangements are possible. Incoming orders are highly uncertain but are processed immediately and the goal is to minimize fulfillment time. High-speed algorithms process the very large stocking location database to generate picklists that allow orders to be fulfilled within hours. This is extreme Brownian flow; you could watch the warehouse for months and never see the same picker travel ever again.

- **Zenni—Prescriptions Eyeglasses:** *Streamline flow*—Man-ufacturers of prescription eyeglasses partner with a network of opticians. The optician is an order aggregator with some customer value-adding services. Customers visit the opti-cian and a streamlined flow of orders are transmitted to the manufacturers and then shipped to the optician for customer delivery. Variances and uncertainty at the customer level are accommodated by the optician. *Brownian Flow*—Zenni com-municates directly with the customer and offers a very large portfolio of frame choices. The order flow is highly uncertain with a very large set of order variables including frame size and selection, customer value-added options, delivery address, and delivery speed. Customer order frequency is very low, and all shipments are unique.

- **Venmo—Peer to Peer Money Flow:** *Streamline flow*—Most consumer level financial transactions occur through checks or credit cards. Financial institutions have streamlined these flows such that these occur instantly and with perfect reliability between millions of pay points. *Brownian Flow*—Venmo provides a money flow process that lets immediate transactions between any pair of users in any amount with full validity. These money flows are highly uncertain in three dimensions, the originator and recipient, the frequency, and the amount.

Brownian Organization—The Why Nots?

A streamlined flow machine will have a higher operational efficiency than a Brownian flow machine but is going to become slower in the face of Brownian demand behavior. The design-build challenge is to minimize the efficiency gap and maximize the speed difference. Let's identify the speed bumps and friction that cause this inefficiency.

1. *Higher Costs*—It's the economies of scale mantra. Brownian flows involve many more process setups, slower processes, greater inventories, and a larger number of points of sale, all leading to higher costs.
2. *Decision Complexity*—When you transition from hundreds to tens of thousands of possible flow paths, there will be a correspondingly huge increase in the number of decisions you need to make. For every online order, you need to decide which warehouse to ship from, which bin to pick the item from, and which transport to use. The common response is, it's too complex we cannot do that. Most likely, both the physical and information technology infrastructure is unable to process the required decision complexity.
3. *Process Complexity*—An increase in the number of product/service options will require a production process that can handle all the possible options. Consider a jeans manufacturer that currently offers jeans in seven waist sizes (28, 30, 32, etc.) and two inseam lengths (short, long). If they need to expand to 28 waist sizes (28, 28.5, 29, etc.) and six inseam lengths, there will be a multifold increase in the process complexity. BOFS fulfillment of grocery products is an inherently complex process. Twenty customers order red onions, and each of them a different quantity ranging from 1 lb. to 4 lbs., you

need to weigh each separately and track it through the fulfillment process.

4. *Delivery Complexity*—More product/service options, plus more delivery locations, plus random behavior requires response flexibility outside the capabilities of the streamlined supply chain. Multiple speed bumps slow down the flow, these include issues with intermediate inventories and transport vehicles.

The previous four causes are the source of reasons that an innovative idea or concept is likely to be put aside. To counter with a why not do it response, start the argument from one or more of these causes.

Brownian Multipliers

To investigate whether these changes in online demand behavior affect a specific business, one needs to look first at the drivers that are forcing this change. I label these drivers as Brownian multipliers and identify four types that are defined in Figure 8.2: *What, When, Where, and Like.* Each of these originates from the market, not the company, and are related to customer events, or product/service transactions that are descriptive of the business's products and services. In a streamlined flow, the multipliers are limited and in the extreme case will have a single answer or outcome. As the number of configurations (what), locations (where), frequency (where), and customer evaluation attributes (like) increase and change with time, the more likely a streamlined flow approach will not be successful. Inability to recognize and/or accept the growing effect of the multipliers has been a key reason many established company brands have faltered—it is the Kraft Heinz paralysis. The company produces a single popular brand of cream cheese: Philadelphia cream cheese. Yes, there are several flavors and channel-driven packaging options, but in a Brownian economy, these choices are insignificant when compared with the very broad range of demand tastes in the online customer.

For most products and services, demand is either growing or shifting. If the business has a great product but still losing market share, it could be because it is unable to fulfill the Brownian demand. In February 2019, Kraft Heinz lost a quarter of its market value due to slow sales. Famed

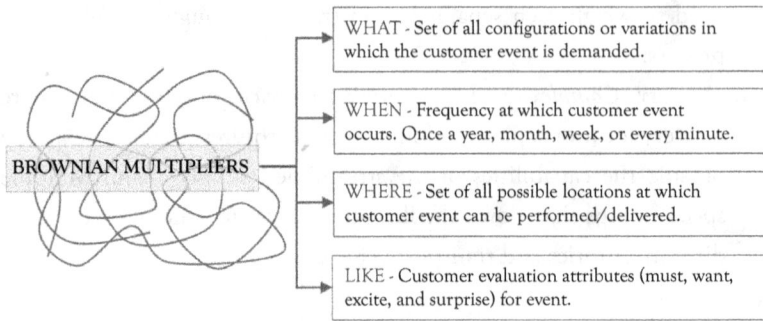

Figure 8.2 The Brownian wants and demand multipliers

investor Warren Buffet observed, "I was wrong in a couple of ways on Kraft Heinz. The ability to price has changed, and that's huge."[77] The growing power of private brands has been a headwind for Kraft Heinz, he said, citing the rising power of Amazon as a brand and the Kirkland brand of Costco. What he did not say, though, and I argue was a critical factor, was that the consumer had many more choices provided by innovative producers with a fast fulfillment machine.

Consider the case of a start-up company looking to disrupt the business of distributing wines to restaurants in a regional market. This is big business in Europe, and during my sabbatical in Italy, this is what I learned from some new upstarts. The company has a set of direct customers, restaurants, and a very large number of indirect customers, the restaurant patrons. The streamlined flow strategy would be to compete on price and service efficiency.

Wine Distributor supplying to restaurants—Brownian Multipliers

WHAT: (i) Catalog of wines unlikely to be stocked in the local store; (ii) Seasonal catalog changes; (iii) Supply in units, not cases; (iv) Half/ Full bottle sizes.

WHEN: (i) Twice a week not once a month; (ii) Minimum quantity of one, not a case.

WHERE: (i) Ship/deliver directly to restaurants; (ii) All restaurants with no monthly minimums.

LIKE: (i) AI-driven wine selection to match restaurant menu and prices; (ii) Sales analytics for optimal price/quality selection; (iii) Custom online page linked to restaurant web page describing wine selection.

The upstarts succeeded, but they made it clear to me, they had to work long hours, develop a new fulfillment infrastructure, and cleverly use information technology to satisfy the multipliers.

Digitizing Brownian Flows

The most effective way to build efficiency in a Brownian organization is digitizing the information and decision flows. At first glance, this seems elementary. Enterprise computing has been the underlying infrastructure of all successful corporations. These systems digitized all business processes, created centralized data repositories, and automated a wide range of decision-making tasks. Most companies already have a significant IT department led by a Chief Information Officer (CIO), and any recommendations to digitize business flows would seem strange and archaic. Smart teams have successfully built and implemented large-scale enterprisewide cost and efficiency optimization models, and the productivity gains are obvious. So, what's the big deal with Brownian flows? Brownian organizations require a much larger number of daily decisions relative to a streamlined organization. Each of these decisions, many of which are relatively minor, has an associated transfer function. Both the inputs and desired outputs from the transfer functions are highly random, which in effect eliminates the use of rule-based decision solutions. It is therefore virtually impossible to manage the decision and process of a Brownian flow model using traditional enterprise flow information technology solutions. Here is an example rule-based decision solution widely used in ERP systems.

Inventory Stocking Rule: Close to 80 percent of the inventory in large retails chains (Walmart, HomeDepot, Kroger, etc.) are commonly controlled by a Base Stock reorder policy. Putting it simply, when the current inventory in a store reaches a predetermined level (R) a replenishment order for a predetermined quantity (Q) is placed by the ERP system. Once every couple of years someone specifies Q and R. Now we transition to Brownian flow and decide that Q and R will be dynamic and derived every day, and for every item in every store. First, you need a transfer function model to derive Q and R in real time, then a system to collect and analyze the transfer function input data, customer data to update the desired likes and dislikes, an IT system to operationalize these functions and models, and finally a logistics chain to quickly restock the inventory. Furthermore, every so often the transfer functions need to be updated with new market knowledge.

In an Amazon fulfillment center, few decisions, if any, are being made by the warehouse employees. But the warehouse is not organized like an ERP style standardized flow process. The warehouse serves a constant stream of highly random customer orders and receives a constant stream of incoming stock. All activities have been digitized, and hundreds of model-based data-driven decisions are continuously being made by the cloud computers running the center.

The digital organization allows for physical disorganization. An Structured Query Language (SQL) relationship between the physical entities lets the disorganization be digitally formalized in the computing view. To digitize a Brownian flow organization, the design-build team must adopt and pursue the following three process digitization strategies:

1. *Explosive Decision Process Mapping*—Start with the assumption that all decisions will be made by a computer and generated dynamically in real time. The fulfillment machine is driven by an explosion in the number of decisions since every action that could potentially affect performance must have an associated decision. The decision process map must reflect this view. Design the network of objectives that will achieve optimal performance, starting from the task level up to the system level. For example, consider the sequence of objectives that link the flow of items through a fulfillment center: Next day order delivery → Prioritized order release → Efficient item picklists →

Higher probability of neighboring picks → Prioritizing item restocking → Higher inventory turnover ratios. If the map is dominated by a few strategic decisions, it's a warning sign that managers assume a deterministic streamlined flow will characterize the business.

2. *Artificial Intelligence (AI) Freedom*—Digitizing the flows will greatly expand the decision space in a fulfillment machine. What does this mean operationally? The decision space is not limited by any physical constraints or memory capability and hence unbounded. Decisions are not limited to a few choices but a very large, possibly infinite, number of possibilities. To exploit these choices, decisions must be made and implemented and cannot be just theoretical recommendations. Compared to an enterprise system, decisions are made more frequently, and the level of control is more specific and detailed. A fulfillment machine cannot be driven by today's state of the art enterprise systems, they are just too slow and dependent on human intervention. The solution is AI, it's real, doable, and profitable. It's not Mars project AI, but rather small AI solutions that automatically make small decisions for the larger collective goal. Digitized flows set the stage for AI freedom—receive data, make any decision immediately, implement it now.

3. *Transfer Function Modeling*—In a fulfillment machine, autonomous AI programs make decisions to optimize the current situation. Building these programs requires quantitative knowledge of the relationship between decisions and objectives, and most importantly the uncertainty in the system. This knowledge transforms into a transfer function model at the heart of the AI programs. Multiple parameters that describe the current situation must be accurately identified. If the parameters are incorrect or inaccurate the decisions are likely not going to be optimal. An amazing feature of the fulfillment machine is decreasing decision granularity. By controlling the flow of the smallest transaction units, one can design systems and processes that were infeasible or even unthinkable just a decade ago. In the normal model, we tend to design for human cognition and memory. In a fulfillment machine, we must transfer more decision responsibility to the computer, why, because it has unbounded memory and processing capabilities.

Let's Get Brownian

To build a fast fulfillment machine, the design-build team must investigate how Brownian demand affects either the current business or generates new customers. The Brown Multiplier to Idea (BM-Idea) generation process is introduced as a tool that can be used to generate physio-digital ideas that can be integrated into the fulfillment machine. The BM-Idea process pushes the team into an exploration of changing customer trends and then sequentially helps create physio-digital innovations ides to support the fulfillment of these trends. The key steps are given as follows:

- *Customer Exploration:* Describe the attributes of the new customer who expects a range of driven services. Four news segments are described: (i) Average-New, (ii) $\pm 3\sigma$ or very different, (iii) $\pm 5\sigma$ or highly different, and (iv) $\pm 7\sigma$ or extremely different customers. Starts with a benchmark description of the current average customer, which is derived from the history data. Next, the team must study how the marketplace is transforming. Internal market study reports are of little value, and very likely past trends will not continue in the Brownian future. Read blogs, online reviews, and insightful trend reports from the big-name experts (Gartner, McKinsey, and others).
- *Identify and Describe Brownian Multipliers in Your Business Context:* Building on the customer exploration step, this step identifies the specifics: the what, when, where, and like drivers of the multiplication process. The team investigates the multipliers that will allow the product/service to successfully fulfill the wide range of new customers.
- *Identify the Why Nots:* Good multipliers will not be easy to implement and should severely challenge the existing fulfillment process. Being aware of why not prepares the team for rigorous BM-Idea meetings and promotes risk transparency.
- *Identify a Digital and a Physical Idea to Serve the Multipliers:* This is a classical ideation step. The multipliers and why not are already known, the team is tasked with formulating ideas that can seed the development process. The task is not a full design process but only the generation of ideas that confirm

the possibility of a doable solution. The ideas are innovation solution statements that later seed the design-build process.

- *What Is the Critical Intelligence?* Identify the required intelligence for optimal decision making in the context of digital and physical ideas. A key issue in systems with many decision points is the risk of performance deterioration due to suboptimal decisions at several points. Several approximate decisions or decisions with weak objective function linkages will lead to performance drift.

The innovation toolbox provides detailed steps and supporting worksheets to complete the BM-Idea generation process. The resulting fulfillment ideas should integrate one or more of the three process digitization strategies. The BM-Idea process and outputs highlight the opportunities and possibilities of disrupting the market, through new fast fulfillment processes.

Chapter Summary

- Brownian process flows are evolving into the new normal, and companies need to organize themselves to efficiently and rapidly respond to the varying demand trends in an online economy.
- Four sequential catalysts are driving the Brownian dispersion of online customer wants and their shifting demands: an unbounded selection, crowdsourced information, end of the normal distribution, and random is the new normal.
- The disruptive innovators are already servicing browning customer flows, thus validating that the trend is real and happening.
- Objectors to the Brownian flow model will identify four speed bumps and frictions: higher costs, decision complexity, process complexity, and delivery complexity. Prepare a counter response at the get go.
- The Brown Multiplier to Idea (BM-Idea) generation process is introduced as a tool to generate physio-digital ideas that can be integrated into the fulfillment machine.

CHAPTER 9

Modeling and Optimization

Brownian models require an explosion in decision points, data points, and transfer functions. Learn how Very Large-Scale Flow (VLSF) models leverage computing technology with decision algorithms. Discover how to build Internet of Things (IoT) driven streaming data models that emphasize—nX data point multiplication, data latency, and decision latency. Focus on the four decision making capabilities—data tracking capability, cloud capability, action capability, and modeling capability.

Numbers, numbers, and numbers—*The quants will rule the business:* Let me repeat, the quants will rule the business. Yes, visionary leaders with great management skills will always be at the forefront of great companies. But at the tactical and operational level, decisions will increasingly be numbers-driven and strategic initiatives must leverage a quantitative decision paradigm. One may well argue that the quantitative view is nothing new—just a recycled cliché! Business school textbooks are filled with chapters on statistical analysis and quantitative modeling. Project teams across industries routinely build and integrate Excel graphs in their PowerPoint presentations and use data analytics to prove their conclusions. Many will counter that quants are already widely participating in business management and the emphasis on numbers only states the obvious. The previous chapter identified four catalysts driving the Brownian dispersion of customers: (i) An unbounded selection, (ii) crowdsourced information, (iii) end of the normal distribution, and (iv) random is the new normal. The net result of these four catalysts is that the existing quantitative view and strategy are simply insufficient to drive an efficient fulfillment process. Why? Without precise flow control, Brownian flows can quickly get chaotic, inevitably leading to fulfillment failures. The incoming data flow are fast and furious, requiring time-sensitive optimization. Most traditional decision models, though, have a planning perspective or long view and are simply not capable of handling the fast-flowing decision needs of a Brownian business. The planning view expects that good frontline managers will make immediate decisions from real-time data. But this only works when the data changes are small or infrequent. In a fulfillment environment with significant uncertainty in order flows, only a series of computerized decision models will maintain orderly flow.

A Brownian flow system will have many intersections between competing flows, and if these intersections are not efficiently controlled you are going to have a multicar pileup. The number of must control intersection points explodes as we transition from a streamlined enterprise view to a Brownian view. The exploding number of decision points requires decision and control systems to undergo an order of magnitude increase in the use of quantitative methods, data analysis, transfer functions, and decision-making models. These are the building blocks of AI, machine learning, and the digital intelligence-driven world being described by futurists. At first glance, the utility of many decisions is clear, and it would be simpler to make it a fixed parameter. But these micro decisions often have macro effects. At first glance, none of this seems any different from current practice, decision models, and optimization algorithms are widely used in business. To explain the difference, we need to first revisit the enterprise view of business and then propose the Brownian view. In classical process flow analysis, there are a series of value-adding activities or tasks, which together represent what the fulfillment process delivers to a customer. We are all familiar with what a business activity entails, but here is a generic definition:

> *Activity:* Execution of a business task that requires resources (such as labor, materials, space, and equipment) and may involve an activity execution time. In some instances, a purely digital activity may have an execution time of zero. From a modeling perspective, an activity represents the time, effort, and resources required to move from a starting to end event.

The operational goal of a business is to manage all enterprise activities such that operational performance is optimized, and the business goal is achieved. Two identical businesses may differ considerably in how activities are described and managed, and as a result, one business could be considerably more profitable and efficient. The previous chapters proposed that fulfillment machines experience high levels of uncertainty and a Brownian view of managing activities can accelerate the process flow rates. In the context of order fulfillment, the transition from an enterprise to Brownian views will require the adoption of several physio-digital innovations. Let us compare the two views in the next sections.

The Enterprise View

The enterprise view of business is salient to the application of large-scale software systems which run 90 percent of Fortune 500 companies today. These systems have been evolving over the last three decades, and in most cases are sourced from established software companies, the most well-known of which are SAP or Oracle. Two critical technology enablers for these enterprise systems have been, first, large relational databases that provided the capability to track all transactions, and second, communication networks, which allowed users in all global locations to access the same enterprise system. An enterprise view streamlined process flows by minimizing the number of decision points, and their surrogate pain and pressure points. This allowed managers to build and implement process flow decision models that very effectively used archived data to achieve productivity and efficiency gains. Two standard elements in the modeling of process flow in the enterprise view are business objects and business processes.

Business Object (B-Objects): An identifiable entity in the business, these could be time static (Employee, Resource, Customer, and Product SKU) or transient (customer order, purchase requisition, and invoices). Objects are typically characterized by one or more attributes (Customer order—Date, Customer, and Delivery Date).

Business Process: A set of co-ordinated tasks and activities performed by one or more resources and involving one or more business objects. The process is intended to achieve a specific operational goal (on-time shipment of a customer order).

Both definitions are well-known to those involved in the design and operation of enterprise systems. The enterprise model drives higher efficiencies by standardizing business objects and processes. Several examples of large-scale enterprise view fulfillment models are household names. In the physical space, FedEx and UPS are exemplary, while in the digital space Visa and MasterCard are widely used. ERP systems are a popular and effective way of institutionalizing the enterprise view across an organization. Such systems have been the underlying software infrastructure for achieving the fulfillment productivity gains in the last 30 years.

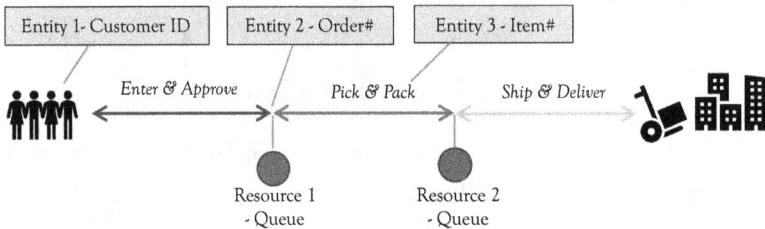

Enterprise View: Item stored in a single warehouse, specific area with a single shipping option

Figure 9.1 Enterprise process flow and entities in an online customer order

To illustrate the streamlining efficiency of the enterprise view, let us consider the process flow of an online customer order for two to three items (Figure 9.1). The fulfillment business process involves three activities and three business objects are required to track the order through the process. The process can be designed with no operational decisions. After confirming the items are in stock, the order is first released to a picker/packer queue (resource-1), and then to a transport queue (resource-2). The ERP system tracks all business objects and guarantees fulfillment within the target date. It's efficient, it's transparent, it's simple, and it works. Everyone wins, everyone is a hero, and there are no errors. Managers go to the SAP Sapphire convention in Orlando, drink a few margaritas, high-five other attendees, and are convinced they are at the frontier of operational excellence and technological innovation. I hate to be the iceberg alert guy, but the fulfillment machine has either already sped past you (more than likely!), or is right behind you on a highway six miles to the west (not in your rearview mirror!!). The enterprise view is yesterday's celebrity, the cloud and AI is here, and you need to explore the risks and opportunities of the Brownian view.

The Brownian View

Consider a system where every business object entering the system can follow any one of several paths to fulfillment. Furthermore, the business is characterized by a high degree of uncertainty in demand arrival (customer orders), deliverables (products/services), pricing and priority, and delivery points (addresses/locations). A stationary perspective is that the situation is efficiently modeled with an enterprise or planning view. A more aggressive perspective is that a Brownian view will allow the business to leverage the uncertainty into business advantage and optimize process flows. In Chapter 3, we discussed the case of Norwegian and Spirit Airlines who model each seat on each flight as a differentiated item. This allows them to create a Brownian capacity utilization model and serve shifting and highly random demand arrivals. The approach is to implement decision control of every resource and activity, thereby eliminating process flow waste by leveraging streaming data. Remember the Lean Principle[78] of waste minimization, this remains valid in the Brownian flow model.

Since every business and its associated fulfillment machine and different, we do not propose here a general modeling solution. Rather we introduce modeling elements and then recommend using readily available modeling tools and skills to develop a model for your specific case. The Brownian view expects that every entering order or object is managed like a project, and every activity has a network or chain effect on fulfillment performance. The good news is that project management is an important subject in the business school curriculum, and in many engineering and computer science programs as well. Many of you are familiar with Project Evaluation and Review Technique/Critical Path Method (PEERT/CPM). Using a work breakdown structure approach, PERT/CPM creates a network flow model in which arc represents an activity. Using activity time estimates and resource availability, PERT/CPM allows a manager to create a project fulfillment schedule and make associated decisions to meet the performance goals. Typically, PERT/CPM has been used very effectively to manage a single project or a small group of projects that share activities and resources.

The Brownian view proposes that every object entering the business be managed as a project. Given the effort to manage a single project, this may sound ludicrous, the business would require an enormous amount of resources to project manage the tens of thousands of entities entering and flowing through to delivery. The solution is to develop very large-scale flow (VLSF) models that leverage computing technology with decision algorithms using immediate data. For every flowing entity, VLSF models can control a series of time-sensitive decisions. The following modeling concepts and data strategies facilitate the successful development of VLSF models.

- **100 percent Digital Models:** Chapter 5 listed six innovative differentiators of an Amazon warehouse, ID#5 was *High Transaction Volumes and Total Digital Control.* This differentiator is a necessary condition for Brownian flow modeling and companies must be prepared to invest in the knowledge, skills, and capital equipment to design-build a 100 percent digital control model. It does not have to be a central model and could easily be a distributed architecture. Why this condition? It is not humanly possible to record and make decisions for every activity in a Brownian flow, they must be transferred to an algorithmic decision process. Digital organization and algorithms allow physical flows and arrangements to be disorganized. The digital models have an SQL-style relationship map that links the disorganized physical entities. This eliminates the underlying constraint of streamlined flows— organize and configure the operations to meet the requirements of the normal distribution customer. Today advances in computing and communication technology coupled with economic availability make 100 percent digital modeling doable, achievable, and necessary. It is the weapon of choice for most disruptors.

- **Fulfillment Object (F-Objects):** The end goal of each flow entering the business system or the last tracked stop or terminating node in the fulfillment flow. Example—Delivery of parcel to a customer address. This is equivalent to the points where the company's supply chain control terminates. If a company has 1,000 customers and makes a single annual delivery to each customer, then the flow model has 1,000 F-Objects. If instead, it makes weekly deliveries, then there are 52,000 F-Objects. If each customer has on average 10 delivery locations, and now demands daily drops to each location then the fulfillment flow expands to 3,650,000 F-Objects. Create a data structure that can handle a very large number (millions) of F-Objects.

- *Origin Object (O-Objects):* One or more triggers that initiate the flow. Example—Customer places an online order on the website. Each O-Object is uniquely associated with an F-Object. Often multiple O-Objects will link to a single F-Object for an M:1 relationship. When the relationship is 1:1, then the O and F-Objects can be the same.

- *Pinball Objects (P-Objects):* Each O-Object will generate one or more physical/digital objects that flow through a series of activities and finally converge into an F-Object. In a fulfillment machine with Brownian flows, a very large number of pinballs are flowing through and being processed by a series of activities. To ensure the fulfillment objectives are achieved, the pinball-activity pair must be monitored and continuously optimized.

- *Flowtime Metric:* Flowtime is a common metric in process optimization and is defined as the interval between the arrival of an O-Object and the completion of the associated F-Object. Minimizing the flowtime must be a priority objective in the design-build of a fulfillment machine. A common cause of longer flow times are resource queues, but simply adding resources is a shortsighted and frequently uneconomical solution. VLSF models must use a data and decision strategy to reduce flow times. What decisions must be made and when so that queues are minimized and possibly eliminated?

A comparison of the Enterprise and Brownian view flow models provides several insights. We revisit the process flow of an online customer order for two to three items and redraw the process flow diagram in Figure 9.2. Several major differences are evident; first, the order is split

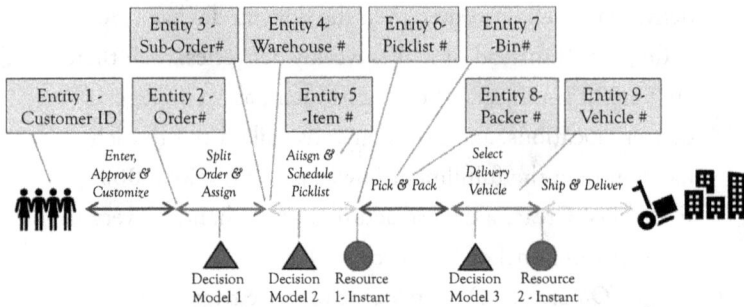

Brownian View: *Item stored in multiple warehouses, multiple areas, with multiple shipping options and immediate resource pairing (no queues)*

Figure 9.2 Brownian process flow of an online customer order

into suborders for each item in the order, so that each could potentially be fulfilled from a different warehouse. Items are stored in many locations within the same warehouse, so the systems could generate unique picklists and item-bin pairs. Since an order could be split over multiple picklists, we need to direct picklists to a specific packer for shipping efficiency. Finally, there are multiple shipping options and the systems need to select a specific vehicle for the completed order package. Comparing the enterprise and Brownian views, the differences are summarized as follows:

- The number of business objects jumps from three to nine.
- The number of controlled activities doubles from three to six.
- Three decision models are needed in the Brownian flow whereas the enterprise flow had none.
- The decision models combined with the detailed flow control eliminate queues and target instant resource pairing with pinball objects.
- Pinballs—Initially there is only one, but after the second activity there are several pinballs for each suborder.

Streaming Data Models

In the enterprise view, data are transactional. What does this mean? The database is updated whenever events related to a business object are processed. When decisions are made, models use current and historical data to predict the future. In a Brownian flow, the system status changes at a high rate, and the fulfillment performance transfer function is highly sensitive to the immediate data. Historical data become less relevant and an increasingly unreliable predictor of the immediate future. Early decision making on P-Objects can and will be suboptimal. A streaming data model focuses instead on making decisions closer to the execution point, with the expectation that this is more likely to generate optimal performance.

Order flows are often competing with each other for the same resources. Streaming data let decision models allocate resources closer to the point of use or need, and achieve faster fulfillment. In Chapter 5, we discussed the impact of the Internet of Things (IoT) on businesses and how it was being leveraged by the disruptors. IoT allows a business to stream data from all points within and outside the business. Smartphones are ubiquitous in society today and are an effective and immediate pathway for seamless tracking of endpoints in the consumer fulfillment supply chain. The advantages of a streaming data model can be measured by data and decision latency, and we define these next.

nX Data Points: How many data points, relative to a business process or activity, are being tracked. In a streaming data model, the detailed or granular view of the process or activity increases the associated datasets by severalfold or *nX* times. This is needed to make the many decisions for the multiple P-Objects.

Data Latency: How old are the data relative to the time when decisions are being made. Generally, decision-making models use two datasets: (i) Passive Data—Archived data that change infrequently and (ii) Active Data—Streaming data that change frequently. The active/passive data ratio is contextual to the problem or industry. In the old or enterprise, datasets are frozen much earlier, the assumption is that fresher data have very little performance value. The enterprise view active/passive data ratio is likely to be quite low.

Figure 9.3 compares the active and passive data flows between old and new view decision models. In a fulfillment machine or new view, the data latency is much shorter. Transitioning from the old view to the new view, not only do we see an *nX* Data multiplication but also a shift to a higher active/passive data ratio. Possibly, even the passive-new data component

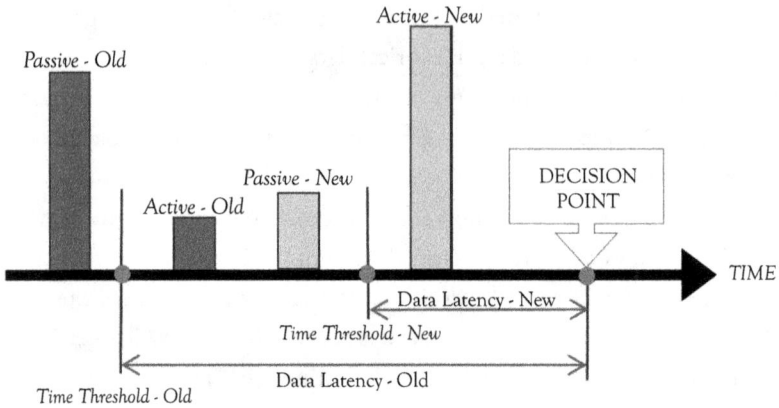

Figure 9.3 Old and new views of data latency

has a shorter latency than the active-old data. Here are four new-old view data questions for the fulfillment machine design-build team to evaluate:

Data Latency Streaming Model Questions:

1. *Old View:* What is the current time threshold? What is tracked in the active *dataset?*
2. *New View:* What should be the target time threshold to achieve optimal data *latency?*
3. *New View:* What is the *nX* data required to control the Brownian flow?
4. *New View:* What active data are critical to achieving fast fulfillment performance?

Decision Latency: The time delay between the arrival of an O-Object and the generation of decisions that ensure timely delivery of the associated F-Object. In a fast fulfillment machine, decisions would be made immediately and the decision latency or delay is zero (Figure 9.4). Commonly, businesses will operate with either (i) negative decision latency—customers are required to submit O-Objects earlier than preferred, basically a preorder or (ii) positive decision latency—actionable decisions are made later, and F-Objects are delivered late or on time with a penalty. The optimal state is zero decision latency, providing customers with full O-Object and F-Object time freedom.

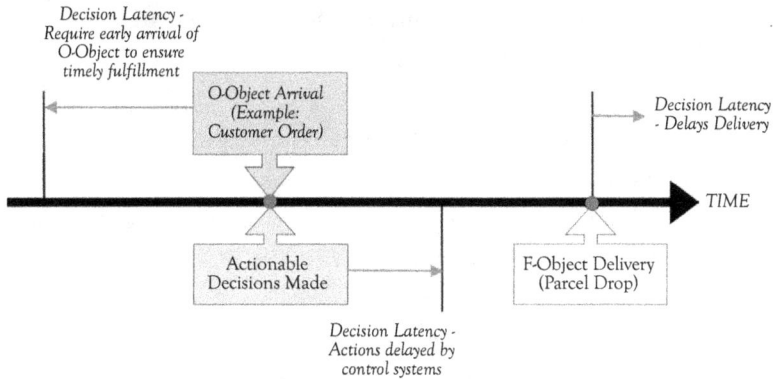

Decision Latency - Require early arrival of O-Object to ensure timely fulfillment

O-Object Arrival (Example: Customer Order)

Decision Latency - Delays Delivery

TIME

Actionable Decisions Made

F-Object Delivery (Parcel Drop)

Decision Latency - Actions delayed by control systems

Figure 9.4 Modeling view of decision latency

Some will argue that decision latency is a business requirement, making it possible for management to plan for the optimal use of business resources. They are partially correct, but an innovative disruptor knows this and builds a competing zero decision latency process. Let's say you have a flight this evening and would like to book a car to pick you up at 5 p.m. today. You call the local limo service and they respond that you should have booked it two days ago (negative decision latency), but that they can arrange it for a $20 premium (positive decision latency). Now let's take the Uber view, you are ready at 4:46 p.m. and enter your order on the Uber App, decisions are made immediately, and you are matched to a driver who arrives at your doorstep at 4:58 p.m. The Uber model is designed with zero decision latency, making it impossible for a traditional taxi or limo service to just build a convenience app and match the Uber service level. Here are three decision questions for the fulfillment machine design-build team:

Decision Latency Streaming Model Questions:

1. What is the O-Object to F-Object interval or optimal flow time that represents zero decision latency? In the Uber example, the latency is a few minutes, while for a same-day delivery order it could be four to six hours.

2. What is the fulfillment value of zero decision latency to the customer?

3. What design aspects of the current resource configuration are road-blocks to zero decision latency?

To illustrate how streaming data models are already being used by innovative disruptors, we take a brief look at three examples:

Uber: A simplistic view of Uber is that it's just an app for calling rides, and possibly in its early years that's what it was. But today it's a highly engineered data-driven ride-fulfillment machine. A static view of the Uber machine shows a set of ride requests and a set of available drivers. It is relatively easy to create a matching algorithm to create an optimal set of rider–driver pairs to minimize travel times. But the problem is not static, the drivers are moving, and new/free drivers are entering the space, similarly, new ride requests are continuously entering the space. Moreover, a rider may not accept a match for either price or waiting time reason, likewise a driver may also reject a match. Its classical Brownian flow, so one way to gain control is to take the view of a flowing particle.

Uber uses the Rider Session State Machine[79] to link the multiple event and data streams from the rider opening the Uber app to ride completion. In lower Manhattan, there may be hundreds of sessions active at any time and they are competing for rides. The session machine allows sequential data streaming models to be efficiently activated at intersecting points in the session. To run their 100+ Petabytes data flow platform, Uber uses many tools, including Marmaray, Kafka, Hudi, and Spark. These are complicated systems requiring deep talent and technology, but they allow the Uber team to create and visualize the active data for optimal instant decision making.

Waze: Finding the shortest route from an origin location to a destination is a common problem in mathematical modeling and commonly called the network routing problem. The applicable map is converted into a weighted network graph, where arcs represent streets and nodes represent intersection points. A well-known and widely applied solution is Dijkstra's Shortest Path First[80] algorithm. In a static view, the weights represent the arc distances and the best routes can be predetermined and stored in a database. But the problem is not static and the traffic flow rate on any street is constantly changing and at each node the previous best route may no longer be valid. A key challenge is where to get the streaming data from. One source could be data partners that provide automatically sensed information, these would include smartphones of other travelers, local traffic feeds, and weather reports. A second source is manually entered data from other travelers.

Waze uses a participatory sensing system (PSS)[81], whereby each traveler is a virtual sensor and periodically transmits contextual information on road conditions through a mobile interface. The PSS data stream is cleansed and validated to be useful. The route network quickly becomes a Brownian flow with every day and every instance being quite different for millions of different origin/destination pairs. Since the route can be updated, a key design issue in the data streaming model is how often data should be reassessed. Waze divides each arc into segments with mini-nodes (small intersections). The streaming data are used to estimate the time slice, or the time for a Wazer to enter and exit the slice. These data are then used to frequently update route travel times.

Ulta Beauty: Here's an amazing statistic, the company's Ultamate loyalty program has 33 million members.[82] Wow! That is 10 percent of the U.S. population. So is this just a bunch of people who signed up for the program or is it a key part of Ulta's growth strategy? Here's amazing statistic number two, more than 95 percent of Ulta's sales go through its loyalty program. The fair question is what's the big deal with Ulta's loyalty program? I get my haircut at Great Clips, and they have a loyalty program that gives me a free cut after 10 cuts stamped on a little card. Ulta, takes this simple activity to an advanced level, it uses a data streaming model to maximize the customer experience and dollar spend at Ulta. Ulta's chief marketing officer states that's the loyalty program that allows them to track all sold items back to an individual, providing the company with a deep understanding of purchasing behavior.

Ulta is leveraging technology to build an innovation ecosystem that is focused on personalization and connecting online and offline experiences to tailor its communications and help consumers navigate the beauty space. Each Ulta customer is unique and needs specific value-adding information and promotions that lead to a sale. Ulta has leveraged the loyalty program with data streaming models that provide promotional e-mails with greater product and time precision. Its Brownian precision is not mass marketing, the model predicts the most suitable mascara for

Janice in the East Village, not Jane Doe in Main Street, USA. For each customer, Ulta tracks, product selection, product retention rate, sales volume, frequency of purchases, and average sales ticket for every customer. All these data are used to increase a specific customer's store visits, the average sales per visit, and most importantly the customer satisfaction after each visit. It's a data-driven fulfillment machine.

Building Decision Capability

You cannot design-build a Brownian decision model if you do not have the skills repository and capital resources to build the required decision capability. Brownian models are not free! If they were, we would all be FANG[83] millionaires. The required decision capability is a function of the complexity of the VLSF model the business plans to build. Certainly, the required complexity of a takeout restaurant is quite different from that of a large online retailer or a 700-bed hospital. To assess the complexity and estimate the required decision capability, the design-build team should first ideate what the Brownian view of the business will be. From this initial idea, the team can estimate the modeling complexity in the following six dimensions:

- *Frequency:* The rate at which O-Objects arrive at the fulfillment machine and the size or content of each arriving object. Set the reference time unit (hourly, daily, weekly, etc.) appropriate for the business and then specify the mean rate for the business times. Example—A restaurant taking online orders through GrubHub expects 25 orders/hour with a mean value of $14/order.

- *Variance:* The variance and 80 percent percentile levels of the O-Object arrival rate and the size/scale variance. Example— The restaurant order arrival rate ranges from 15 to 38 orders/ hour and the order value ranges from $11 to $18/order.

- *Fulfill Locations:* The number of different locations (address zones) to which the associated F-Objects are delivered. Example—The restaurant has two locations, but delivery is made by GrubHub to 30 local zones, so from the restaurant's perspective the number of order fulfill locations is only 2.

If the restaurant decides not to use GrubHub and instead takes over the delivery process then the fulfill locations would be 30. In another example, a hospital organized into 25 patient care departments, the fulfill locations would be 20.

- **Entity Count:** The average number of pinball entities or P-Objects that will flow through the business to fulfill an F-Object. Example—The restaurant operates in a short-order flow model and the entity count is 1/F-Object. The restaurant updates to a parallel flow model with partial batch processing of menu items in each order, the entity count jumps to 6/F-Object.

- **Resource Load:** The average capacity utilization rate for the top three bottleneck resources in the business process. If the loads are low, then the decision models are less stressed since flow performance is less sensitive to nonoptimal decisions.

- **Flowtime Slack:** The time gap between the cumulative processing time for an F-Object and the targeted flowtime. The target flow is what the team estimates are required for business success. Example—The restaurant direct order prep time is 16 minutes, and it promises GrubHub a 60-minute pickup time, the slack time then is 44 minutes. Longer slack times reduce complexity, and possibly a streamlined enterprise view can meet the fulfillment needs.

Brownian complexity increases with increasing levels of each of the previous dimensions except for flow time slack. With increasing complexity, a larger number of decision control points will be needed. Relative to an enterprise view, a VLSF model may require 20 to 100 multiplication in decision control points. Companies need to build a physio-digital system that can monitor and control all these decision points. We call this the fulfillment machine decision capability. It's the difference between a future expectation of what can be controlled, and the ability to optimally make and execute decisions today. Decision capability is the critical component of the digital infrastructure in a physio-digital system, and the design-build team needs to prioritize this in all their activities and initiatives.

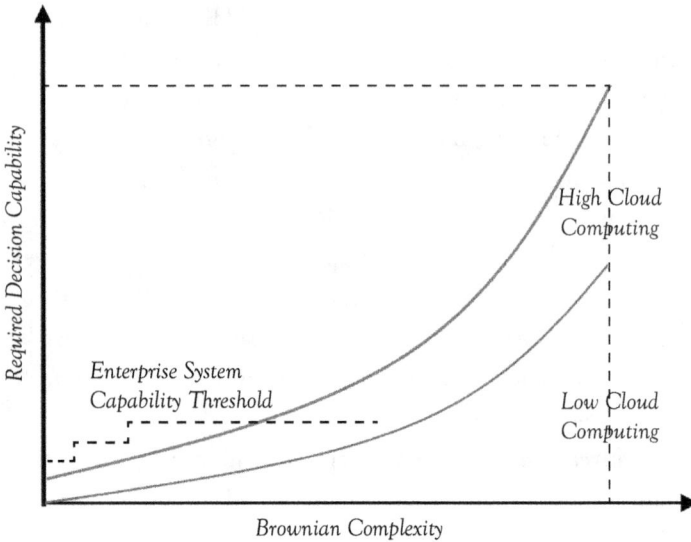

Figure 9.5 Required decision capability increases with Brownian complexity

The required decision capability increases exponentially with Brownian complexity (Figure 9.5). Initially, as complexity increases a business can upgrade its enterprise IT systems and meet the required capability. But after a few iterations, this strategy will hit a threshold and the associated resource costs and staffing needs are longer economically feasible. Cloud computing has been growing rapidly for over a decade now, and it is a necessary condition for building a complex Brownian model. Amazon Web Services (AWS) was born from the cloud computing capability the company built to support its fulfillment machine.[84] Today's innovator and disruptor are blessed, they have readily available technologies from AWS and Microsoft Azure. This provides them with efficient and immediate access to the needed cloud computing technology to build the required decision capability.

Let's be realistic, not every business is going to require high model complexity. Nor are they going to see a steep increase in the associated decision capability. For these, a low cloud computing technology is sufficient. There is no explicit boundary but low cloud and high cloud computing. But here is an operational threshold—high cloud computing requires the company to have a significant in-house computing technology skills repository. This means the company needs to have an IT team with deep knowledge of machine learning, data-driven optimization, which implies the team includes several computer scientists with advanced Computer Science degrees. Companies and teams must determine early on whether they are looking to design-build a high or low cloud solution, and then partner with enabling vendors accordingly.

From the initial VLSF idea, the team should sketch out the needed data and decision flows. From these flows, the team should estimate four needed capabilities, and plans and initiatives to build these capabilities must be started.

1. ***Data Tracking Capability:*** The VLSF model will require constant tracking of the streaming nX data points that drive the model. Ensure that the data flow process can achieve the target time threshold and minimizes data latency. Capability must include data sourcing, action to data immediacy, and data flow to decision associated repositories. In general, you want to minimize human input dependency since that is often a critical source of data latency.

2. ***Cloud Capability:*** Significant computing infrastructure will be required, further, it will be quite different, both in size and structure, from your existing enterprise capabilities. Ensure that the databases and computing resources are configured to meet the needs of the decision models that will form the VLSF backbone. Capability must include data manipulation, access to enabling software, machine learning, and AI tools, and network access. Accessing cloud resources from one of several ready to serve vendors can enable the business to leapfrog the technology learning curve, reduce dependency on consultants, and overall reduce the capital expenditures.

3. ***Action Capability:*** Implementing a much larger number of decisions than what the business currently implements, and achieving very low decision latency, is going to require the ability to make decisions, transmit them to the decision point and execute the needed action. This is the decision-to-action chain is a necessary condition for the physio-digital innovation to succeed. Identify the actions that are likely to occur, and what capability is needed to link them to an operating environment where each action is controlled by a streaming flow of decisions engineered for a specific P-Object.

4. ***Decision Modeling Capability:*** Numbers, numbers, and numbers—VLSF models are going to be hardcore quantitative

businesses, a team of skilled people who can understand the natural law mathematics that rule the physio-digital physics of the operations. Capabilities must include transfer function modeling and build skills, multidimensional querying of data, formulating performance equations that can be mathematically linked to decision optimization. Either your models must match your decision capabilities, or you need to expand your capabilities to meet the model complexity.

A good exercise is to visit the career websites of companies at the forefront of building fulfillment machines, the Amazons, Ubers, and Teslas of the world, and investigate what skill sets they are looking for in new hires. Your business needs the same skills to build the needed decision capability. Table 9.1 shows some skills collected from several openings for decision-modeling engineers at Amazon. Read the list and do an audit to confirm what skills the team has and what it needs to match the leaders. For the most part, these are hard skills requiring specific knowledge and training. They are not necessarily very sophisticated, nor do they always require advanced degrees.

Table 9.1 Skillsets of an Amazon decision sciences engineer

- Leverage the wealth of Amazon's information to build a wide range of probabilistic models, set up experiments that ensure that we are thriving to reach global optimums and leverage Amazon's technological infrastructure.
- Instituting processes to reduce redundancy and improve data acquisition and data quality at scale.
- Scale econometrics through Amazon and beyond by incorporating science into internal facing tools and making it easier for others to do so as well.
- Creating analytical services and products that solve business problems and drive effective decision making at scale.
- Comfort dealing with ambiguity and work backward from the customer to solve their problems.
- Track record of building either analytical OR reporting/visualization solutions using standard business intelligence tools: Tableau, PowerBI, QuickSight (Reporting); R, Python (Analysis).

Some Physio-Digital Ideas

We end this chapter with three examples of Brownian flows and streaming data models that integrate physio-digital innovation. For all three ideas, IoT is a prerequisite. The first (Peloton) has gone through the design-build cycle and already a proven success. The second (Healthcare) is going through the design cycle and we should see build-out in the not-so-distant future. The third (Hospitality) is just an idea, but a disruption that adds value to both guests and businesses.

> *Interactive Exercising (Peloton)*—People all over the world enjoy exercising and they do so one of two ways, either they visit a Gym, or they make a trip to their basement where they have their tread-mill/bike. Gyms have become a fast-growing business and people love going there. They are an interactive and social place, where you can get a trainer, attend classes, and be motivated to work-out. The downside you need to follow the gym's schedule and you need to go there. Could we, instead, build a digital solution that brings the gym to the home and fulfills your class require-ments anywhere, anytime, and with hundreds of instructors and multiple levels of difficulty? Yes! Peloton is already doing it by live streaming workouts and on-demand classes to a special IoT exercise machine in your home. Their innovative equipment and software infrastructure give every rider, no matter what their pro-file, the feeling they are in a gym class of peers. A key part of the model is the built-in social-interactive competitive element deliv-ered through a leader board. It collects streaming data of everyone in the class and provides the user with real-time feedback. Their logic models deliver targeted motivation to each customer via verbal and onscreen messages.

> *Hospital Patient Stay (Healthcare)*—Patient care is a highly Brown-ian flow process. The progression of a disease, the response to medical treatment, the physical and psychological characteristics, and social support are unique for every patient entering a hospital. Hospitals, though, have a streamlined design that directs patients

into treatment classified channels. A common measure for hospital performance is Length-of-Stay (LOS), and for each channel, there is a target LOS. A big challenge of hospitals is the large variety of resources a patient will access during their stay. Patients in a hospital are often waiting for test results, insurance approvals, physicians, a bed, or surgical facilities. All of this leads to delayed patient care, longer LOS, and higher costs. This fulfillment system is ripe for data streaming and Brownian modeling. It's going to happen, and we should see transformative changes in health care within the next decade. This example also illustrates the frequent battle between enterprise solution vendors and the disruptive Cloud/App-based vendors. In a recent battle (Add CNBC Ref) between Epic (the largest hospital enterprise system in the US) and the cloud kings (Amazon, Microsoft, and Google), Epic CEO Judith Faulkner e-mailed hospital CEOs urging them to oppose proposed regulation which would make it easier to share patient data. Her key argument is that interoperability and data sharing will result in patients losing control of their confidential health information, basically, privacy issues. The counterargument is that streaming data would spawn a broad range of application programming interface (API) apps that would increase patient control, analytics-driven patient care models, and better utilization of health care resources.

Continuous Time Room Bookings (Hospitality)—The are a little over five million hotel rooms in the United States alone, and every day millions of people check-in and check-out of these rooms. The streamlined hospitality industry limits your check-in/out times, typically 3 p.m. for check-in and 11 a.m. for checkout. Why? Hotels need to clean rooms between guests and the check-in/out window allows for efficient staff scheduling. Additionally, enterprise booking systems can provide reliable room availability to customers. The reality, though, is that customer arrivals/departures are widely dispersed throughout the day and each customer has a unique travel plan. Front desks will frequently receive requests for early check-in and late check-outs and depending on loyalty status they may occasionally accommodate these requests. A Brownian model can use streaming data to project arrival/departure time behavior on a future date. An incoming booking query, with preferred arrival departure times, could be uniquely processed against these projections to provide a custom quote providing price and time ranges. Hotel management systems will also need to follow a Brownian model, with staff getting continuous time room clean instructions. Assuming there are 25 million daily booking queries, then we need very large-scale models to efficiently respond to all these queries. Enterprise models with daily room price data repositories will become a thing of the past.

The challenge for all businesses and organizations is to have their innovation lookout teams constantly surveying the technology landscape, and identify how the disruptors are using modeling and optimization ideas to achieve process innovation. Ideas are not trends, they are precision interventions, which means magazines and advisery consultant are only going to give you latent information. Extend the innovation lookout teams to your existing employees. *Employee of the Month* programs have outlived their utility, and we need to transition to an *Idea of the Month* culture culminating with the *Annual Grand Slam Idea*.

Chapter Summary

- The incoming data in Brownian flows are fast and furious. The exploding number of decision points requires decision and control systems to undergo an order of magnitude increase in the use of quantitative methods, data analysis, transfer functions, and decision-making models.
- A Brownian view leverages uncertainty into a business advantage. Very large-scale flow (VLSF) models control every resource and activity. VLSF modeling concepts and data strategies were presented.

- Introduced streaming data models that make decisions closer to the execution point. Data and decision latency are defined.
- Six dimensions by which the design-build measures model complexity is defined: Frequency, variance, fulfill locations, entity count, resource load, and flow time slack.
- The required decision capability increases with complexity. Four capabilities are needed: data tracking, cloud, action, and decision modeling.

CHAPTER 10

Machine Building

The utopic machine will have zero fulfillment time and an infinite variety of product options. Fast fulfillment is not easy and requires huge capital investments and deep modeling knowledge. Existing assets frequently are a disadvantage. Proceed with seven investigations to initiate the fast fulfillment project: Speed, Brownian Uncertainty, Physio-Digital Innovation, Streaming Data, Transfer Function Math, Automation Segments, and Decision Models.

Fast, faster, fastest. Smart, smarter, smartest. Choices, more choices, most choices. These are the goals of a design-build fulfillment team. In the preceding chapters, we investigated and explained strategies pursued by the innovators and disruptors to build some of the fastest, smartest, and most choice fulfillment machines. Now it's your turn, and this chapter describes activities to maximize the probability of success.

Zero-Infinity: The Utopic Machine—Fulfillment occurs instantly or in zero time. All possible configurations of the deliverables are possible, or an infinite product/service selection.

For most businesses, a zero-infinity machine is neither possible nor is it necessary. The first step in machine building, actually step zero, is to describe the zero-infinity target for your business. Do not expect this to be a precise or specific target, rather plan for a moving target that takes shape as you learn more about disruptive trends, technologies, and the possible pathways to achieve customer pivots. Assemble a zero-infinity team to collaboratively investigate and calibrate the zero-infinity target for the business.

Business and the management teams are generally organized to view all new initiatives or innovations as a project. This is a proven strategy that is easily implemented through well-known project planning tools. The team is focused on a specific endpoint, has a specified execution timeline, and a development budget. But this strategy does not play out well in a fast fulfillment innovation project. The endpoint is fuzzy in that the team may only have a 10 percent idea of what the endpoint and its associated processes are. This makes timelines, budgets, and even skill requirements just a set of guesses. Frequently, we will read stories of how successful founders innovated continuously and changed the scope and endpoint when a better idea or pathway came along. In contrast, established businesses operate in a more structured setting. To increase the probability of innovation success, it is, therefore, necessary to first increase endpoint visibility. This can be achieved through a series of step-zero investigations. These are designed to collect data and knowledge that are then used to fertilize the design-build innovation process.

The Seven Investigations

Earlier we learned that functional and process innovations, as opposed to inventive innovations, are the primary value creation drivers in a fulfillment machine. A necessary condition, therefore, for building a fulfillment machine are deep insights and knowledge into what functionalities excite your customer base, and what process inefficiencies or even lack of capabilities are limiting market growth and opportunities. Here are two mistakes that can derail our machine building efforts: *Mistake #1*—we institutively assume that we know the answers, the reality though is we only have a historical or experience view, not an outside or disruptor view. *Mistake #2*—we tend to focus on the product/service as opposed to the process for fulfilling the customer need.

Collectively, the earlier chapters introduced and presented methods and strategies for building a fast fulfillment machine. These methods and strategies are the focus theme for seven investigations (Figure 10.1) businesses must conduct as they initiate their fast fulfillment project. These investigations define and shape the unknown knowledge space within which the design-build team will conduct their zero-infinity innovation explorations.

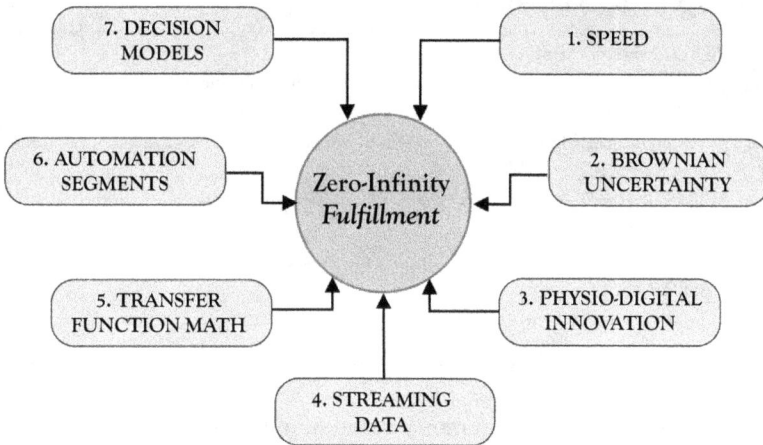

Figure 10.1 Fast fulfillment—Seven investigations

The first two investigations, SPEED and BROWNIAN UNCER-
TAINTY, provide an initial specification of the target endpoints and
associated performance goals for the fulfillment machine. Meeting these
targets will be a necessary condition for the project to succeed. The subse-
quent investigations identify the knowledge needed, available technology,
and the underlying transfer functions.

The investigations are organized into a set of four to six questions and
are intended to probe how the current business operations can be transformed or expanded through disruptive innovations. Each investigation
includes a prospective view sourced from a proven disruptive innovator or
innovation. This is not the time to study retrospective views, history can
be a handicap in innovative machine building.

Investigation 1: Speed

The primary seduction of the physical-internet-of-things is speed. It
allows customers to do things immediately, from anywhere, and at any
time. The six investigative questions (Table 10.1) focus on identifying the
speed, which will disrupt the current business environment and ensure
fulfillment success. The investigative results are critical in setting the target
endpoints. A conservative approach will only provide only incremental,
the investigation must be aggressive in their approach to identify the correct innovative speed targets. The speed targets must be backed up with
data and projections that convince the doubters and excite the innovators.

Table 10.1 Speed investigation

1. SPEED: Investigative Questions
A. What is the necessary speed for success? Quantified in four themes: (i) Time Efficiency, (ii) Cost Efficiency, (iii) Quality Enhancement, and (iv) Provider Expansion.
B. What is the speed limit at which customers will start pivoting to the fast fulfillment product/service?
C. What is the optimal position for the product/service in the frequency/immediacy map?
D. What are the key friction points limiting our current processes?
E. What are the major speed bumps limiting our current processes?
F. What are the incremental or enterprise solutions? What is the confessional rational for why this solution does not meet necessary speed?

Prospective View: The operational speed of a fulfillment machine is the culmination of many innovative ideas. If the target speed is high, then the innovators will be driven to design-build the needed ideas. Sir Jonathan Ive was chief design officer at Apple and worked closely alongside Steve Jobs in developing the iPhone. Here is what he has to say about the idea to reality journey.

> *How Does a New Product Come About At Apple?*[24]—What I love about the creative process, and this may sound naive, but it is this idea that one day there is no idea, and no solution, but then the next day there is an idea. The nature of having ideas and creativity is incredibly inspiring. There is an idea that is solitary, fragile, and tentative and does not have form. What we have found here is that it then becomes a conversation, although remains very fragile. When you see the most dramatic shift is when you transition from an abstract idea to a slightly more material conversation. But when you made a 3D model, however crude, you bring form to a nebulous idea, and everything changes—the entire process shifts. It galvanizes and brings focus from a broad group of people. It is a remarkable process.

Investigation 2: Brownian Uncertainty

Uncertainty and a multiplicity of options are inherent in modern fulfillment systems. The machine must recognize and respond rapidly to all requests that enter the system. The three investigative questions (Table 10.2) identify the range of options and the associated uncertainty that characterize the new normal customer base. The innovative ideas, design constructs, and structural elements of the fulfillment machine will be motivated by the results of this investigation.

Table 10.2 Brownian uncertainty investigation

2. BROWNIAN UNCERTAINTY: *Investigative Questions*
A. How are the Brownian catalysts changing or creating new customer needs? Described in terms of the four catalysts: (i) An unbounded selection, (ii) Crowdsourced information, (iii) End of the normal distribution, and (iv) Random is the new normal.
B. What is the Brownian multiplier effect on the existing/proposed business process or system? Described in terms of the four multipliers: (i) What, (ii) When, (iii) Where, and (iv) Like.
C. How are streamlined flows limiting responsiveness to Brownian flows? Describe the speed bumps and friction in terms of: (i) Higher costs, (ii) Decision complexity, (iii) Process complexity, and (iv) Delivery complexity necessary.

Prospective View: Shopify has been a powerful innovator in online retailing and over one million businesses in more than 175 countries have used it as a disruptive tool to take their business online. The founder Tobi Lutke has designed a fulfillment machine that adapts to the unique needs of each of its million retailers. In terms of fulfillment efficiency, Shopify is possibly the closest competitor to Amazon. In a recent interview, Tobi provided insights on seeking process improvements and make trendline predictions in an Internet-driven uncertain market.

> *Build an Online Business—No Matter What Business You Are In: Three kinds of processes*[85]—There is a kind of process that makes things that were previously impossible to do, possible. That is good. Then there is a kind of process that makes something that was previously possible significantly simpler, which is also good. And then there is everything else. I bet you 99.9 percent of all process that exists in corporate America is the third category, which is just telling people to behave slightly different from what common sense tells them to do. *Programmatically predict the unpredictable*[86]: How am I going to predict the future? What I am going to do is I'm going to work very hard on understanding what

everyone else, everywhere in the world, has already figured out. And then take those trendlines and try to spin them into the future and figure out what possibility space I have for the future. And then I am trying to figure out how the idea of entrepreneurship fits into that, and how does retail fit into that. What expectations change once some of those things that might currently be very nascent but are sharply increasing in steep trendlines; once they grow into something that everyone does? I think if people were honest about the future, they would admit that that is exactly what they are doing because, again, the future, itself, is completely chaotic and is unpredictable. It is just that you can extrapolate it sometimes.

Investigation 3: Physio-Digital Innovation

Fast fulfillment requires an intelligent and controllable cyber-physical infrastructure that adds intelligence to the machine. The four investigative questions (Table 10.3) identify the touchpoints and entry ramps that link the machine to the Internet of things. This is a critical investigation that will seed the innovation pathway and map key data and decision waypoints. Current methods and solutions promote incremental progress and equilibrium, the investigation must circumvent the current status-quo and motivate innovators to put on their disruptor hats.

Table 10.3 Physio-digital innovation investigation

3. PHYSIO-DIGITAL INNOVATION: *Investigative Questions*
A. What are possible physical pathways a disruptor/disintermediator can follow to efficiently respond to the effects of the Brownian multipliers?
B. How could subscription plans to optional products/services facilitate an effective leveraging of the Brownian catalysts?
C. Is there a ready compensator idea that incorporates one or more physio-digital innovations based on identified physical and digital pathways?
D. Is there a Nash equilibrium driving innovation complacency among the existing industry leaders?

Prospective View: Softbank and its founder Masayoshi Son is among the most significant funders of innovative disruptors. This is their plan for the utopic future, review, and discusses it in the context of your business as part of investigation 3:

Softbank Vision—The World 30 Years from Now[87]—You can own storage that can store a virtually infinite amount of information, knowledge, and wisdom. Digital will become the norm for information vehicles. Not only every electrical appliance but also shoes, glasses, everything will have embedded chips. They will be connected to each other through a limitless cloud and a super-high-speed network. This will provide a whole other level of emotional experiences through "seeing," "learning," "meeting," and "playing." Not only education but also medicine and work style will change fundamentally. Under such circumstances, the SoftBank Group is committed to accumulating all knowledge and wisdom of humans and artificial intelligence in the cloud, making it the largest asset of humankind. We want to revolutionize people's lifestyles by working with like-minded companies with cutting-edge technologies and superior business models.

Investigation 4: Streaming Data

The quants will rule, and the fulfillment machine will be data-driven. But data are like bread in a bakery, it becomes stale and hard by the end of the day. It is best when warm and fresh, and that is what you need fresh streaming data. The five investigative questions (Table 10.4) explore how data streams will power the disruptive processes of fast fulfillment. All data have hidden value or utility that needs to be discovered. The disruptors are magicians who know how to conjure this value, and you need to learn this trick too.

Table 10.4 Streaming data investigation

4. STREAMING DATA: *Investigative Questions*
A. For which business processes has latent or limited data availability restricted decision capability? What was the performance impact of these restrictions?
B. Specific to the identified business processes, what are the needed nX data points and their associated active data frequency?
C. What are possible additive business objects (B-Objects) and controllable activities that would accelerate fulfillment times of the targeted business processes?
D. What crowdsourced data streams could be integrated as speed catalysts in the fulfillment machine?
E. What technological constraints may be experienced in collecting the data streams?

Prospective View: Venky Harinarayan and Anand Rajaraman are two well known, but not publicly famous, data capitalists in Silicon Valley. Why do I call them data capitalists? They used data as the currency to build the machine and ultimate success. Working alongside Jeff Bezos, they innovated many of the data-driven models that are integral to the Amazon fulfillment machine. Summarized in the following are some of their data capitalization strategies. Review and investigate if they can be applied to leverage streaming data in your business.

> *Venky and Anand Data Capitalists: Model lite and data rich[88]*— More data almost always beats better algorithms, so when you have developed your parameterized model don't throw the data away. Make decisions in a collaborative approach with both the model and data, this will provide unique solutions for every instance in a Brownian world. *Data dashboard*—Provide process innovators with grab-and-go data and keep collecting more data including complementary data. Data provide instant proof, the idea is already validated in the first presentation. The naysayers and doubters with soft roadblocks cannot stop the data-backed ideas. *Materialize Decisions[89]*—Partition the problem into a hyperspace. Then use heuristics to materialize or precompute the decisions for the most common subproblems. This will allow the system to make the instant decisions required to operate the VLSF models.

Investigation 5: Transfer Function Math

The well-known design principle, KISS: Keep it Simple Stupid, later also became a management mantra. But KISS has limited applicability in today's data and Internet-driven world. MATCH: Model and Transfer Complexity to Algorithms is the mantra of fast fulfillment. The four investigative questions (Table 10.5) are designed to explore input variables, output parameters, and management's ability to control the relationship through the right decisions at the right time.

Prospective View: Uber disrupted one of the oldest service industries, taxis, or the ride-hailing business. Later, Uber expanded into the food delivery business. These have historically been very low technology

Table 10.5 Transfer function math investigation

5. TRANSFER FUNCTION MATH: Investigative Questions
A. What input process variables will enhance our ability to model the transfer function, which describe the underlying physics of current and future business processes?
B. What controllable decision variables will enhance our ability to manage and improve the output performance of transfer functions driving current and future business processes?
C. How could probability theory be integrated into decision control methods so as to leverage the process uncertainty into a competitive advantage?
D. Is there an immediate example of a Lite-AI solution that could significantly the performance of a current and future business processes?

businesses with almost no innovation (except for Pizza delivery). Uber used the full power of technology including advanced math modeling to radically disrupt the industry. Described in the following is how the seemingly mundane task of food delivery is controlled by a complicated transfer function model.

Michelangelo—Uber's Machine Learning Platform[90]—Predicting meal estimated time of delivery (ETD) is not simple. When an UberEATS customer places an order, it is sent to the restaurant for processing. The restaurant then needs to acknowledge the order and prepare the meal, which will take time depending on the complexity of the order and how busy the restaurant is. When the meal is close to being ready, an Uber delivery partner is dispatched to pick up the meal. The delivery partner needs to get to the restaurant, find parking, and walk inside to get the food, then walk back to the car, drive to the customer's location (which depends on route, traffic, and other factors), find parking, and walk to the customer's door to complete the delivery. The goal is to predict the total duration of this complex multistage process, as well as recalculate these time-to-delivery predictions at every step of the process. On the Michelangelo platform, the UberEATS data scientists use gradient-boosted decision-tree regression models to predict this end-to-end delivery time. Features for the model inputs include information from the request (e.g., time of day and delivery location), historical features (e.g., average meal prep time for the last seven days), and near-real-time calculated features (e.g., average meal prep time for the last one hour).

Investigation 6: Automation Blocks

Human capital costs are a constant focus of Chief Financial Officer (CFOs) simply because they represent for most businesses the largest discretionary costs. For a zero-growth company, a common management strategy is cost reduction through headcount reduction, followed by a short-term cheer on Wall Street. Here the quest for automation is directionally opposite to a headcount reduction, or to put it bluntly, a retreating strategy. Automation is the way to design-build those high-growth process. Furthermore, humans are bounded by their decision-making speed and the ability to process a set of fast-changing variables. The four investigative questions (Table 10.6) are designed to first look at what previous ideas were limited by headcount constraints. This ensures that future ideas are not a casualty of the same constraints. Innovators view automation as an opportunity and the investigators will find those opportunities as they answer the questions.

Table 10.6 Automation blocks investigation

6. AUTOMATION BLOCKS: *Investigative Questions*
A. What activities in planned/future business processes were not pursued due to the projected need for high levels of manual labor or manual decision control?
B. What situation attributes are likely to generate automation challenges in the face of Brownian uncertainty associated with future business processes? Described in terms of the four attributes: (i) Randomness, (ii) Factor Complexity, (iii) False Signals, and (iv) Congestion.
C. What technology enablers could facilitate alpha and sigma automation solutions, which in turn result in faster fulfillment speeds?
D. Are there any disruptive moonshot opportunities or canopy blossom ideas that can only be operationalized with an accompanying automation project?

Prospective View: Marc Andreessen is a legendary venture capitalist in Silicon Valley and has been involved with several very successful innovators, including Facebook, Lyft, and Slack. Marc created the highly influential Mosaic Internet browser and cofounded Netscape. In a 2011 Wall Street Journal essay, he coined the phrase *software is eating the world.* Summarized as follows is a 2019 revisit of the phrase and future disruptive trends. It says if it can be automated, then automate it, else someone is going to do it first.

Software is Eating the World[91]—So there is a 70-year journey to basically get everybody on a computer, and everybody on the internet. OK, how does this unfold from here, across industries? I describe it in three claims. First *claim is that any product or service in any field that can become a software product, will become a software product. And* so, if you are used to doing something on the phone or paper, that will go to software. If you have had a physical product, answering machines, or tape players, boom boxes, like, all the things Radio Shack used to sell. They are all apps on the phone. If it can become bytes, it becomes bytes. Bytes are zero marginal cost, so they are easy to replicate at scale, and become much more cost-effective. *The next claim is that every company in the world that is in any of these markets in which this process is happening, must become a software company.* Any company that deals with customers, especially consumers, is going to have to radically up its game, in terms of its ability to build the kinds of user interfaces and experiences that people expect these days. And *then the most audacious claim is, as a consequence of one and two, in the long run, in every market, the best software company will win.* And that does not necessarily mean that a new company that starts as a software company entering an existing market will win, but it also does not necessarily mean that an incumbent that adapts to being a software company will win.

Investigation 7: Decision Models

Speed is a necessary condition for fast fulfillment. Multiply that with complex transfer models and streaming data, and you have a decision-making system that is outside the realm of the human envelope. The only solution is a computerized network of intelligent decision models driven by smart algorithms. The four investigative questions (Table 10.7) list specific challenges the business faces in developing an automated decision system. Next, the questions identify the likely speed acceleration the system will provide. A multitude of solution providers are willing to help with tools and application knowledge and the investigation must shortlist those most likely to help with building the innovative machine.

Table 10.7 *Decision models investigation*

7. DECISION MODELS: *Investigative Questions*
A. What are the likely complexity challenges in building decisions models for fast fulfillments? Discussions should be in the context of (i) frequency, (ii) variance, and (iii) fulfill locations.
B. What resources queues will slow down the fulfillment speed and cumulatively increase flow time slack? How can automated process control decision models shrink these queues without additional resources?
C. What are the needed data tracking and cloud computing capability needed to build and implement fast decision control models? Described in terms of software tools, hardware needs and service vendors.
D. What manpower skills do we need immediately if we are going to build a fast fulfillment machine?

Prospective View: Tesla and its founder Elon Musk are revolutionary, and at times arrogant, disruptors in the biggest industry of them all, automobiles. Full Self-Driving (FSD) vehicles are possibly the most complex decision problem in engineering. The autopilot system experiences a hyper Brownian environment and the consequences of a decision error are severe. Tesla plans to achieve FSD soon and plans to distribute FSD as a software upgrade to all recently built Teslas. Their game plan shows how disruptors simplify complex problems through decision models.

Tesla Autopilot Game Plan:[92]—We develop and deploy autonomy at scale. We believe that an approach based on advanced AI for vision and planning, supported by efficient use of inference hardware is the only way to achieve a general solution to full self-driving. Autonomy algorithms drive the car by creating a high-fidelity representation of the world and planning trajectories in that space. To train the neural networks to predict such representations, algorithmically create accurate and large-scale ground truth data by combining information from the car's sensors across space and time. Use state-of-the-art techniques to build a robust planning and decision-making system that operates in complicated real-world situations under uncertainty.

What, Who, and How?

Before starting the investigations, a few questions must be answered. The first is what? The investigation must be directed by a threat or opportunity-driven business purpose, or an aspiration, typically associated with an internal or external product/service. It could be small or big, abstract or specific, but it must provide a broad not focused direction for the investigation. Here is one big and one small purpose statement for two of the largest companies in the world, at the start of their machine building journey.

> Amazon was launched in 1995, with the mission "to be Earth's most customer-centric company, where customers can find and discover anything they might want to buy online, and endeavors to offer its customers the lowest possible prices."

> Mark Zuckerburg created Facebook in 2004 with the design goal of a campus wide social media website to connect Harvard students with one another.

The second question is who should be on the zero-infinity team? Greg Christie, who led the software development team for the first iPhone, recalls that it was a shockingly small team.[93] Likewise, many start-ups developed their first ideas with less than five members. Small teams can achieve higher levels of communication and are far more likely to have the same level of investigative focus. Listed here are the ideal specification for the zero-infinity team:

- Team size should be between three and five members. The same team must do all seven investigations, but associates should be added as needed to complement a specific investigation.
- Members should have complementary not overlapping skills. Three skill sets must be covered by the team, domain knowledge, technology insight, and data processing.

- Members should not have a confirmatory bias. That is, they are likely to seek and interpret information in a way that supports their existing beliefs.

The third question is how the team should proceed. There is no right way and the recommendation is to follow an approach that works with team dynamics. Here, though, are a few process suggestions:

- The seven investigations should be done sequentially. The sequence was designed for information rollover.
- There should be frequent meetings, ideally every day. Many disruptive innovators were collocated. If this is not possible, all possible online tools should be used for effective interactions.
- The process should be relatively short. The target should be to complete each investigation in one week and the entire activity wrapped up in two months.
- Investigations should be democratized, and all member views and investigative results must be reviewed and analyzed.
- The answers should be brief, one to two pages per question. Data should be generously used to illustrated trends and projections.
- Avoid the boundaries of key performance indicators (KPIs) they can be false signals that steer the investigation away from the disruptive innovations.

The final output is an investigation report that identifies and confirms there are disruptive opportunities in the business. The report also confirms that these disruptions are doable, possibly requiring tools and methods that we have never used before. The report should have a summary page upfront, which presents the findings in a sort of VC (Venture Capitalist) pitch mode. Briefly stated, (i) Market Opportunities, (ii) Technology Enablers, and (iii) Potential Value. The next chapter provides additional details on how the investigation and accompanying report integrates with the overall design-build project.

Chapter Summary

- In the Utopic Machine, fulfillment occurs instantly or in zero time. All possible configurations of the deliverables are possible. The first step in machine building is to describe the zero-infinity target for the business.
- Seven investigations that initiate the fast fulfillment project are introduced. These investigations define and shape the unknown knowledge space within which the design-build team will design-build their zero-infinity innovation.
- Specifications and action plans for the investigation team are presented.

CHAPTER 11

Team Innovation

Product innovation usually results in a new product or new technology, and the innovators can visualize the singular outcome. Process innovation on the other hand is cumbersome, it is not immediately brilliant and the disruption is not obvious. A three-team sequential plan to design and build your fast fulfillment machine is introduced. This plan deploys the concepts and methods presented in the preceding chapters.

Team innovation is not looking for incremental ideas but rather ideas that lead to hyper-disruptive high-impact innovations. Ideas come from people, and people make the team. Who is on the team and who leads the team is what ultimately determines success. In start-ups, innovation teams are like rock bands, the business has a few employees, and everyone is creative and passionately driven by the disruption. But in all successful start-ups, some key innovators stayed through all the failures and earned that coveted knighthood of founder or cofounder. Numerous books are describing the innovation stories of these companies, plus many other books listing innovation traits and how companies can acquire these traits.

A key goal of this book is that companies will deploy the presented concepts and methods to create their fast fulfillment machine. Disruptive process innovations are what companies need to build the machine, but the underlying ideas and their disruptive value are not easily seen and realized. So, we introduce a three-team sequential plan.

1. *Innovation Lookout Team*: Would serve as a surveillance force that ensures the company is not blindsided by the disruptors.

2. *Zero-Infinity Investigation Team*: Would confirm the machine building opportunities and pathways.
3. *Team Innovation*: Would be tasked with designing and building (design-build) the fast fulfillment machine.

In the previous chapter, we described the investigation process and provided suggestions for putting together the zero-infinity investigation team. In this chapter, we do the same for the lookout team and team innovation. These formal or assigned teams serve as a surrogate for the natural teams that form in start-ups. Make no mistake, these formal teams will be challenged to match the drive and passion of the start-ups. The knowledge tactics of this book will help close the gap. Read and access the innovation team-building knowledge provided by many experts to close the gap further.

We all want that innovation recipe, a step-by-step plan or process that will get us to the endpoint. There is a library full of textbooks and management books on New Product Development, but the reality is that the disruptors never used any of these. The fulfillment machine is driven by process innovation, and the classical approaches do not work very well when you are looking to disrupt the current process or business. So, my recommendation is to construct a plan that is best suited to the team, the nature of the business, and the company's aspirations. Rigid or highly structured plans are likely to be innovation hurdles, so keep it fluid.

In the previous chapter, we introduced the role of the zero-infinity investigation team in machine building, and earlier we had talked about the innovation lookout team. In this final chapter, we bring it all together and recommend a three-team sequential process (Figure 11.1). The first team, innovation lookout, is on all the time in a sort of constant surveillance mode. The other two, zero-infinity investigation and team innovation, are activated in response to an identified threat/opportunity.

Chapter 10 described in detail the tasks and outputs of the zero-infinity investigation team. Here we focus on the other two teams. Unlike the zero-infinity team, we do not provide a specific list of tasks, rather, this chapter proposes features and flavors that will drive team success.

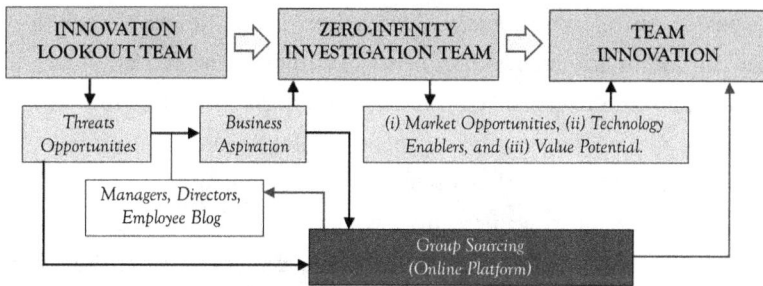

Figure 11.1 Three-team sequential innovation process

Innovation Lookout Team

The classical view of innovation is periodic, that is, great things happen every *N* years. The reality though is that technology enablers are being created continuously, and more importantly, these are external to the company. A business, therefore, needs to be on a constant lookout for these creations and be prepared to immediately innovate products and services. The innovation lookout team is charged with seeding these innovations. Do not assume that you can skip the team and it will happen organically, or that technology officers, marketing departments, and data analytics will do the job. Here are the attributes of the lookout team:

> *Purpose:* Constant survey of the business landscape to innovation derive threats and opportunities which could disrupt or current product/service portfolios.
>
> *Formation:* Small team of one to three members. Rotating membership with a new team every quarter or semi annually.
>
> *Lookout Intelligence Report:* A three- to five-page report prepared by the team and submitted to management and other key parties once every quarter. The report should include the following sections: (i) Technology enablers, (ii) Disruptors and/or potential disruptions, (iii) Customer shifts or trends, and (iv) Threats and Opportunities, which are the cumulative or summary effect of the previous three.

A report is only valuable if it is used effectively and generates necessary action. The obvious reviewers of the Lookout Intelligence Report are senior managers and stakeholders who will decide if a zero-infinity team should be activated. But often this group is not a sufficient group to ensure innovation success. Crowdsourcing information is a great way to reach out to a wider group of company employees and we introduce the Group Idea Sourcing method, as an additional tool.

The review must evaluate first, whether any further investigations are required, and second formulate business aspirations from the report intelligence. It is unlikely that every iteration of the report will generate follow-up action. The more threats and opportunities the team identifies, the more actionable the report. The biggest risk of an ineffective team is Titanic latency. Remember the lookout team on the crow's nest of the Titanic, they saw the iceberg and alerted the captain, but the warning was too late to save the ship. Looking out at the innovation disruptor landscape there are four possible situations:

Situation #0: There are no disruptors and no technology enablers that could challenge the existing machine.

Situation #1: There are no disruptors, but technology enablers were identified and you have first-mover advantage.

Situation #2: The disruptors have built the machine and are ready to set sail.

Situation #3: The disruptors are at the gate! You need to build a machine at warp speed.

Apart from situation #0, all others should get the ball rolling on some kind of action. If situation #2 or 3# are detected, then you have Titanic latency, and you need an all-hands-on deck plan. When management decides to activate a zero-infinity team, then they must synthesize the intelligence report into a brief business aspiration.

Business Aspiration: A sketchy idea of process solutions or products/ services that could counter the threats or leverage the opportunities.

This would include inputs of all reviewers, plus the comments submitted in the group sourcing platform. Let's take a look at what the lookout team at a financial services firm would have reported

(Table 11.1), and the resulting business aspiration. If done correctly and at the right time, the firm would have been able to innovate faster than upstarts like Robinhood[94], and not just been copycat followers.

Table 11.1 Example Output of the Innovation Lookout Team

Innovation Lookout—A Financial Services Firm
Opportunity: An increasing population of young investors with small capital (less than $2,000) are looking for zero-cost solutions to fulfill their stock market investment plans. New programming and communication technologies make it possible to provide advanced services as a self-service utility.
Threats: A few companies have already built and deployed a first-generation zero-cost investment fulfillment solution.
Business Aspiration: Offer a broad service fast execution investment solution through an ultra-low-cost platform. Small capital investors are provided large capital services and utilities with no service fees.
Robinhood—On a mission to democratize finance for all[94]
Founders realized that big Wall Street firms pay effectively nothing to trade stocks, while most Americans are charged up to $10 for every trade and decided to build products that would provide everyone with access to the financial markets, not just the wealthy. They built Robinhood—a company that leverages technology to encourage everyone to participate in our financial system.

Group Sourcing

Those most vested in the current system are least likely to propose an innovative disruption, which implies that a business must reach out to individuals less vested in the current system to promote, propose, or validate innovative disruptions. Wired magazine introduced the term *crowdsourcing*, and it can be a powerful tool for distributing the innovation process through the company and more importantly among those less vested.

Crowdsourcing is a sourcing model in which individuals or organizations obtain goods and services, including ideas, from a large, relatively open, and often rapidly evolving group of participants. Crowdsourcing typically involves using the internet to attract and divide work between participants to achieve a cumulative result. Some forms of crowdsourcing, such as in "idea competitions" or "innovation contests" provide ways for organizations to learn beyond the "base of minds" provided by their employees (Wikipedia Definition).[95]

The intelligence report includes valuable information that the business plans to transform into an innovative idea, so it is not something you want to share with a public crowd. Group sourcing using a forum style platform can limit participation to selected employees. The approach expands the numbers of participants, who can then add supporting, critical, and/or alternative viewpoints to the report. Additionally, they can tap and foster ideas from insightful individuals in the business. Here are some industry examples to show how group sourcing can be implemented.

What's your Starbucks Idea?[96]—Revolutionary or simple, we want to hear it. This is a basic crowdsourcing idea platform, but it works.

L'Oreal Innovation Runway 2020[97]—Open call for start-ups from the many fields of deep tech and various industries to shape the future of beauty together. Let's cocreate revolutionary solutions that are scalable, sustainable, and environmentally friendly to transform the industry! Proposals are judged by LOreal innovation experts based on the following: (i) Technology description, (ii) Differentiation and Impact of the Value proposition, (iii) Business/revenue model, and (iv) Traction: KPI metrics and milestones. The program is run on Agorize[98]—an open innovation challenge platform.

Idea Drop[99]—An intuitive idea management software—Group sourcing can use many modes, includes e-mail, or a digital wall where participants can add notes to specific features of the proposed innovations and disruptions. You can also use a readily available platform such as Idea Drop.

Team Innovation

Team innovation is tasked with the detailed activity of designing and building the fulfillment machine. The innovation lookout and zero-infinity teams have collected key data and information needed to give the team focus and direction. Similar to the lookout report, the zero-infinity report is reviewed by a management team, and a decision is made on whether to activate team innovation. Capital and talent resources required by team innovation could be substantial. A swift and democratic review of the seven investigative questions and the associated summary page is critical.

> *Machine Building Goal:* Design-build a fast fulfillment solution that delivers the company's current and future products/services in new innovative ways that disrupt the current process. The solution would involve process innovations that build on the identified: (i) Market Opportunities, (ii) Technology Enablers, and (iii) Value Potential.

Team innovation would formulate a more detailed goal that specifies products/services or functional parts of these products/services. The keywords in the goal are disruptive and process innovations and the team has a stated consensus on how these keywords are evaluated.

How the team functions and how the team is comprised will be different for every business, and no specific process or method is proposed here. The number of members and the required process skills will be determined by the business aspiration and process innovation scope. But here are some recommendations to consider as the team is put together. Remember the resulting innovations are only as good as the team.

XYZ Leadership

Teams have leaders, and their leadership style will be reflected in the output. Traditionally, businesses have followed a classical style of leadership, which I will call the ABC style. Vision, focus, and inspirations are the key elements of ABC leaders and this style works perfectly at the highest levels of the business organization. But this is not the style of leadership we see in successful start-ups or innovation projects. Rather, an XYZ leadership style seems to be the more popular and effective. Figure 11.2 compares the traits of the two leadership styles. Innovators need to channel their excitement, they need to validate their achievements and be democratic participants in the process, and they know new technologies make big innovations possible. The XYZ style promotes and facilitates innovations, and leaders should pivot to it.

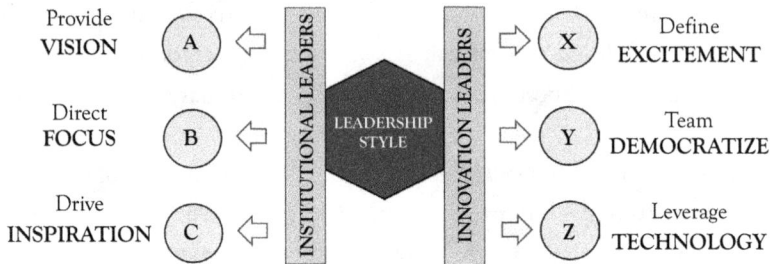

Figure 11.2 Two leadership styles—ABC and XYZ

Technology will be an integral part of the fulfillment machine, and team innovation leaders and members must collectively have significant knowledge about the technology enablers. Outsourcing the technology role to a contractor, or assuming there is some plug-and-play vendor supplied solution is not going to generate disruptive innovations. The team leadership must view technology as a core process and a necessary strength for the business.

Flavors of the Team

Innovation projects are very different from traditional improvement projects. Why? Because the team has to assume and expect that process innovations are likely to discount all the strengths of the current system. Having a team with the right attitude is critical to success, and here we identify four flavors or characteristics, that are required of team innovation.

#1 Good Bones Good Soul—All teams have good bones: they have domain knowledge and expertise, the requisite analytical skills, and insightful curiosity. But the soul, ah! It does not come easily. The soul is the passion

that drives the desire to build that disruptive innovation solution, and for most start-ups, it comes naturally. For a formal team, the risk is that we end up with *Good Bones No Soul*. I have no solution to transitioning from No Soul to Good Soul. Maybe that special canopy growth smoothie or that organic hyper botanical premium gin and tonic is what team innovation needs to create that collective passion.

> Do what you love. Passion is everything. Innovation doesn't happen without it. Dig deep to identify your true passion. Steve Jobs was not passionate about computers; he was passionate about building tools to help people unleash their potential. One of the most profound remarks Jobs ever made occurred at the end of one of his last major public presentations. Jobs said, "It's the intersection of technology and liberal arts that makes our hearts sing."
> —*The Innovation Secrets of Steve Jobs, Carmine Gallo*[100]

#2 No Reservations, No Limitations—Legendary chef journalist Anthony Bourdain made food into a discovery journey, which was portrayed on his iconic TV show, *No Reservations*. He disrupted the structured recipe view of food shows and instead introduced millions to the innovative and unknown cuisines and cultures from all over the world.

> Bourdain described his initial pitch for the show to The New Yorker: "I travel around the world, eat a lot of s***, and basically do whatever the f*** I want."[101]

Overlooking the profanity, team innovation must adopt the same attitude. A great thing about process innovations is that they are often portable. The team should be ready to look far and wide, study a lot of innovations, and say whatever they want at team meetings. That's what the business needs, not the 99 percent same as other innovations.

#3 Light my Fire—Missed opportunities; didn't see it coming; or passed by that great idea. These are all common phrases used by businesses, teams, and individuals to describe a disruption. The greatest risk to team innovation is that even though all members have the needed skills, information,

and experiential background, and the innovation trends and technology enablers are obvious, it still does not light an innovation fire.

> *The time to hesitate is through. No time to wallow in the mire.*
> *Try now we can only lose. And our "ideas" become a funeral pyre*
> —Robby Krieger and Jim Morrison, The Doors

The ability to scan and process the information and then spark it into an idea is a necessary flavor condition for the team. As the song says, hesitation, or waiting for more information, or looking for that certain winner is not going to light any innovation fires. In the absence of this ability or characteristic, team innovation will struggle to design-build a fast fulfillment machine. The 1979 visit to Xerox PARC by Steve Jobs[102] is now folklore in innovation history. In one short visit, Jobs saw ideas that immediately lit a fire in his innovative mind and greatly influenced the design of the Macintosh.

#4 Front Loaded Optimism—A good team will be democratic and analytical, and should quickly progress on the design-build path. Legacy companies often correctly identify threats and opportunities, respond with an innovative design-build team, but ultimately end up with a weak dead-on-arrival product or service. Why? Innovation experts have a long list of reasons, but one frequent reason is the team shoots down its own great ideas. The net result, they end up with mediocre ideas.

> *Optimism Rule: For* the first 20 minutes, anyone speaking about the idea has to be positive, contributing only to the bullish case. Say anything critical and you're swiftly escorted from the room. The optimism rule is designed to thwart what the partners believe is the natural tendency for smart people to be skeptical and shoot down ideas prematurely—*Baillie Gifford Investment Partners*[103]

No idea will pass all the analytical discussions, so the team must follow the optimism rule and focus on why the idea will work, not why it will not work.

How you determine whether the team has these flavors is a matter of judgment. But start by asking the candidates themselves and then those who have worked with them. If all four flavors are not strongly present in team innovation, STOP, these are necessary conditions.

Disruption Icebreaker

Disruptive innovation is already happening and throughout the book, we have reviewed many examples. A great way to get team innovation started is to have them meet some disruptors. Since arranging actual meetings with disruptors could be a challenge, an easier and more efficient way is to learn about the disruptors, is from magazine reports and TV shows.

CNBC Disruptor 50 Companies[104]—CNBC identifies private companies whose breakthroughs are influencing business and market competition at an accelerated pace. The start-ups making the 2020 Disruptor list are at the epicenter of a world-changing in previously unimaginable ways, turning ideas in cybersecurity, education, health IT, logistics/delivery, fintech, and agriculture into a new wave of billion-dollar businesses. A key disruptor selection criterion is the ability to disrupt established industries and public companies. Scalability and user growth were the most important criteria plus a list of the key technologies driving their businesses.

Feature Company: Lemonade[105]—Offers homeowners and renters insurance in the United States, through its full-stack insurance carriers. Powered by artificial intelligence (AI) and behavioral economics, Lemonade set out to replace brokers and bureaucracy with bots and machine learning, aiming for zero paperwork and instant everything. Eliminates the conflict of interest between insurers and the insured. It offers insurance—powered by AI, chatbots, and behavioral economics—to renters and homeowners. Process innovations are given as follows: (i) Customers are guided by a chatbot through the application process in under a minute; (ii) AI optimizes insurance for what the customer wants to pay; and (iii) API integration of Lemonade into any other service fulfillment process.

Forbes Next Billion-Dollar Start-ups[106]—Forbes has teamed up with TrueBridge Capital Partners to search the United States for the 25 fastest-growing venture-backed start-ups most likely to reach a $1 billion valuation. TrueBridge asked 300 venture capital firms to nominate the companies they thought were most likely to become unicorns, while Forbes reached out directly to more than 100 start-ups. Then came the deeper look, financial analysis, user/customer count, and founder interviews.

Feature Company: Capsule[107]—Free, same-day prescription delivery from the safety of your home. Patients request to transfer their prescriptions to Capsule, schedule a same-day delivery time, and wait for a courier to deliver medication to their door via bike, subway, or other modes of public transit, all within two hours and free of charge. Process innovations are given as follows: (i) Pharmacy warehouse located in a dense urban area; (ii) Army of UberEats-style couriers; and (iii) App-based digitization of the physician to the pharmacy to the patient communication process.

A good start for team innovation is an icebreaker meeting where members share innovation stories and strategies. Each member can be assigned one company from the previous lists, and they can then present the disruptive innovations the company has developed and deployed.

Prepare for the Fulfillment Machine

Driven by the ubiquitous Internet, a host of new technologies, and an entirely new customer delivery expectation, fulfillment machines are being created by innovators in every industry and every country. We started this book by describing the Amazon fulfillment process and how it disrupted the retail supply chain. Progressively, we presented the building blocks of fast fulfillment: the physical machines and the intelligent fuel. The first goal was to convince you that fast fulfillment is spreading across industries. But the final goal was to describe a pathway for building your fast fulfillment machine with organically generated disruptive innovations.

Fast fulfillment machines are radically different from current business processes. New forms of process automation and Lite-AI-driven decision models will often challenge the business, and the workforce must be prepared for this dramatic process change. Executive involvement and C-Suite visibility are cliché requirements for team innovation, but more importantly, the workforce and stakeholders most closely associated with the fulfillment machine must be prepared with the needed training and educated on the what, why, and how. These preparations should start as early as possible. The zero-infinity report provides sufficient intelligence to initiate the training and learning programs. Amazon had the luxury of time and could develop its fulfillment machine at an evolutionary pace. Today businesses need to have an instant solution, and team innovation, and everyone else must work at warp speed. The preparation must introduce all participants to failure tolerance. The machine is not going to work flawlessly on day one, but we should be confident that the team is smart and robust enough to quickly recognize stress points and design-build a solution.

Failure is an option. If things are not failing, you are not innovating enough.
— Elon Musk, CEO of SpaceX and Tesla Motors[108]

Pandemic—Victorious

As I wrote the final chapters of this book, one of the most significant events of our lifetime occurred, starting from a market in the city center of Wuhan, China, a virus affected every country, every industry, every company, and every individual on earth. While we're all overcome by the tragic news of case counts and deaths, I was simultaneously surprised and amazed by the remarkable design-build innovations that companies across the globe deployed to respond and sustain their business. In the most unusual Berkshire Hathaway annual meeting ever, the greatest investor of our lifetimes Warren Buffett proclaimed you just had to believe that the American miracle was intact.

Yes, Warren was right, but possibly not the way he thought. Over a period of five months, companies across the United States, and the globe, built fulfillment machines at lightning speed. It was Brownian uncertainty at its extreme: every family ordered a unique grocery list with several strange items that they needed in two hours; every patient wanted a virtual meeting with their preferred doctor at a convenient time tomorrow; every stuck at home do-it-yourself builder needed that special order flooring in an odd quantity in two days; and there were many more with their unique demands.

In August 2020, a full five months after the virus shut down the U.S. economy, several companies reported remarkable growth numbers: Home Depot (100 percent increase in digital sales with 60 percent fulfillment from stores), Walmart (97 percent increase in digital sales), Target (273 percent increase in same-day fulfillment digital sales), Best Buy, Chillis Restaurants all excelled. One remarkable innovation during the pandemic is the new restaurant concept: It's Just Wings:

> *It's Just Wings: The birth of ghost kitchen fulfillment*[109]—As the pandemic closed restaurants across the United States, innovators at Brinker International (owner of the Chillis chain) were busy in the design-build of a new virtual restaurant. A purely delivery restaurant concept that leveraged the under-utilized kitchen capacity of associated restaurants and the fulfillment network of Doordash. Analytics and smart modeling prescribed a menu, preparation schedule and ready to deliver inventory. This was not simply a take-out expansion, it was a textbook disruptive innovation in food fulfillment.

Developments that would have occurred over the next five years were completed in five months. Jim Cramer the effervescent CNBC host created the *Covid-19 Stock Index*[110], this was a list of companies who were either building fast fulfillment machines or providing technology enablers that made the machines possible. On the flip side, many companies, particularly small businesses, struggled in the pandemic economy and some would not survive. Speed—the necessary condition—is what determined the victors. The fulfillment innovators were victorious against the pandemic and progressively their solutions helped a resolute economy.

Chapter Summary

- A three-team sequential plan to develop disruptive process innovations and design-build the fulfillment the machine is presented: Innovation Lookout Team, Zero-Infinity Investigation Team, and Team Innovation.
- Leadership styles and the four flavors or characteristics that make a good team innovation are presented.

It's raining ideas! Hallelujah!

Appendix

Innovation Toolbox

Here are three readily and easily applicable tools that facilitate the implementation of one more methods presented in the chapters.

For completed examples and detailed presentations on the toolbox worksheets, please visit the accompanying website www.fastfulfill.org

A. Process Speed Analyzer (PS-Analyzer)

What Information Does It Provide?

Focus is on a specific fulfillment process. The PS-Analyzer evaluates whether the process is fast enough to survive in an Internet-driven world, and identifies the slow causes that are reducing process speed. A quick investigation of the causes projects whether the team can come up with a set of innovative ideas that can eliminate or accelerate the causes. The final decision is whether to *Fix-It:* Reengineer the process or *Design-Build-It:* Build a fresh new process.

Definitions

Specific Fulfillment Process: The specific process with defined start and end. Example: (1) Start—Order receipt at the warehouse; End—Package shipped from the warehouse. (2) Start—Ride request confirmed in the system; End—Ride assigned to a driver. Multiple entities (e.g., customer orders) will flow through the process over a period of time.

Process Speed: Time for a single entity to flow through the specific process from start to end. The shorter the time the faster the speed. Use Figure A.1 to calibrate the process at four speed levels: (i) T^L—Speed at which the business will start losing customer rapidly, (ii) T^S—Speed at which the customer count remains steady, (iii) T^B—Best speed among current competitors also a pivot point for customers, and (iv) T^D—Speed at which an innovator will disrupt the business.

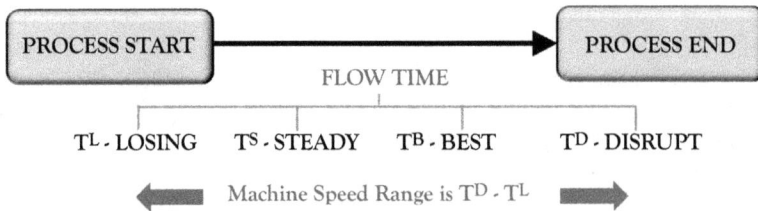

Figure A.1 Process speed calibration

The machine speed range must be based on market information and customer behavior trends. The speed T^B is a critical speed and must accurately reflect the customer pivot factor.

Slow Cause: An identified behavior of one or more activities in the process that is slowing the fulfillment speed. Benchmark is the best speed (T^B), and any cause that slows the process below this speed should be listed. There two types of slow causes:

- **Type-F: Process Friction**—Slows down the fulfillment process flow by the insertion of decisions, activities, or uncertainties that impede the throughput efficiency. There are four sources of friction.
  i. *Skill Inefficiency:* Workers/Machines not optimized for fast activity times
  ii. *Data Search:* Data needed to complete activity not readily available
  iii. *Process Design:* Requires many steps or a suboptimal flow
  iv. *Time Waste:* Unnecessary or redundant steps and activities
- **Type-S: Speed Bump**—Temporarily stops the fulfillment process by creating a queue or holding stage for the flowing entities. The delay time is typically a function of one or more internal or external factors. There are four sources of speed bumps.
  i. *Resource Shortage:* Queue formation due to fully utilized resources
  ii. *Decision Optimize:* Process control delays, waiting for assignment or reset
  iii. *Batch Process:* Processing occurs at fixed intervals or quantities
  iv. *Low Priority:* Waiting for resource attention

Speed Effect: Use Figure A.2. to calibrate effect of the slow causes on process speed. Calibrated at four levels: Low, Medium, High, and Mega. The effect is benchmarked against the machine speed range. Low indicates the cause is slowing the process by 10 percent, Mega indicates a 60+ percent effect.

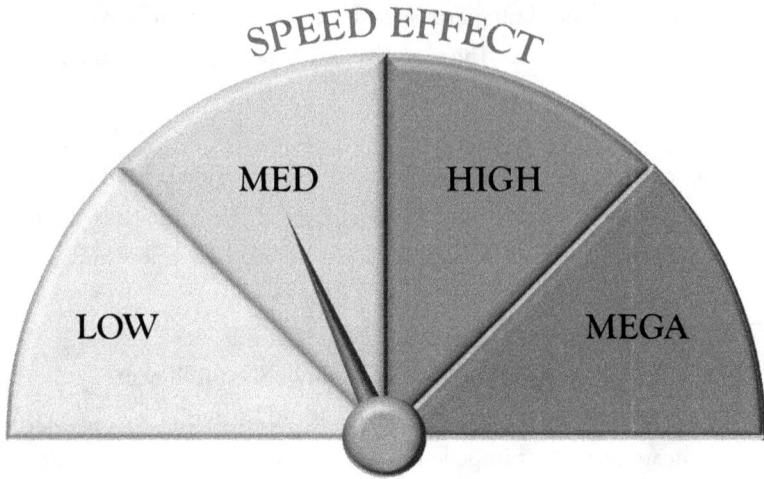

Figure A.2 Speed effect calibration

Innovation Idea: A solution for countering the speed effect of the slow cause. These innovative ideas either eliminate the cause or accelerate the process flow. There are six innovation idea drivers: (i) Data Streaming, (ii) Decision Modeling, (iii) Process Time, (iv) Automation, (v) Resource Cloud, and (vi) Uncertainty Analytics.

Fix-It or Design-Build-It: The critical question in fast fulfillment is whether an existing process can be fixed so that it runs and speeds that are higher than T^B and with the potential to achieve T^D. If this process acceleration is not possible, then the business needs to design-build a new process that integrates several disruptive innovations.

PS-Analyzer Steps:

1. Describe the specific fulfillment process that is to be analyzed. Identify the process start and endpoints and the entity flowing through.
2. Investigate current and future market trends that determine customer process speed expectations.
3. For the specific process record the four speed levels: T^L, T^S, T^B, and T^D.

4. Review the current process and create a list of slow causes. Limit to 5, more than that, design-build a new process.
5. For each slow cause complete the PS-Analyzer worksheet (Table A1).
6. Investigate and create a list of innovation ideas.
7. For each idea complete the PS-Analyzer worksheet (Table A2).
8. Review the tables, analyze the causes, ideas, and associated data, and decide whether to Fix-It or Design-Build-It.

When innovative disruptions are successful, they commonly follow one of four performance themes: (i) Time Efficiency—Activities are done faster or quicker, (ii) Cost Efficiency—Fewer or cheaper resources are used, (iii) Quality Enhancement—Products satisfy higher levels of customer wants, or (iv) Provider Expansion.

PS-Analyzer—Header

Specific Fulfillment Process :

Process Start :

Process End :

Process Speed :   ○ Days   ○ Hours   ○ Minutes

T^L- Losing =

T^B- Best =

T^S- Steady =

T^D- Disrupt =

Speed Range =

Table A.1 PS-Analyzer

No.	SLOW CAUSE	TYPE	SOURCE	SPEED EFFECT
1		○ Friction	□ Skill Inefficiency □ Data Search □ Process Design □ Time Waste	
		○ Speed Bump	□ Batch Process □ Low Priority □ Resource Short □ Decision Optimize	
2		○ Friction	□ Skill Inefficiency □ Data Search □ Process Design □ Time Waste	
		○ Speed Bump	□ Batch Process □ Low Priority □ Resource Short □ Decision Optimize	
3		○ Friction	□ Skill Inefficiency □ Data Search □ Process Design □ Time Waste	
		○ Speed Bump	□ Batch Process □ Low Priority □ Resource Short □ Decision Optimize	
4		○ Friction	□ Skill Inefficiency □ Data Search □ Process Design □ Time Waste	
		○ Speed Bump	□ Batch Process □ Low Priority □ Resource Short □ Decision Optimize	
5		○ Friction	□ Skill Inefficiency □ Data Search □ Process Design □ Time Waste	
		○ Speed Bump	□ Batch Process □ Low Priority □ Resource Short □ Decision Optimize	

Table A.2 PS-Analyzer

No.	INNOVATION IDEA	LINK SLOW CAUSES	IDEA DRIVER	SPEED EFFECT
1			□ Data Streaming □ Decision Model □ Process Time □ Resource Cloud □ Automation □ Uncertainty Analytics	□ + 10% □ +20% □ +40% □ +60%
2			□ Data Streaming □ Decision Model □ Process Time □ Resource Cloud □ Automation □ Uncertainty Analytics	□ + 10% □ +20% □ +40% □ +60%
3			□ Data Streaming □ Decision Model □ Process Time □ Resource Cloud □ Automation □ Uncertainty Analytics	□ + 10% □ +20% □ +40% □ +60%
4			□ Data Streaming □ Decision Model □ Process Time □ Resource Cloud □ Automation □ Uncertainty Analytics	□ + 10% □ +20% □ +40% □ +60%

B. Lite-AI Builder

What Does it Do?

AI (Artificial Intelligence) adds complexity to decision problems by increasing the number of dynamic input variables and the controllable decision variables. The Lite-AI Builder captures and operationalizes the intelligence linking these inputs and decisions to a target performance metric. It prepares the team for the next stage where computer and data scientists get involved in creating an operational model.

Definitions

Specific Fulfillment Activity: A specific activity within the fulfillment process for which an AI model is being developed.

Performance Metric: The activity outcome you are focused on achieving, or literally, the performance target or goal. It is critical to ensure that the right goal is identified, else you will be efficiently progressing in the wrong direction. In a fulfillment machine, this metric will likely be defined in terms of activity speed and could be associated with listed friction and speed bump causes from an associated PS-Analyzer worksheet.

Process Variables (Dependent Inputs): Physical and digital attributes of the process activities that are changing or changeable. These inputs are known determinants of the performance metric, which implies that as they change the process performance changes. Variables should be described at the functional level with as much precision as possible.

Decisions or Controllable Variables: Decisions could be either stationary (design) or dynamic (operational) in nature. Stationary decisions are made occasionally and have a much lower frequency, while dynamic decisions are real-time and have a higher frequency. Take a disruptive approach to identify the decisions, often we assume something is fixed or cannot be changed, challenge this assumption.

Performance Transfer Relationships: This is the guts of the analysis and comprises the intelligence driving the AI solution. The intelligence team projects the effect of each input on the performance target. Described by two effect measures: (i) Steady-State Effect (Linear assumption)—For each variable what is the likely percentage increase in the performance metric for a unit/category change if all other variables are fixed and (ii) Paired Effect—Identify variable pairs that have an additive/multiplicative effect on performance, then estimate the likely combined effect of the pair for a unit/category change.

Data Curation: Starts with the ROC (Recorded, Optimized, and Controlled) principle, the variables specify the datasets that need to be collected and stored. These datasets will be used to learn from the data and then train your decision-making models. Over time they will validate the performance transfer relationships. All data is time-variant and readily recorded in a transactional database. Curation is the process of cleaning up and referencing this data so that it will be useful in creating decision intelligence.

Feature Engineering Variables: Selecting the variables that are most critical to performance. Set an effect threshold and only focus on modeling those variables with either a steady-state or paired effect above the threshold.

Supervised Learning Notes: In many decision problems the performance transfer relationships are not exact or readily understood. AI can apply the previous information to a curated dataset, to learn and propose a model for better decision making. Record here what are the strategies or tactics in the AI learning process. These will be used by the computer/data scientist to develop an applicable model.

Lite-AI Builder Steps:

1. Describe the specific fulfillment activity for which an AI-based decision-making program is being developed.
2. Identify the target performance metric that is being optimized.
3. Investigate the current and future operational designs for the activity, to understand the activity variables and their effect on the performance metric.

4. List the input process variables and for each variable complete the Lite-AI Builder worksheet (Table B1).

5. List the decision variables, and for each decision complete the Lite-AI Builder worksheet (Table B2).

6. For each process and decision variable complete the Lite-AI Builder worksheet (Table B3) single variable effect section.

7. Review the variables and list variables pairs that have a significant combined performance effect. For each pair complete the Lite-AI Builder worksheet (Table B3) paired variable effect section.

8. Review the tables, analyze the variables and effects, and summarize the training notes.

Lite-AI Builder—Header

Specific Fulfillment Activity:

Performance Metric:

Table B.1 Lite-AI Builder

No.	INPUT PROCESS VARIABLE	DATA MEASURE	DATA SOURCE	UNCERTIANITY RANGE
V1			□ Flow Entity □ System State	
V2			□ Flow Entity □ System State	
V3			□ Flow Entity □ System State	

Table B.2 Lite-AI Builder

No.	DECISION VARIABLES	MADE BY	FREQUENCY
D1		□ Human □ Computer Rule □ Analytical Program	□ Time - Interval: _____ □ Batch - Size: _____
D2		□ Human □ Computer Rule □ Analytical Program	□ Time - Interval: _____ □ Batch - Size: _____

Table B.3 Lite-AI Builder

	WHY - EFFECT INTELLIGENCE	STEADY STATE / PAIRED EFFECT	DATA CURATION	FEATURE SELECTION
No.	*Single Variable Effect*		*Threshold % =*	
V1				□ Yes □ No
V2				□ Yes □ No
V3				□ Yes □ No
D1				□ Yes □ No
D2				□ Yes □ No
Pair	*Paired Vairable Effect*		*Threshold % =*	
				□ Yes □ No
				□ Yes □ No
				□ Yes □ No

Supervised Learning Notes:

C. Brown Multiplier to Idea Generator (BM-Idea)

What Information Does it Provide?

In the Internet-of-Things (IoT) world, fulfillment processes need to adapt efficiently to a wide range of product/service level uncertainties and a broad range of customer preferences. The BM-Idea generator identifies what range of uncertainties and how it affects the fulfillment process. This information is used to generate physio-digital ideas that can be integrated into the fulfillment machine.

Definitions

Specific Product/Service: The specific product or service that is going through a design innovation update to meet the new customer market.

Customer Exploration—Segment and Attributes: A customer segment is defined by an aggregate view of the specific product/service. Each segment is described by a set of attributes or product/service features. Five segments are studied: (i) Average-Now, (ii) Average-New, (iii) ±3σ or very different, (iv) ±5σ or highly different, and (v) ±7σ or extremely different customers. Average-Now is the default and represents the current market and serves as a benchmark. Most likely the ±3σ to ±5σ segments are not served in the current situation. Note the ±3σ to ±5σ segments are relative to the Average-New.

Customer Exploration—Research: Investigating how the product/service is being transformed in the marketplace, with a specific focus on digitization and the IoT. Internal market study reports are of little value since many past trends are unlikely to continue in the digitized future. Online blogs, customer reviews, and insightful trend reports from big-name experts (Gartner, McKinsey, and others) are valuable sources. An exploratory investigation of what the Internet allows the customer to do in the context of existing/future products is also recommended. The market knowledge will describe the Average-New segment and the ±3σ to ±5σ segments. These should together be disruptively different from the Average-Now.

Brownian Multipliers: Four types of market of driven multipliers will affect the fulfillment process of the new customer: *What, When, Where, and Like* (see definitions in Chapter 8). There can be several multipliers of each type. A multiplier is described by specific fulfillment requirements to meet the customer order range. A good multiplier should be easily associated with the attributes of the product/service.

Why Nots: There are four common reasons that an innovative idea or thought is put aside. The why not counter-response links each multiplier to one of the four reasons. Identify which of these applies to each of the multipliers. To counter with a why not do it response, start the argument from one or more of the previous causes. Good multipliers will not be easy to implement and should severely challenge the existing fulfillment process. Being aware of the why nots prepares the team for rigorous BM-Idea meetings and promotes risk transparency.

Digital Idea: A primarily digital solution that will let the fulfillment process rapidly and efficiently respond to the multipliers. This is a classical ideation step. The multipliers and why nots are already known, the team is tasked with formulating ideas that can seed the development process. The task is not a full design but seed ideas that confirm the possibility of a doable solution.

Physical Idea: A primarily digital solution that will let the fulfillment process rapidly and efficiently respond to the multipliers. The digital and physical ideas could be combined into a physio-digital innovation. Integration of the ROC principle is encouraged.

Critical Intelligence: Required intelligence for optimal decision making in the context of the digital and physical ideas. This intelligence will be in the form of data that will be required by associated models or algorithms.

BM-Idea Generator Steps:

1. Describe the specific product/service for the fulfillment machine that is being developed or rebuilt.

2. Customer Exploration—Now: describe the attributes of the Average-Now customer and record them in the worksheet (Table C1).

3. Customer Exploration—Research: Investigate the disruptive transformation occurring in the market.

4. Customer Exploration—New: describe the attributes of the Average-New segment and the $\pm 3\sigma$ to $\pm 5\sigma$ segments and complete the worksheet (Table C1).

5. List one to three multipliers for each of the four types: what, when, where, and like. Record in the worksheet (Table C2).

6. For each multiplier identify which of the why not reasons can be used to build an innovative idea. Record in the worksheet (Table C2).

7. For each multiplier generate one digital and physical idea that can be used to create an effective fulfillment solution. Record in the worksheet (Table C2).

8. Identify the required critical intelligence for each pair of physio-digital ideas. Record in the worksheet (Table C3).

BM-Idea—Header

Specific Product/Service :

Table C.1 BM-Idea

SEGMENT	ATTRIBUTES
AVERAGE - NOW	
AVERAGE - NEW	
± 3 Sigma	
±5 Sigma	
±7 Sigma	

Table C.2 BM-Idea

BROWNIAN MULTIPLIERS		WHY NOT?	DIGITAL IDEA	PHYSICAL IDEA
WHAT				
1.1		o Higher Costs o Decision Complexity o Process Complexity o Delivery Complexity		
1.2		o Higher Costs o Decision Complexity o Process Complexity o Delivery Complexity		
WHEN				
2.1		o Higher Costs o Decision Complexity o Process Complexity o Delivery Complexity		
2.2		o Higher Costs o Decision Complexity o Process Complexity o Delivery Complexity		
WHERE				
3.1		o Higher Costs o Decision Complexity o Process Complexity o Delivery Complexity		
3.2		o Higher Costs o Decision Complexity o Process Complexity o Delivery Complexity		
LIKE				
4.1		o Higher Costs o Decision Complexity o Process Complexity o Delivery Complexity		
4.2		o Higher Costs o Decision Complexity o Process Complexity o Delivery Complexity		

Table C.3 BM-Idea

BROWNIAN MULTIPLIERS		DIGITIZATION STRATEGY	CRITICAL INTELLIGENCE
WHAT			
1.1		o Explosive Decision Map o Artificial Intelligence o Transfer Functions	
1.2		o Explosive Decision Map o Artificial Intelligence o Transfer Functions	
WHEN			
2.1		o Explosive Decision Map o Artificial Intelligence o Transfer Functions	
2.2		o Explosive Decision Map o Artificial Intelligence o Transfer Functions	
WHERE			
3.1		o Explosive Decision Map o Artificial Intelligence o Transfer Functions	
3.2		o Explosive Decision Map o Artificial Intelligence o Transfer Functions	
LIKE			
4.1		o Explosive Decision Map o Artificial Intelligence o Transfer Functions	
4.2		o Explosive Decision Map o Artificial Intelligence o Transfer Functions	

D. Automation Challenge Analysis (AC-Analysis)

What Information Does it Provide?

Focus is on a set of tasks or a process, within the fulfillment machine, that are to be automated. Successful development and implementation of the automation project is a dependent on several attributes that describe the task. The AC-Analysis helps the team to investigate the challenges associated with an innovation automation idea. The analysis then relates these challenges to target performance and the resource constraints. The analytical results will help determine how to prepare for the project and increase success probability.

Definitions

Automation Tasks or Process: The set of tasks or an entire process with defined start and end. Example: (1) Start—Pick order released to the storage area; End—Picked item in tote (2) Start—Ride request confirmed in the system; End—Ride assigned to a driver. Multiple entities (e.g., customer orders) will flow through the process over a period of time.

Input Factor: A task/process variable that determines the difficulty by which the task can be automated. The factor value/state varies between each incidence of the task and often determines the specificity of the task and differentiates it from a fixed automation machine. In a fixed automation program there are no input variables, the machine repeats the same task.

Situation Attributes: These describe the behavior of the input factor in the context of the automation task as presented sequentially to the machine.

1. Complexity—The range of possible input values, including small variances (continuous variables or shades of gray) in each factor. Example: How many different colors plus variations of the same product (red, blue, dark blue, light blue)?
2. Randomness—Uncertainty in the input factor as presented in each automation event. Variance and centralization of the uncertainty behavior are measurable dimensions. Example: The number of dark

blue boxes in stock ranges from 5 to 50 but 80 percent of the time there are only 20 boxes (centralized) as opposed to the case where it is 20 percent each for 10, 20, 30, and 40 boxes (uniform).

3. Congestion—The decision granularity in each automation event, as measured by the number of presented entities. Density and overlap in the physical or data situation are measurable dimensions. Example: The average customer order is for six items (congestion) and order arrival times of many items are highly correlated (overlap).

4. False Signals—Errors in reading or receiving an input value, possibly due to environmental errors. Frequency of the errors and the effect on successful completion of the automation task. Example: Likelihood the wrong item (color or size) is picked, possibly due to lighting conditions.

5. Unknowns—Factors or situations that are unknown but could become an automaton issue. The probable risk and their effect on the automation project are the measured dimension. Examples: The box is damaged, or there is a high volume of returned items with different packaging.

Machine Capability: The required machine capability to complete the automation task with given situation attributes. Describe the associated machine building challenge, and identify the related input factors. Estimate the building effort required to overcome the challenge, ranging from minimal to very difficult. Consider the situation score of the input factors in estimating the building effort.

1. Sense—Ability to identify the presence of an entity and/or its attributes. How many boxes are on the shelf?

2. Vision—Ability to capture and digitize a picture of the situation or analog data. Where the boxes are located and what is the positional arrangement?

3. Motion—Ability to move entities or objects from one point to another. Pickup and move a box from the shelf to the cart.

4. Manipulation—Ability to change the position or arrangement of an entity. Rotate a box to change its position or orientation.

5. Memory—Ability to immediately access data about past events or transactions. What boxes were placed and removed from this rack in the past 30 days?

Capability Challenge Score—Derived by summing the three highest capability score and then dividing by 3. Indicates on a 0 to 10 scale the capability challenge.

Performance: Identify the required performance level or targets for the automation to be deemed a business success, and describe in the notes column. Three performance metrics are evaluated. Define both the minimum to succeed and the target performance levels. Estimate the probability that each performance level will be achieved.

1. Speed—The task completion rate.
2. Accuracy—Percent of tasks completed correctly.
3. Quality—Relative to a human benchmark the output quality.

Constraints: Explain why reasonable and/or justifiable resources may constraint the success of the automation project. Three constraint categories should be evaluated. Back up the explanation with the likely effect of the constraint on the target performance levels. The explanations and effects make it easier for management to either assign additional resources or explore alternative automation pathways.

1. Costs—The capital cost to build and implement the automation solution.
2. Technology—Availability and feasibility risk of the needed automation technologies.
3. Talent—Availability and sustainability of the talent pool to support the automation effort.

AC-Analysis Steps:

1. Describe the task/process that is the focus of the automation project.
2. Define the start and end points of the automation task/process.
3. Identify and describe the three most important inputs factors. Record in the worksheet (Table D1).
4. Evaluate each input factor in the context of the five situation attributes using the associated scale. Compute the situation score by adding the five attribute scores. Record in the worksheet (Table D1).
5. Required machine capability—Analyze each capability in the context of the input factors. Identify the challenges and estimate the building effort. Record in the worksheet (Table D2).

6. Performance Analysis—Complete and record in Table D3.

7. Team review of Tables D1 to D3 with goal of synthesizing the project opportunities and challenges.

8. Estimate the resources needed for success and translate into constraints. Complete and record in Table D4.

AC-Analysis—Header

Automation Task/Process :	
Process Start :	
Process End :	

Table D.1 AC-Analysis

No.	INPUT FACTOR	DESCRIPTION	SITUATION ATTRIBUTES	SITUATION SCORE
1			1. COMPLEXITY / 2. RANDOMNESS / 3. CONGESTION / 4. FALSE SIGNALS / 5. UNKNOWNS	
2			1. COMPLEXITY / 2. RANDOMNESS / 3. CONGESTION / 4. FALSE SIGNALS / 5. UNKNOWNS	
3			1. COMPLEXITY / 2. RANDOMNESS / 3. CONGESTION / 4. FALSE SIGNALS / 5. UNKNOWNS	

Table D.2 AC-Analysis

No.	CAPABILITY	CHALLENGES	CRITICAL FACTORS	BUILDING EFFORT	
1	SENSE		□ Input Factor #1 □ Input Factor #2 □ Input Factor #3	□ Minimal (Score=1) □ Normal (Score=3) □ Difficult (Score=7) □ Very Difficult (Score=10)	
2	VISION		□ Input Factor #1 □ Input Factor #2 □ Input Factor #3	□ Minimal (Score=1) □ Normal (Score=3) □ Difficult (Score=7) □ Very Difficult (Score=10)	
3	MOTION		□ Input Factor #1 □ Input Factor #2 □ Input Factor #3	□ Minimal (Score=1) □ Normal (Score=3) □ Difficult (Score=7) □ Very Difficult (Score=10)	
4	MANIPULATION		□ Input Factor #1 □ Input Factor #2 □ Input Factor #3	□ Minimal (Score=1) □ Normal (Score=3) □ Difficult (Score=7) □ Very Difficult (Score=10)	
5	MEMORY		□ Input Factor #1 □ Input Factor #2 □ Input Factor #3	□ Minimal (Score=1) □ Normal (Score=3) □ Difficult (Score=7) □ Very Difficult (Score=10)	
CAPABILITY CHALLENGE SCORE =					

Table D.3 AC-Analysis

No.	PERFORMANCE	NOTES	TARGET LEVELS	
1	SPEED		*Minimum to Succeed* → _____ *Likelihood its Met:* □ 50% □ 80% □ 90%+	*Disruption Tartget* → _____ *Likelihood its Met:* □ 50% □ 80% □ 90%+
2	ACCURACY		*Minimum to Succeed* → _____ *Likelihood its Met:* □ 50% □ 80% □ 90%+	*Disruption Tartget* → _____ *Likelihood its Met:* □ 50% □ 80% □ 90%+
3	QUALITY		*Minimum to Succeed* → _____ *Likelihood its Met:* □ 50% □ 80% □ 90%+	*Disruption Tartget* → _____ *Likelihood its Met:* □ 50% □ 80% □ 90%+

Table D.4 AC-Analysis

No.	CONSTRAINT	EXPLAIN WHY	EFFECT ON THE PROJECT
1	COST		*Likelihood the constraint will effect:* SPEED: □ Low □ Average □ High ACCURACY: □ Low □ Average □ High QUALITY: □ Low □ Average □ High
2	TECHNOLOGY		*Likelihood the constraint will effect:* SPEED: □ Low □ Average □ High ACCURACY: □ Low □ Average □ High QUALITY: □ Low □ Average □ High
3	TALENT		*Likelihood the constraint will effect:* SPEED: □ Low □ Average □ High ACCURACY: □ Low □ Average □ High QUALITY: □ Low □ Average □ High

Bibliography

1. Smith, A., and M. Anderson. 2016. "Online Shopping and E-Commerce." *Pew Research Center*, https://pewresearch.org/internet/2016/12/19/online-shopping-and-e-commerce/

2. Mims, C. September 20, 2018. "The Prime Effect: How Amazon's Two-Day Shipping Is Disrupting Retail. The Quest to Offer Fast, Free Delivery has Triggered an Arms Race Among the Largest Retailers. *The Wall Street Journal*, https://wsj.com/articles/the-prime-effect-how-amazons-2-day-shipping-is-disrupting-retail-1537448425

3. Bell, D., S. Gallino, and A. Moreno-Garcia. 2014. "How to Win in an Omnichannel World." *MIT Sloan Management Review* 56, no.1. https://sloanreview.mit.edu/article/how-to-win-in-an-omnichannel-world/

4. New York Times. October 2012. "The Story of a FreshDirect Order." *New York Times*, https://archive.nytimes.com/nytimes.com/interactive/2012/10/10/dining/the-story-of-a-freshdirect-order.html?_r=0

5. HBS Digital Initiative. 2015. "Whole Foods Market: Healthy Products with a Healthy Profit." *Technology and Operations Management Challenge*, https://digital.hbs.edu/platform-rctom/submission/whole-foods-market-healthy-products-with-a-healthy-profit/

6. Bradmer Foods. n.d. "Note to Start-ups: Whole Foods can't be your Whole Plan," https://bradmerfoods.com/note-to-start-ups-whole-foods-cant-be-your-whole-plan/

7. Huddleston, T. 2018. "How Instant Pot Became a Kitchen Appliance with a Cult Following and a Best-Seller on Amazon." *CNBC Make It*, https://cnbc.com/2018/11/26/how-instant-pot-became-a-kitchen-appliance-with-a-cult-following.html

8. About Amazon. 2021. "Getting Packages to Customers." https://aboutamazon.com/workplace/facilities

9. MWPVL International. 2021. "Amazon Global Supply Chain and Fulfillment Center Network." https://mwpvl.com/html/amazon_com.html

10. Supply Chain Digest. 2010. "Number of Warehouse Workers Continues Significant Rise." *Supply Chain News*, http://scdigest.com/ontarget/17-02-27-1.php?cid=1

11. Christensen, C.M., M.E. Raynor, and R. McDonald. December 2015. "What Is Disruptive Innovation?" *Harvard Business Review Magazine*, https://hbr.org/2015/12/what-is-disruptive-innovation

12. ARK Investment Management. n.d. "ARK Disruptive Innovation." *Investment Strategy Description,* https://ark-invest.com/strategy/ark-disruptive-innovation/

13. Stone, B. 2013. *The Everything Store: Jeff Bezos and the Age of Amazon, Little, Brown and Company.*

14. Harrington, C. 2018. "The Wired Guide to Online Shopping." *Wired,* https://wired.com/story/wired-guide-to-online-shopping/

15. U.S. Department of Commerce. n.d. "Quarterly Retail E-Commerce Sales 3rd Quarter 2020." *U.S. Census Bureau News,* https://census.gov/retail/mrts/www/data/pdf/ec_current.pdf?.

16. Amazon Inc. n.d. "Annual Reports, Proxies and Shareholder Letters." *Data Sourced from Several Years of Amazon Annual Reports,* https://ir.aboutamazon.com/annual-reports-proxies-and-shareholder-letters/default.aspx

17. Amazon Inc. n.d. "Non-Product Revenues are Primarily from Services and the Largest Component of that is Amazon Web Services."

18. Bezos, J. n.d. "2018 Letter to Shareholders." *Amazon Inc.,* https://aboutamazon.com/news/company-news/2018-letter-to-shareholders

19. Amazon Inc. n.d. "Annual Report—Results of Operations—Operating Expenses." *Fulfillment Costs Represent Costs Incurred in Operating Fulfillment and Customer Service Centers, Including Costs Attributable to Buying, Receiving, Inspecting, and Warehousing Inventories; Picking, Packaging, and Preparing Orders for Shipment,* https://s2.q4cdn.com/299287126/files/doc_financials/2020/ar/2019-Annual-Report.pdf

20. eMarketer. February 2020. "Top 10 US Retail eCommerce Sales by Company." *Reported in Tech Crunch,* https://techcrunch.com/2020/02/24/target-breaks-into-the-top-10-list-of-u-s-e-commerce-retailers

21. Supply Chain Digest. 2015. "Amazon Ponders Ninth Generation Fulfillment Center Design." *Supply Chain News,* http://scdigest.com/ontarget/15-03-03-1.php?cid=9051

22. MWPVL International. 2020. "The Walmart Distribution Center Network in the United States." https://mwpvl.com/html/walmart.html

23. Karlgaard, R., and L. Bloomers. 2019. "The Power of Patience in a World Obsessed with Early Achievement." ISBN-10 : 1524759759: Currency.

24. Prigg, M. 2012. "Sir Jonathan Ive: The iMan cometh." *Evening Standard—London Life,* https://standard.co.uk/lifestyle/london-life/sir-jonathan-ive-the-iman-cometh-7562170.html

25. Julia La Roche—Correspondent. 2019. "Bill Ackman thanks Warren Buffett for Pershing Square's Turnaround." *Yahoo Finance,* https://finance.yahoo.com/news/bill-ackman-thanks-warren-buffett-for-funds-turnaround-125338678.html

26. KPMG International. 2017. "The Truth About Online Consumers." *Global Online Consumer Report,* https://assets.kpmg/content/dam/kpmg/xx/pdf/2017/01/the-truth-about-online-consumers.pdf

27. Walmart Inc. 2017. "Walmart Launches Free Two-Day Shipping on More Than Two Million Items, No Membership Required." *Walmart Newsroom,* https://corporate.walmart.com/newsroom/2017/01/31/walmart-launches-free-two-day-shipping-on-more-than-two-million-items-no-membership-required

28. Nguyen, D.H., S. de Leeuw, and W.E.H. Dullaert. 2016. "Consumer Behavior and Order Fulfilment in Online Retailing: A Systematic Review." *International Journal of Management Reviews* 20, no. 20, pp. 255–276.

29. Murfield, M., C.A. Boone, P. Rutner, and R. Thomas. 2017. "Investigating Logistics Service Quality in Omni-Channel Retailing." *International Journal of Physical Distribution & Logistics Management* 47, no. 4, pp. 263–296.

30. Lieber, E., and C. Syverson. 2012. "Online versus Offline Competition." *The Oxford Handbook of the Digital Economy,* ed. Peitz, M., and Waldfogel, J. Chapter 8, Oxford University Press.

31. Li, Z., Q. Lu., and M. Talebian. 2015. "Online versus Bricks-and-Mortar Retailing: A Comparison of Price, Assortment, and Delivery Time." *International Journal of Production Research* 53, no. 13, pp. 3823–3835.

32. Zhang, J., S, Onal, and S. Das. 2019. "Fulfillment Time Performance of Online Retailers – An Empirical Analysis." *International Journal of Retail & Distribution Management* 47, no. 5.

33. Meller, R. January-February 2015. "Order Fulfilment as a Competitive Advantage." *Supply Chain Management Review,* pp. 40–45.

34. Teixeira, T., and E. A. Watkins. August 2015. "Building an e-Commerce Brand at Wayfair." *Harvard Business School Case,* pp. 516–028

35. Berthene, A. February 13, 2020. "Wayfair.com Dominates Online Furniture Sales." *Digital Commerce 360,* https://digitalcommerce360.com/2020/02/13/wayfair-com-dominates-online-furniture-sales/

36. Fein, A.J. June 2017. "Latest Data on Pharmacy Market's Evolution: The Real Story Behind the Retail vs. Mail Battle." *Drug Channels,* https://drugchannels.net/2017/06/latest-data-on-pharmacy-markets.html

37. IMS Institute for Healthcare Informatics. 2016. "Annual Use of Medicines report: US Sales Reach $424.8 Billion." Pharmaceutical Commerce, https://pharmaceuticalcommerce.com/business-and-finance/ims-2015-use-medicines-report-us-sales-reach-424-8-billion/

38. CB Insights. n.d. "The 9 Industries Amazon Could Disrupt Next." https://cbinsights.com/research/report/amazon-disruption-industries/

39. Hübner, A., H. Kuhn, and J. Wollenburg. 2016. "Last Mile Fulfilment and Distribution in Omni-Channel Grocery Retailing: A Strategic Planning

Framework." *International Journal of Retail & Distribution Management* 44, no. 3, pp. 228–247.

40. Ladd, B. July 2019. "What If General George Patton Was the CEO of Walmart?" *Observer,* https://observer.com/2019/07/walmart-ecommerce-strategy-amazon-ceo-george-patton/

41. Beketov, M., K. Lehmann, and M. Wittke. 2018. "Robo Advisors: Quantitative Methods Inside the Robots." *Journal of Asset Management* 19, pp. 363–370.

42. Caro, F., and J. Gallien. 2010. "Inventory Management of a Fast-Fashion Retail Network." *Operations Research* 58, no. 2, pp. 257–273.

43. Simon, H. 1978. "Rational Decision-Making in Business Organizations." *The Nobel Prize Lecture,* https://nobelprize.org/prizes/economic-sciences/1978/simon/lecture/

44. Acimovic, J., and S.C. Graves. 2015. "Making Better Fulfillment Decisions on the Fly in an Online Retail Environment." *Manufacturing & Service Operations Management* 17, no. 1, pp. 34–51.

45. Onal, S., J. Zhang, and S. Das. 2018. "Product Flows and Decision Models in Internet Fulfilment Warehouses." *Intl Journal of Production Planning & Control* 29, no. 10, pp. 791–801.

46. Marr, B. 2018. "The Key Definitions Of Artificial Intelligence (AI) That Explain Its Importance." *Forbes Enterprise Tech,* https://forbes.com/sites/bernardmarr/2018/02/14/the-key-definitions-of-artificial-intelligence-ai-that-explain-its-importance/#5d3618d84f5d

47. Onal, S., J. Zhang, and S. Das. 2017. "Modelling and Performance Evaluation of Explosive Storage Policies in Internet Fulfillment Warehouses." *International Journal of Production Research* 55, no. 20, pp. 5902–5915.

48. QuickBooks Commerce. 2018. "Zara Supply Chain Analysis—The Secret Behind Zara's Retail Success." *Supply Chain Management,* https://tradegecko.com/blog/supply-chain-management/zara-supply-chain-its-secret-to-retail-success

49. Pan, S., E. Ballot, G.Q. Huang, and B. Montreuil. 2017. "Physical Internet and Interconnected Logistics Services: Research and Applications." *International Journal of Production Research* 55, no. 9, pp. 2603–2609.

50. CNBC News. June 2018. "Amazon Shakes Up Drugstore Business with Deal to Buy Online Pharmacy Pillpack." *CNBC Health & Science News,* https://cnbc.com/2018/06/28/amazon-to-acquire-online-pharmacy-pillpack.html

51. Gao, F., and X. Su. N.d. "Omnichannel Retail Operations with Buy-Online-and-Pick-up-in-Store." *Management Science* 63, no. 8, pp. 2478–2492.

52. Gallino, S., A. Moreno, and I. Stamatopoulos. 2017. "Channel Integration, Sales Dispersion, and Inventory Management." *Management Science* 63, no. 9, pp. 2813–2831.

53. Yahoo Finance. February 2018. "Amazon should be Having Trouble Sleeping At Night." *Interview on The Final Round,* https://aol.com/news/ron-johnson-amazon-walmart-target-192845878.html

54. Merriam-Webster Dictionary. n.d. "Definition of Innovation." https://merriam-webster.com/dictionary/innovation

55. SKillicorn, N. April 2016. "Infographic: 15 Experts on What Innovation Actually Means." *Inc. Innovate,* https://inc.com/nick-skillicorn/9-defining-characteristics-of-successful-innovation.html

56. CNBC News. n.d. "Shark Tank." Video Stories from the Featured Innovative Entreprenerus, https://cnbc.com/shark-tank/

57. Perry, M.J. July 2017. "Saturday Afternoon Links, All Graphic Edition— Chart of the Day V -." AEIdeas—American Enterprise Institute, https://aei.org/carpe-diem/saturday-afternoon-links-all-graphic-edition/

58. CNN News. 2010. "Inside One Of Amazon's Busiest Days." *Tour Provided to CNN Reporters at Amazon's Fernley, Nevada Fulfillment center,* https://youtube.com/watch?v=Z2Bs0nqVyqs

59. CNBC News. 2019. "How Amazon Delivers On One-Day Shipping." https://youtube.com/watch?v=Yiafb0-gqF4

60. D'Andrea, R. 2012. "Guest Editorial: A Revolution in the Warehouse: A Retrospective on Kiva Systems and the Grand Challenges Ahead." IEEE Trans. on Automation Science and Engineering 9, no. 4, pp. 638–639.

61. Boysen, N., R. De Koster, and F. Weidinger. 2018. "Warehousing in the E-Commerce Era: A Survey." *European Journal of Operational Research* 277, no. 2, pp. 396–411.

62. Lopp, M. 2008. "Apple's Design Process—Presentation at SXSW." *Blommberg Business,* https://bloomberg.com/news/articles/2008-03-07/apples-design-process

63. Oches, S. January 2019. "How Blaze Ignited a Pizza Revolution." *QSR,* https://qsrmagazine.com/reports/how-blaze-ignited-pizza-revolution

64. Wikipedia. n.d. "Nash Equilibrium." https://en.wikipedia.org/wiki/Nash_equilibrium

65. Nichols, M. November 2018. "Why Memphis? Fred Smith Talks about Picking the Perfect Hub for FedEx, Global Trade." *Memphis Business Journal,* https://bizjournals.com/memphis/news/2017/10/30/why-memphisfred-smith-talks-about-picking-the.html

66. Galloway, S. 2017. *The Four: The Hidden DNA of Amazon, Apple, Facebook, and Google.* New York, NY: Portfolio – Penguin.

67. CNBC News. 2018. "Trump Claims the Post Office is Losing Billions Because of Amazon, But It's a Lot More Complicated." *Politics—Jaden Urbi,* https://cnbc.com/2018/04/06/trump-claims-amazon-is-ripping-off-post-office-but-its-complicated.html

68. Task Force on the United States Postal System. 2018. "United States Postal Service: A Sustainable Path Forward." United States Postal System, https://home.treasury.gov/system/files/136/USPS_A_Sustainable_Path_Forward_report_12-04-2018.pdf

69. Bowes, P. 2019. "Global Shipping Volume Predicted to Reach 200 Billion Parcels by 2025." *Pitney Bowes Parcel Shipping Index,* https://pitneybowes.com/content/dam/pitneybowes/us/en/shipping-index/shipping_index_release_2019_final_100919_v2.pdf

70. ATKearney & Council of Supply Chain Management Professionals. 2018. "US E-Commerce Trends and the Impact on Logistics." https://kearney.com/consumer-retail/article?/a/us-e-commerce-trends-and-the-impact-on-logistics

71. Walmart Inc. 2017. "Who is Parcel? What This Delivery Company Means to Walmart." *Walmart Newsroom,* https://corporate.walmart.com/newsroom/business/20171003/who-is-parcel-what-this-delivery-company-means-to-walmart

72. Wood, C. 2020. "Food delivery Apps are a Lifeline for Restaurants During the Pandemic, But at a High Cost." *Berkeleyside NOSH,* https://berkeleyside.com/2020/11/05/third-party-food-delivery-apps-pros-and-cons-for-restaurants

73. Buffett, W.E., and L.A. Cunningham. 2015. *The Essays of Warren Buffett: Lessons for Corporate America.* The Cunningham Group & Carolina Academic Press.

74. Uber Marketplace. N.d. "How does Uber Match Riders with Drivers?" *Uber Inc.* https://marketplace.uber.com/matching.

75. Romano, R. 2004. "Everybody Loves Raymond (TV Series)." Season 8, Epsiode 23.

76. Mountz, M. December 2012. "Kiva the Disrupter." *Harvard Business Review Magazine,* https://store.hbr.org/product/kiva-the-disrupter/r1212e?sku=R1212E-PDF-ENG

77. Reuters News. 2019. "Warren Buffett Says Berkshire Overpaid for Kraft Heinz." https://reuters.com/article/us-berkshire-buffett-kraft-heinz/warren-buffett-says-berkshire-overpaid-for-kraft-heinz-idUSKCN1QE1F0

78. Womack, J.P., D.T. Jones, and D. Roos. 2007. *The Machine That Changed the World: The Story of Lean Production.* Free Press.

79. Uber Engineering. 2018. "Sessionizing Uber Trips in Real Time." *Uber Inc.,* https://eng.uber.com/sessionizing-data/, 2018.

80. Navone, E. September 28, 2020. "Dijkstra's Shortest Path Algorithm—A Detailed and Visual Introduction." *Free Code Camp,* https://freecodecamp. org/news/dijkstras-shortest-path-algorithm-visual-introduction/

81. Tomasic, A. J. Zimmerman, A. Steinfeld, and Y. Huang. February 2014. "Motivating Contribution in a Participatory Sensing System." *CSCW '14: Proceedings of the 17th ACM conference on Computer supported cooperative work & social computing,* http://citeseerx.ist.psu.edu/viewdoc/download?doi=10.1.1.431.5963&rep=rep1&type=pdf

82. Pillar, M. June 2015. "Ulta Beauty's Quest For The Ultimate Omni-Channel Experience." *Retail Supply Chain Insights,* https://retailsupplychaininsights. com/doc/ulta-beauty-s-quest-for-the-ultimate-omni-channel-experience-0001

83. Investopedia. n.d. "In Finance, The Acronym "FANG" Refers to the Stocks of Four Prominent American Technology Companies: Facebook (F), Amazon (AMZN), Netflix (NFLX), and Alphabet (GOOG)."

84. Miller, R. July 2016. "How AWS Came to Be." Tech Crunch, https:// techcrunch.com/2016/07/02/andy-jassys-brief-history-of-the-genesis-of-aws/

85. Lutke, T. n.d. "The Trust Battery [The Knowledge Project Ep. #41]." Farnam Street Newsletter, https://fs.blog/knowledge-project/tobi-lutke/

86. Motley Fool Staff. 2018. "The Motley Fool Interviews Tobi Lutke, CEO of Shopify." *The Motley Fool,* https://fool.com/investing/2018/09/11/the-motley-fool-interviews-tobi-lutke-ceo-of-shopi.aspx

87. SoftBank Inc. n.d. "SoftBank's Next 30-Year Vision." *Softbank Vision & Strategy,* https://group.softbank/en/philosophy/vision/next30.

88. Winslett, M., and V. Braganholo. December 2013. "Anand Rajaraman Speaks Out on Startups and Social Data." *SIGMOD Record* 42, no. 4. https://sigmod.org/publications/sigmodRecord/1312/pdfs/07.profiles. rajaraman.pdf?189db0

89. Harinarayan, V., A. Rajaraman, and J. Ullman. June 1996. "Implementing Data Cubes Efficiently." *ACM SIGMOD Record* 25, no. 2, https://sfu-db. github.io/cmpt884-fall16/Papers/implementing_data_cube.pdf

90. Uber Engineering. 2017. "Meet Michelangelo: Uber's Machine Learning Platform." Uber Inc. – Hermann, J., and Del Balso, M. https://eng.uber. com/michelangelo-machine-learning-platform/

91. Andreessen, M., and J. Conde. 2019. "Why Marc Went From 'We'll Never Do Bio' to Betting on Bio Founders." *Andreessen Horowitz,* https://a16z. com/2019/08/23/software-eats-healthcare-bio-next/

92. Tesla. 2021. "AutopilotDescription and Elements—Hardware, Neural Networks and Autonomy, Code and Evaluation Infrastructure." *Tesla Inc.* https://tesla.com/autopilotAI

93. Wakabayashi, D. March 25, 2014. "Apple Engineer Recalls the iPhone's Birth—Jobs's Ultimatum: Lay Out a Vision Fast or Lose the Project." *The Wall Street Journal*, https://wsj.com/articles/SB10001424052702303949704579461783150723874

94. Robinhood Inc. 2021. "Our Mission and Our Story." *About Robinhood—As Reported on their Corporate Website*, https://robinhood.com/us/en/support/articles/our-mission/

95. Wikipedia. 2021. "Crowdsourcing Description." *From Wikipedia, The Free Encyclopedia*, https://en.wikipedia.org/wiki/Crowdsourcing

96. Strabucks inc. 2021. "What's your Starbucks idea? Revolutionary or Simple—We Want to Hear It." *Starbucks.com*, https://ideas.starbucks.com/

97. L'Oreal Inc. 2020. "L'Oreal Innovation Runway 2020—a partner competition with Slingshot 2020." *L'Oréal Research & Innovation*, https://lorealinnovationrunway.sg/en

98. Agorize. n.d. "Agorize Helps Businesses to Innovate and Identify the Best Talent by Connecting them with a Global Community of 5 Million Innovators." https://agorize.com/en

99. Idea Drop. 2021. "The Leading Idea Management Platform for Global Innovation." *2021 Idea Drop Ltd*, https://ideadrop.co/

100. Gallo, C. 2010. *The Innovation Secrets of Steve Jobs: Insanely Different Principles for Breakthrough Success*. McGraw-Hill Education.

101. Keefe, P.R. February 6, 2017. "Anthony Bourdain's Moveable Feast—Guided by a Lusty Appetite for Indigenous Culture and Cuisine, The Swaggering Chef has Become a Travelling Statesman." *The New Yorker*, https://newyorker.com/magazine/2017/02/13/anthony-bourdains-moveable-feast

102. May 9, 2011. "Creation Myth—Xerox PARC, Apple, and The Truth About Innovation." *The New Yorker—Annals of Business*, https://newyorker.com/magazine/2011/05/16/creation-myth

103. Gara, A. 2020. "The Don't Worry Make Money Strategy Trouncing the Stock Market by-30 % Points." *Forbes*, https://forbes.com/sites/antoinegara/2020/05/19/the-dont-worry-make-money-strategy-trouncing-the-stock-market-by-30-percentage-points/?sh=582a7ffd2028

104. CNBC News. June 2020. "These are the 2020 CNBC Disruptor 50 Companies." *CNBC DISRUPTOR 50*, https://cnbc.com/2020/06/16/meet-the-2020-cnbc-disruptor-50-companies.html

105. Lemonade Inc. 2021. "Forget Everything You Know About Insurance—Instant everything. Incredible prices. Big heart." *Lemonade Website*, https://lemonade.com/

106. Feldman, A. 2020. "Next Billion Dollar Startups." *Forbes has Teamed up with TrueBridge Capital Partners to Search the Country for the 25 Fastest-Growing Venture-Backed Startups Most Likely to Reach a $1 Billion Valuation,* https://forbes.com/sites/amyfeldman/2020/05/28/next-billion-dollar-startups-2020/?sh=6621dbf33f9f

107. Capsule Inc. 2021. "The Pharmacy in your Phone—Free, Same-Day Prescription Delivery from the Safety of your Home." *Capsule Website,* https://capsule.com/

108. Satara, A. April 2018. "In 2 Sentences Elon Musk Explains Why the Key to Success Is Failure If You're an Entrepreneur You Should Follow Elon Musk's Rule of Thumb." *Inc. Magazine—Icons & Innovators,* https://inc.com/alyssa-satara/in-2-sentences-elon-musk-explains-why-key-to-success-is-failure.html

109. Brinker International Inc. 2021. "The Story Behind the Killer Wings—Born in the Kitchen." *It's Just Wings Website,* https://itsjustwings.com/aboutus.html

110. CNBC News. 2021. "Cramers COVID-19 Stocks." *CNBC Markets,* https://cnbc.com/cramer-covid-19-stocks/

About the Author

Sanchoy Das is Professor of Mechanical and Industrial Engineering at the New Jersey Institute of Technology where he teaches graduate classes in supply chain engineering, operations management, and decision modeling. He received his PhD from Virginia Tech. His research passion is supply chains, that remarkable cocktail of logistics, industrial engineering, business operations management, and data-driven information technology that brings the world of products and services to our neighborhoods and now to our doorsteps. Today that passion is focused on Fast Fulfillment— How disruptive innovators are getting online orders delivered to you immediately—today, tomorrow, or at the latest the day after tomorrow. He has published numerous research articles on the topic and his research continues to investigate how companies are developing and pivoting the supply chains to meet the needs of the online customer.

Index

OTHER TITLES IN THE MARKETING COLLECTION

Naresh Malhotra, Georgia Tech, Editor

- *Branding & AI* by Chahat Aggarwal
- *Stand Out!* by Brian McGurk
- *The Coming Age of Robots* by George Pettinico and George R. Milne
- *Market Entropy* by Rajagopal Rajagopal
- *Decoding Customer Value at the Bottom of the Pyramid* by Ritu Srivastava
- *Qualitative Marketing Research* by Rajagopal
- *Social Media Marketing* by Alan Charlesworth
- *Employee Ambassadorship* by Michael W Lowenstein
- *Critical Thinking for Marketers, Volume I* by David Dwight, David Soorholtz, and Terry Grapentine
- *Critical Thinking for Marketers, Volume II* by David Dwight, David Soorholtz, and Terry Grapentine
- *Relationship Marketing Re-Imagined* by Naresh Malhotra, Can Uslay, and Ahmet Bayraktar
- *Marketing Plan Templates for Enhancing Profits* by Elizabeth Rush Kruger
- *Launching New Products* by John C. Westman and Paul Sowyrda
- *Market Sensing Today* by Melvin Prince and Constantinos-Vasilios Priporas

Concise and Applied Business Books

The Collection listed above is one of 30 business subject collections that Business Expert Press has grown to make BEP a premiere publisher of print and digital books. Our concise and applied books are for...

- Professionals and Practitioners
- Faculty who adopt our books for courses
- Librarians who know that BEP's Digital Libraries are a unique way to offer students ebooks to download, not restricted with any digital rights management
- Executive Training Course Leaders
- Business Seminar Organizers

Business Expert Press books are for anyone who needs to dig deeper on business ideas, goals, and solutions to everyday problems. Whether one print book, one ebook, or buying a digital library of 110 ebooks, we remain the affordable and smart way to be business smart. For more information, please visit www.businessexpertpress.com, or contact sales@businessexpertpress.com.

www.ingramcontent.com/pod-product-compliance
Lightning Source LLC
Chambersburg PA
CBHW061154220326
41599CB00025B/4477